Prayer
for the Day

Prayer for the Day

VOLUME II

More Reflections for Daily Inspiration

WATKINS

Sharing Wisdom Since
1893

This edition first published in the UK and USA 2016 by
Watkins, an imprint of Watkins Media Limited
19 Cecil Court
London WC2N 4EZ

enquiries@watkinspublishing.com

By arrangement with the BBC
The BBC and Radio 4 logos are trade marks of the British Broadcasting Corporation and are
used under licence.
BBC logo copyright © BBC 2005
Radio 4 logo copyright © Radio 4 2011

10 9 8 7 6 5 4 3 2 1

Typeset by JCS Publishing Services Limited

Printed and bound in Europe

A CIP record for this book is available from the British Library

ISBN: 978-1-78028-966-3

www.watkinspublishing.com

Publisher's Note: Scripts may not be exactly as broadcast, but are always substantially so.

Contents

Foreword

by Bishop James Jones

There's a spiritual instinct in us all, and very few people do not at some stage in their lives find themselves praying, in one form or another. Often, it's a crisis that brings us to our knees. But sometimes it's the sheer joy of being alive that makes us want to find someone to thank for our good fortune.

I love *Prayer for the Day*. You never quite know where the day's chosen prayer will take you. There's a serendipity about it, and I'm often surprised by the prayer's relevance not just to the day's events but also to my own personal life.

The programme suits early-risers like myself. I catch it as I surface from slumber and lie there, half-asleep and half-awake, while my soul catches up with my body. But this book is also for those whose body clock works differently! If you're not up in time for the radio broadcasts, these pages show you what you're missing.

All religions teach us about praying. Whatever else they tell us about the mysteries of life, they all agree that to be human is to pray. The prayers and reflections in this collection are geared to equip us to face whatever life throws at us each day. They give us words to respond to the vagaries of being alive. They connect us to our common world, at the same time lifting us above it to become a little less attached and slightly more objective about our circumstances. And, in doing so, we begin to discern some values and principles of universal application.

I often pray aloud when I'm out walking. With the proliferation of mobile phones and earpieces, the whole world now looks as if it's talking to itself, so I don't feel quite so self-conscious! But people have been praying aloud for generations. In fact, it was when the disciples of Jesus heard him praying out aloud that they asked him to teach them how to do it. He famously told them to start their prayers by calling on God as Father. Now, that's not an easy concept if you've had a bad experience of fatherhood. But what Jesus was driving at was that, at the heart of creation, there is not just a force but a being capable of love.

When you think about the greatest gifts we have as creatures, it is to love and to be loved. Presumably the one that made us can do what we can do, so it's not such a giant leap to believe that the Creator can also love and be loved.

This is what gives our praying such beauty: the thought that the one with whom we are communing might not only hear us but love us and want the best for us.

That's not always easy to believe, especially in a world that can appear so random and destructive. I heard one writer say that faith is like holding on to a length of string that disappears up into the clouds and every now and again tugs a little.

You might just find that the prayers in these pages get the string tugging a little. If they do, they'll have done their job.

The Right Reverend James Jones was Bishop of Liverpool from 1998 to 2013, and Bishop of Hull from 1994 to 1998. He chaired the Hillsborough Independent Panel, and he speaks, writes and broadcasts on a range of issues, including the environment, ethics in business, regeneration and faith and its impact on the future.

January 1

Leslie Griffiths

The slate is clean and all's to play for. 'Ere we go, 'ere we go, 'ere we go. A new year stretches out ahead of us and we have no way of knowing quite what it's going to contain. It's a time for making resolutions, promising ourselves and our loved ones that we'll make every effort in this new year of grace to pull our socks up and to get our act together. A lovely idea, though we all know how short-lived these declarations of intent can be.

Methodists begin the New Year with what we call a covenant service. We put our good intentions in a context where we remember the God who has always kept the promises he's made to us. Our New Year resolutions don't depend on our being strong enough to keep them, but are seen as a response to the unfailing and unfathomable love of our maker. So we make our commitments knowing that God will help us to keep them. 'I am no longer my own,' we'll say, 'but Yours. Your will, not mine, be done in all things, wherever You may place me, in all that I do and in all that I may endure; when there's work for me and when there's none; when I'm troubled and when I'm at peace. Your will be done when I'm valued and when I'm disregarded; when I find fulfilment and when it's lacking; when I have all things, and when I have nothing. I willingly offer all I have and am to serve You as and where you choose.'

Dear Lord, on this New Year's Day, we ask You to help us keep our promises and to hold fast to us in love, through Jesus Christ our Lord, Amen.

BROADCAST WEDNESDAY 1 JANUARY 2014

January 2

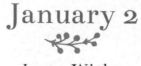

Jenny Wigley

This is the week that Christians celebrate the feast of the Epiphany, the visit of the Wise Men to present their gifts to the Christ-child. They are travellers who come from a place that *we* don't know – somewhere in 'the East' – to a place that *they* don't know – first to Jerusalem and then to Bethlehem, one the birth place and the other the royal seat of David, Israel's most celebrated king. But the Wise Men were in search of the future, not the past, seeking the one the carol calls 'Great David's greater son'.

For many pilgrims today, a place is made holy by its rootedness in the past. They kneel in reverence in a building like my own parish church, where God has been worshipped for centuries. It is, as TS Eliot says, a place 'where prayer has been valid'.

Or it can be the landscape itself that offers that experience – Bardsey Island, off the west coast of Wales, is said to be the burial place of 20,000 saints. It's what the Celtic Christians called a 'thin place', where the divine and natural worlds are so close together that we can catch a glimpse of God beyond the veil that elsewhere hides him from our sight.

The Celts used to say that heaven and earth are only three feet apart, but in the 'thin' places, the distance is much smaller. For the Wise Men in the Gospel story, heaven came so near that they could reach out and touch it. For Christians, God had come to earth in the form of a tiny babe.

Holy God, Your love enfolds us; You are before us and behind; You are the light that shines in our darkness. Hear our prayer that those who seek You may find You, and those who find You may rejoice in that knowledge always; in the name of Jesus Christ, who is the Way, the Truth and the Life. Amen.

BROADCAST SATURDAY 2 JANUARY 2010

January 3

Graham Forbes

It was pitch black. I could make out the beach — just — and could certainly hear the thundering surf beyond it. We were told we just had to watch and wait. And that's what we did. Being stranded on Ascension Island in June for four days was not part of the plan, but it did mean I got to know this volcanic outcrop, near the equator, miles from everywhere. We watched and waited. Then things began to happen. A shape appeared from the surf and began to struggle up the beach. The noise from above confirmed the arrival, as flocks of skua birds circled in anticipation of a meal.

The arrival was a mother turtle scraping her way up the beach and away from the Atlantic surf to lay her young. The sand was scooped away, the eggs laid, and then the exhausted mother tried to cover them and her tracks as the skuas flew closer and closer. This reptile did what mothers all over the world do: worked tirelessly to protect her young, regardless of the cost to herself.

There will be many mothers in all parts of the world today, waking up as we do, but fearful for their young and what this day will bring. In the days after the birth of her first child, Mary must have woken up fearful too — far from her home in Nazareth, confused by visits of shepherds and stories of angels in the pitch-black sky above Bethlehem.

All young mothers deserve a prayer this day.

Lord God, bless all mothers as they care for their newborn. Watch over them and protect them; and help us to see in every child the face of Your Son. Amen.

BROADCAST THURSDAY 3 JANUARY 2013

January 4

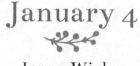

Jenny Wigley

According to the Gospel story, the Wise Men who came searching for Jesus had two guides: the star they'd followed from the East, and the holy books which the Jewish scribes consulted at the court of King Herod. The Messiah, they said, was to be born not in Jerusalem but in Bethlehem, for so it had been written by the Prophet.

For many people, such predictions are as strange and unnerving as the origins of the Wise Men themselves. And yet Christians claim their scriptures to be divinely inspired. 'Listen to the word of the Lord,' we often say in church at the end of a Bible reading. Perhaps we'd be clearer if we said 'listen *for* the word of the Lord', seeking to discern God's will in and through those ancient texts. For there's an ongoing conversation between the words on the page and those in the hearts and minds of those who listen to them.

There are so many ways of interpreting scripture, and Christians have not always agreed with one another about what principles to follow. And yet, we *are* agreed that the Bible is more than just of historical interest. In it we can discover how God wants his people to live their lives.

Christians are continually revisiting the scriptures, discovering how to hear God speaking to them in their own situation. So the stories of God's rescue of his people from slavery in Egypt, or from their exile in Babylon, have come to speak powerfully to those on the margins. These ancient texts have become 'founding documents' for those excluded by the prejudice of others against their race, class or gender. They have become words of power, as the scriptures continue to comfort and challenge all who 'listen for the word of the Lord'.

Lord God, You reveal Yourself anew to every generation; help us to trust in Your promises, that in the written word and through the spoken word we may come to see the Living Word, our Lord and Saviour Jesus Christ. Amen.

BROADCAST MONDAY 4 JANUARY 2010

January 5

Andrew Graystone

Today – or at least this evening – is Twelfth Night, the twelfth day of Christmas and the end of the season's festivities. Some people may already have taken the Christmas decorations down and settled back into their normal routines. But, traditionally, today was marked with one last bout of feasting and mischief-making, with all social roles and behavioural norms temporarily suspended before the cold realities of the New Year finally kicks in. Shakespeare's comedy *Twelfth Night* was written for this feast, with its carnival of fun, laughter and practical jokes, mixed with a dash of cruelty and insanity.

The 21st-century descendant of this unbridled madness is probably the office Christmas party. And there will be more than a few people who will be looking back ruefully to the pre-Christmas revelries as they head back to work after a long Christmas break.

The upside-downness of Twelfth Night has theological roots. It's a declaration that at the first Christmas God was born a baby, kings knelt down in a stable and so all heaven and earth was turned on its head. It's madness of course – scandal even – and fully deserves all the opprobrium of rationalists. But if it's true, then it's divine madness that will send us into the day laughing in the knowledge that wise men can be fools, the poor can be rich, and God who sometimes seems so distant is actually as close as a breath away.

God incarnate, we thank You again for this season of Christmas. Today, as I pull my suit out of the cupboard and head back to the office, help me to carry in my heart some transforming sense of the joyful, revolutionary madness of Your incarnation, for Jesus's sake. Amen.

BROADCAST MONDAY 5 JANUARY 2009

January 6

Sharon Grenham-Thompson

Many of you will have heard the song 'Bless this House', written by Helen Taylor and May Brahe. Published in 1927, it's been recorded by a number of artists including Perry Como and Dame Vera Lynn. The opening lines are: 'Bless this house, O Lord, we pray, make it safe by night and day.'

Our homes are where we're supposed to feel safe and secure. Sadly, there are many people of all ages for whom 'home' is a dangerous and unhappy place. The very British notion of our house being our 'castle' — a firmly segregated stronghold — has its good and bad sides. It's good for us to have a measure of privacy, shutting out the world after a long and difficult day; but on the other hand, we're reluctant to be seen as interfering, so we don't get involved with our neighbours or colleagues and maybe miss the signs that all's not well.

In Western Christianity, today is the feast of the Epiphany. It's the day when the Wise Men are traditionally supposed to have arrived at the house of Mary and Joseph after their long search for the child Jesus. They brought their gifts and knelt before the Infant King, recognizing in him the Light of the World.

There are some ancient customs associated with this festival, but perhaps one of the best is the tradition of 'blessing the house' on Epiphany night. Members of the household gather, light a candle and walk around the house saying prayers, asking for love and light, peace and comfort to reign in their home.

Lord, may those gifts be granted to our homes today, as the Light of the World shines in — and even more so to those who are struggling behind closed doors. Amen.

BROADCAST TUESDAY 6 JANUARY 2015

January 7

Bishop Angaelos

Today, many Christians throughout the Middle East who still follow the ancient Julian calendar will be celebrating the birth of Christ, who chose to be born of a simple family in a humble manger. He was not born in a palace, or surrounded by servants of the angelic host, but shared the life that many Christians still live this very day.

For their part, the many thousands who will spend today in refugee camps or in war-torn villages and cities will remember with particular significance that the Infant Christ literally did not have a place to lay His head.

Whether it be our sisters and brothers in Syria, the Palestinian territories, Libya, Egypt or elsewhere in the Middle East, they will have to contend with matters that for us will occupy a three-minute slot on today's news, but for them is the reality of their lives.

During a season when the more privileged are focusing on gifts and feasts, it will be good to remember those for whom the most significant gift today, besides the birth of the Incarnate Word, is the hope that they may be able to wake up healthy and still surrounded by their families and whatever remains of their communities.

We remember all those in the many communities of the Middle East whose lives have been torn apart by war and violence, praying peace and comfort upon them all, and that the spirit of joy will enter into their hearts, homes and communities. Amen.

BROADCAST MONDAY 7 JANUARY 2013

January 8

Sharon Grenham-Thompson

This coming weekend the Christian Church celebrates the festival of the Baptism of Christ. Jesus was baptized as an adult by his cousin John, and as he came up out of the water he was named by God, speaking from heaven: 'This is my beloved Son.'

The giving of a name (usually at birth), and all the rituals that go with it, is a universal human experience. A name marks us out as an individual (even if millions share the same one!), and gives us our place in a family and in society.

The now receding practice of giving a prisoner a number and using only that instead of a name is deeply symbolic of the separation and broken relationship with the community as a result of crime – think of Jean Valjean in *Les Misérables*: 'prisoner 24601'.

In the course of my ministry as a prison chaplain I've met a number of prisoners who not only have a number but have also had to change their name. Sometimes this is because of their notoriety and the crimes they've committed, and sometimes it's because they've given information to the authorities and need to be protected. I remember regularly visiting one man over the course of several months and gradually learning his story. The reasons for his name change were totally understandable, but there was no doubt it had a profound effect on him, cutting him off from his sense of his place in the world and who he was. It was enormously moving when, shortly before his release, he told me his real name.

So, Heavenly Father, help us remember that You've called each of us by name, knowing us inside out, so precious are we to You. With that knowledge lodged in our hearts, may we treat each other with dignity and care. Amen.

BROADCAST THURSDAY 8 JANUARY 2015

January 9

Krish Kandiah

Right now, parents and carers around the country are trying to grab a few more precious moments of sleep before they're dragged kicking and screaming into consciousness by a child desperate to go out into the cold and do some kicking and screaming of their own. While most of us are still in our pyjamas, there is a dedicated minority who have an icy start to the day, struggling to keep warm on a touchline.

I've seen some of the benefits of early morning football training with my birth children, but it was with one particular foster son that I really witnessed the transforming power of sport. He'd had a difficult start to life and struggled with almost everything — concentrating, coordinating, anxiety attacks, poor eyesight, socializing and behaviour. I took him to burn off some energy, and as the coaches invested time and attention in him, he grew in confidence and self-esteem — precious things for a young footballer likely to spend his entire childhood in the care system.

Unlike Bill Shankly, I'm not convinced that football is more serious than life or death, but I do believe sport can be a force for good in the world. For my foster son, sport was the stage for kind words to be spoken. Sport was the social context to receive a rare pat of affirmation, a cheer of celebration or an embrace of commiseration.

But praise needn't be confined to a cold field on a Saturday morning. Let's kickstart a new habit in life-building affirmation and practice today, commending those we rub shoulders with.

Lord God, father to the fatherless, protector of widows and orphans, awaken us today to the opportunities to offer kindness and hope in the lives of those around us. Amen.

BROADCAST SATURDAY 9 JANUARY 2016

January 10

Richard Hill

'On and after the 10th of January a letter, not exceeding half an ounce in weight, may be sent from any part of the United Kingdom to any other part, for one penny if paid when posted, or for two pence if paid when delivered.' These regulations of 1840 mark the birth of the universal postal service that we take for granted.

Sadly, in 2015, handwritten letters are becoming a thing of the past. We now live in a world of emails and social media; more often than not, post means packages and packets that we have ordered over the internet.

I penned a thank-you letter in my spidery script to a friend who had helped me with some work last year: I wanted him to know I'd not simply asked someone to input it for me. He sent me a reply message on social media. He said he was delighted to receive a handwritten letter, he didn't think anyone did that anymore!

Perhaps we should. My emails are regularly archived, but there's something permanent and tangible in having the physical copy in original handwriting. I still treasure my late father's last letter to me sent in 1989 when a 1st-class stamp was 19 pence.

Much of the New Testament consist of letters. Love letters, thank-you letters, letters recording events and letters of warning. Copied and recopied still, evidence of the art with which they were written remains.

At the end of one letter, St Paul writes: 'see what large letters I write with my own hand'. He has taken the pen from the scribe and makes his mark to make his point: this is from me and it matters.

Heavenly Father, in our world of changing and ever faster communications, help us to know and by every means share the permanence of Your love. Amen.

BROADCAST SATURDAY 10 JANUARY 2015

January 11

Michael Ford

January can be a difficult month; one when we find ourselves confronting spells of outer and inner darkness.

With tougher screening at airports and unemployment expected to peak at 2.8 million, many will have to face radical changes to their lives this year. Some may already be coping with other forms of loss — finding themselves bereft after losing a partner, family members or friends, or facing serious illness or perhaps sight problems that will seriously affect their lifestyles during the year, while some older members of society will have to give up their homes to receive full time nursing care.

It's natural and proper to feel compassion for those on the losing end, and yet, in the spiritual life, less is always *more*. It's a paradox I first learned as a young newspaper reporter when my copy was subbed back to make it have more impact; and it's one I'm more conscious of as I grow older. The 13th-century German mystic Meister Eckhart once said that God isn't found in the soul by adding anything, but by a process of subtraction. Perhaps this is why we sometimes feel closer to God through silence or simple monastic chant than in wordy church services.

The late film director Anthony Minghella once told me that he was drawn to Quarr Abbey on the Isle of Wight because it was simultaneously a place of austerity and of beauty. There was little decoration but great attention had been paid to the brick, which provided warmth and welcome. There, too, less was more.

Let us pray for all those facing diminishment of one kind or another at the start of this year. As they embrace their personal difficulties and disappointments, may they discover inner resources and riches from which to uphold their dignity and live each day in trust and hope. Amen.

BROADCAST MONDAY 11 JANUARY 2010

January 12

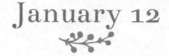

Nick Papadopulos

One of my most hotly anticipated Christmas presents was the DVD box set of a television series that I enjoyed in the mid-'80s. It hasn't disappointed.

I've been relieved to discover that, despite the irrefutable arrival of middle age, my memory is still in reasonable working order. Characters and plots, even specific lines, are as I remember them. And I've been relieved to discover that my sense of humour hasn't morphed beyond recognition. The jokes still make me laugh out loud.

And yet, watching a series I last saw 25 years ago, I've noticed changes too. It's not just that the cars, clothes and hairstyles are often hilariously different. It's not just that the actors all look much younger. It's that the stories provoke reactions in me that I don't think they did then. An account of a failed relationship; a depiction of a dysfunctional team; the development of an unlikely friendship: all these have an impact on a viewer who has experienced them that is different from their impact on a viewer who has not.

My Christmas present has given me a glimpse of who I am and of who I am not. Twenty-five years have passed like the blinking of an eye. I am who I was then. And yet I am different – a tiny bit wiser, perhaps; a little more forgiving, I hope; and possessing just a few more shreds of compassion.

God, You are our beginning and our end and in You we live and move and have our being. Affirm in us those things that are good, perfect in us those things that need perfecting and help us become the people You long for us to be. Amen.

BROADCAST THURSDAY 12 JANUARY 2012

January 13

Richard Hill

Today is the birthday of Michael Bond, the celebrated children's author and creator of Paddington Bear.

I was one of those children who adored his Paddington books when growing up, which explains why I loved the Paddington Bear trail in London last year: 50 Paddington statues in prominent positions close to museums and key landmarks. Each bear was created by an artist, a designer or a celebrity. I was sorry when it finished at the end of December.

As people queued to take their selfies, the idea that a Peruvian immigrant bear got a warm, friendly welcome seemed quite believable.

The reality for some migrants here in parts of Northern Ireland is quite different. No welcome. Told to leave. Their property attacked.

The Bible tells us that Mary and Joseph fled with Jesus into Egypt after Epiphany. It is silent on what happened there, but apocryphal legends captured in Italian paintings tell us how, on the way, dragons bowed, lions and leopards adored, palm trees bent down to give them dates and the journey was miraculously shortened. Stories and legends have a neat way of idealizing and sanitizing the reality of what it is like to be an outsider.

In the Old Testament book of Leviticus it says, 'When a stranger lives with you in your land, don't take advantage of him. Treat the foreigner the same as a native. Love him like one of your own. Remember that you were once foreigners in Egypt.'

Lord God, we were separated from You and You came and sought us. We were outsiders but You prepared a place for us and made us welcome. Help us to reflect Your welcome in our lives. Amen.

BROADCAST TUESDAY 13 JANUARY 2015

January 14

Mark Coffey

As a teacher I seem to be on a treadmill of report writing. Glowing reports cluttered with compliments are the easy ones to polish off. It's finding the words to give a tactful kick up the backside that takes the time. Yet help is at hand in the published reports of the great and the good of the past. Philosopher AJ Ayer's form master from Eton wrote on his report: 'A bumptious, aggressive, difficult boy too pleased with his own cleverness.' Paddy Ashdown's games teacher remarked that he was 'a good fellow, if a bit excessively Irish at times.'

One report written in the school I presently teach at – The Manchester Grammar School – dates back to 1946. 'Though he seems to view his schoolmasters with amused and Olympian contempt,' wrote the boy's form master, 'the present illusion of superior mind is usually shattered by a display of abominable ignorance. He is a lazy observer and lazy in acquiring the solid factual foundations of knowledge.' The pupil was a certain John Polanyi. He went on to be a Nobel Prize-winning chemist.

When I began as a teacher, they had a phrase: 'Catch them being good.' It meant, don't write any student off. Don't blame and anticipate failure. Expect and encourage achievement. It can become a self-fulfilling prophecy. And you never know, it might be their surgical scalpel I fall under, or their political whims that govern the country in my retirement.

So it's important to praise loudly - and blame softly.

Gracious God, slow to anger, abounding in love, thank You that You treat us with compassion and not as our sins deserve. Help us this day to be eager to encourage and slow to point the finger of blame. Amen.

BROADCAST MONDAY 14 JANUARY 2008

January 15

Gordon Gray

It was the title that grabbed my attention: 'Joy Unspeakable in an Unspeakably Joyless World' — an article by a black American female theologian in a journal that arrived in my first post of the New Year. 'An unspeakably joyless world!' — well, that fits, I thought, as the news brought the same sad stories: Iraq; Somalia; global warming; trolley-waits in local hospitals. 'Joyless' indeed. But it was the original source of the quotation that really surprised me: George Bernard Shaw, just over a hundred years ago! But he was reflecting positively on where 'joy' is to be found in such a world as his — and ours! So where is unspeakable joy to be found in an unspeakably joyless world?

This is the true joy of life, Shaw wrote, 'of being used up for a purpose recognized by yourself as a mighty one, being a force of nature instead of a feverish, selfish little clot of ailments and grievances, complaining that the world will not devote itself to making you happy. I am of the opinion that my life belongs to the community, and so long as I live, it is my privilege to do for it what I can.'

Jesus invited people to follow him as individuals and so find 'life in all its fullness'. But he brought them into a community of shared faith and common aims: the Church. True joy in this world is to be found, not in selfish isolation, but in the giving of that self to others and to God.

Lord God, lead me today beyond the suffocating boundaries of my own self interest, that I may find joy in others. Amen.

BROADCAST MONDAY 15 JANUARY 2007

January 16

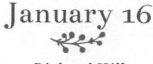

Richard Hill

On 16 January 1920, the United States introduced the nationwide constitutional ban on the sale, production, importation and transportation of alcoholic beverages. We know it better as 'Prohibition'.

The unintended consequences were enormous: the rise of the Mafia and organized crime; widespread corruption in the police forces in every large city in the US; the courts overwhelmed.

Winston Churchill visited the US during Prohibition. He's reputed to have said that Prohibition 'is an affront to the whole history of mankind'. While in New York, he was involved in a car accident and subsequently secured a prescription which reads, 'This is to certify that the post-accident convalescence of the Hon. Winston S Churchill necessitates the use of alcoholic spirits especially at meal times.'

Widespread use of medical permissions made a mockery of Prohibition.

We do, I think, need to take care how we use our freedoms and how we curtail the freedoms of others. I know I find the idea of grace more compelling than compulsion of law. I understand that we need both.

St Paul says, 'It is absolutely clear that God has called you to a free life. Just make sure that you don't use this freedom as an excuse to do whatever you want to do and destroy your freedom. Rather, use your freedom to serve one another in love; that's how freedom grows.'

Heavenly Father, we take our freedoms for granted. We do not pause often to consider the unintended consequences of our words or deeds. Teach us how to use the freedom You have given wisely and graciously. Amen.

BROADCAST FRIDAY 16 JANUARY 2015

January 17

Andrew Graystone

Eight hundred years ago this week, King John was holed up in the Temple Church off Fleet Street in London. He was under intense pressure from the barons of England to recommit himself to the values of the Coronation Charter, which essentially placed limits on the King's powers and providing some basic rights for individuals, especially the barons themselves.

The idea that the King was anything other than supreme was distinctly unattractive to John. And he might well have taken comfort in this from his reading of the Bible. On a superficial reading it seems to place great weight on the authority of kings and on the subjection of commoners. In the Old Testament, many kings were directly appointed by God and anointed by his prophets, and even the bad kings seemed to rule with God's blessing.

But there's another side to the story — a side that the barons pressed but John was less willing to hear. The Old Testament prophets consistently railed against those kings who used their power for self-aggrandisement or to oppress the poor. Above all, it was to be recognized that God was King of Kings and Lord of Lords.

The Bible's understanding of kingship has resonance for any one of us who exercises leadership; whether we're a king or queen in our own workplace, community, business or family.

King of Kings and Lord of Lords, where we have power over the lives of others by virtue of our wealth or talents or position, give us grace to exercise that power with care and compassion, knowing that all authority comes from You. Amen.

January 18

Mark Coffey

A story is told of a bitter feud between two noble families of medieval Ireland, the Butlers of Ormond and the FitzGeralds of Kildare.

Fleeing from Earl FitzGerald's soldiers, the nephew of the Earl of Ormond took sanctuary in the chapter house of St Patrick's Cathedral in Dublin. Surrounding him, FitzGerald had the upper hand, yet he wished to end the bloody feud peaceably. He pleaded with his enemy through the chapter house's oak door, but since the nephew suspected treachery, all negotiations were rejected. FitzGerald then ordered his soldiers to cut a hole in the centre of the door, thrusting his arm through it to shake hands. With heavily armed men inside, it was a risky venture. The nephew however, shook his hand in friendship and ended the dispute.

This 'Door of Reconciliation' is on display in the Cathedral to this day. Beside it are the words of Paul in his second letter to the Corinthians: 'God was reconciling the world to Himself in Christ. And He has committed us to the message of reconciliation.' In any conflict we can lock ourselves up behind walls of past hurts or resentment or have the courage to chance our arm in peacemaking. Jesus taught his own disciples to take up their cross daily and follow him. He knew to his cost the realities of speaking peace to a violent world. It may be in the politics of the workplace, the rage of the road, domestic disputes or long-standing grudges, but the work of reconciliation is all around us.

Prince of peace, may we find in You the strength to avoid fuelling conflicts and to forgive. Amen.

BROADCAST FRIDAY 18 JANUARY 2008

January 19

Johnston McKay

Some years ago now, when I was a producer in religious broadcasting, I took three leading churchmen to the Holy Land. John was a Roman Catholic priest, Richard an Episcopalian bishop and Gilleasbuig a Church of Scotland minister. We were all friends, and we arrived in Jerusalem on a Saturday afternoon. I was anxious to get on with recording but I was aware my colleagues might want to go to worship the next day. So as dinner ended, I asked them anxiously if they wanted to go to church the next morning. Gilleasbuig asked if John, the Roman Catholic priest, would give us communion in his room the next morning. Priests aren't officially allowed to give Communion to those who aren't Catholics, but immediately he agreed, gathered up the remains of a bread roll, took what was left in his glass of wine and we all went off to bed.

At eight o'clock the next morning we all perched on the edge of Father John's bed, beside the crumpled bedclothes. He read a passage from the Bible, talked a wee bit about it and then led us through the mass, the Holy Communion, the Eucharist, the Lord's Supper, call it what you will, and we shared the stale bread roll and the dregs of wine.

It was the most real act of worship I have ever attended. And what made it real was that, although it was intensely moving, none of us said so. We simply went down to breakfast and went out to start recording. Christian faith for me isn't about spiritual 'highs', it's what quietly sustains me as I get on with what I have to do.

I think of that moment at this time of year, for this is the Week of Prayer for Christian Unity. I've seen it and it works.

Loving God, show us how to bring all together in the one Kingdom of Yours, where no sword is known but the sword of truth and no strength known but the strength of love. Amen.

BROADCAST WEDNESDAY 19 JANUARY 2011

January 20

Richard Frazer

Slavery is a curse on humanity that has not entirely gone away. Human trafficking, enforced prostitution and mental imprisonment still happen today, even here in Britain.

Solomon Northup was a free man who lived quietly in upstate New York until he was lured away and sold into slavery. His story is told in the film *12 Years a Slave*, a visceral and heart-rending account of the extent to which slavery harmed all who were caught up in it. Not only were slaves brutally treated, slave owners descended to a shocking level of depravity in order to maintain the system.

On this day in 2009, Barack Obama was inaugurated as President of the United States. At his inauguration he spoke about how his own father would have been barred from many public places even a generation ago. The idea of an African American rising to the heights of Presidency was almost unthinkable until recently.

So much has been achieved but much still needs to be done. Our own freedom actually depends on the liberation of others. That is what Northup's story tells us.

When Nelson Mandela became President of South Africa, he reserved a special place at the inauguration for his jailers. His liberation was also theirs.

The legacy of slavery and oppression lingers on, haunting us with a cruel past that disfigured all those involved. Working to overcome slavery and oppression will make better people of all of us.

Lord Jesus Christ, you were cruelly beaten as a prisoner and executed as an innocent man; and yet you spoke words of forgiveness from the cross. Teach us the grace that enlarges our humanity and remakes the world. Amen.

BROADCAST MONDAY 20 JANUARY 2014

January 21

Leon Litvack

Today is the anniversary of the death of George Orwell, the famed author of *Animal Farm*. This is an allegorical text in which the animals adopt seven commandments to distinguish themselves from humans. These include 'All animals are equal' and 'No animal shall kill any other animal.' Later, however, their leaders change them, manipulating language and situation to suit their own selfish ends. So some animals would become 'more equal than others', and they are not to be killed 'without cause'!

I like what Orwell does in this book. He's playfully and insightfully recalling the Seven Laws of Noah — a set of moral imperatives for all humankind. There is the establishment of a court of law and prohibitions against idolatry, murder, theft, immorality, blasphemy and eating live animals. These precepts are embedded not only in the Ten Commandments, but also in the 613 commandments, or *mitzvot* in Hebrew, that Jewish people are expected to perform — some daily, others on special occasions in their lives.

Many *mitzvot* entail the performance of good deeds — charity, for example, or the visiting of the sick. We don't expect material recompense for these actions; but one *mitzvah* brings another in its train. Indeed, the *Ethics of the Fathers* (a central Jewish text) counts acts of loving-kindness as one of the three pillars upon which the world stands.

O Lord, God of all, help us to live up to the standards we set ourselves. Give us insight into the needs and concerns of all whom we meet this day. Make us conscious of our obligations, and how they can add richness and meaning to our lives. Amen.

BROADCAST SATURDAY 21 JANUARY 2012

January 22

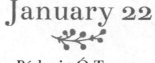

Pádraig Ó Tuama

When I was a school chaplain an 11 year old once said to me: 'I have one important question for you, and I'd like you to answer. I know that God loves us and God made us, but I want to know why God made Protestants.'

This was a Catholic child from West Belfast. The story of a people is present in the question of a child.

I asked her what she meant and why she wanted to ask it, and she said that she'd heard that Protestants hate God and hate Catholics.

She was easily put right. She was magnificent at football and I told her that every Protestant I knew would want her on their team, and she was delighted at the thought.

But still. The story of a people is present in the question of a child.

Joe Liechty and Cecelia Clegg, two researchers from the Irish School of Ecumenics have described sectarianism as 'belonging gone bad'. This girl came from a lively and thriving community, yet somehow that belonging had, for a while, taught her terrible untruths about those who were different. Where else has belonging gone bad in our society today?

Often it seems like we need to make one identity superior to others; it seems like the borders of belonging can be more hostile than necessary.

In Irish, there's a phrase: 'It is in the shelter of each other that the people live.' The word 'shelter' in Irish can also mean 'shadow'. Belonging can turn both beautiful and bad.

God of all belonging, help us see beyond the borders of our belonging so that we might see beauty in faces as yet unfamiliar to us. Amen.

BROADCAST THURSDAY 22 JANUARY 2015

January 23

Calvin Samuel

I grew up in Antigua, a tiny island in the Caribbean. Measuring 14 miles at its longest point and 11 miles at its widest, its coastline includes 365 white sandy beaches, one for each day of the year.

However, I live in Durham in the northeast of England, which also boasts a coastline of white sandy beaches, a number of which are stunning. Unless you know these two locations, you have no idea how much they have in common.

The similarities run deeper than coastlines. The population of Antigua is around 80,000. Coincidentally, the population of the city of Durham is of a similar order.

Perhaps precisely because of this small population, the cultural distance between people of the northeast of England and people of the eastern Caribbean is not as great as you might think. Though less ethnically diverse than Manchester or London, where I have previously lived, the northeast feels far more like home to me. We even speak the same language of cricket, for heaven's sake! Perhaps best of all, I grew up in Antigua's capital city, St John's, and the name of the Durham college in which I work each day is also St John's.

What is the point of this comparison? Durham and Antigua seem unlikely bedfellows. Yet once you get beyond obvious differences, it is possible to find common ground. One obvious difference is the temperature: Antigua is 30 degrees warmer than Durham! In this Week of Prayer for Christian Unity, may we too find common ground.

Merciful God, forgive us when we fail to recognize in the other that there is more that binds us together than keeps us apart. Help us to see in the one who is different from us, one who is equally a child of God. Amen.

BROADCAST WEDNESDAY 23 JANUARY 2013

January 24

Leon Litvack

Anyone who thinks of Britain's role in World War II will immediately mention Sir Winston Churchill, who died on this day in 1965. His political career began in 1900, when he was just 25. By that time, he bragged, he had written 'as many books as Moses'.

Churchill was fascinated with Moses, and wrote about him in 1931 for the *Sunday Chronicle*. He took issue with those who believed that Moses was only an allegorical figure. He added: 'We believe that the most scientific view ... will find its fullest satisfaction in identifying one of the greatest human beings with the most decisive leap forward ... in the human story.' He meant, of course, the Exodus from Egypt. Churchill also praised Jewish monotheism and the ethical code transmitted at Mount Sinai. These, Churchill said, were central factors in the development of modern civilization.

Jewish ethics derive first and foremost from the Torah, the Hebrew Bible. We transcend our limited natural vision and aspire to perfection. In the Torah it's not sufficient that we don't harm others: we're also obliged to assist our fellow human beings, because that's our higher mission, given by God, the basis of all morality. Churchill disagreed that it was easier for the ancient Israelites to feel God's presence, and hence the force of His moral code, than it is for us. They were, he said, 'not so very different from ourselves', and they communicated their impressions across the centuries 'with far more accuracy than many of the ... accounts we read of the goings-on of today'.

God and God of our ancestors, make us understand our higher goals and aspire to perfection, guided by You, who were there at the beginning, and will be, always. Amen.

BROADCAST TUESDAY 24 JANUARY 2012

January 25

Julia Neuberger

It's Burns Night tonight, held in honour of Scotland's most famous poet, Robert Burns. There will be Burns Night suppers all around Scotland to celebrate, with whisky, haggis and poetry readings. And, if it's the full thing, participants will be piped in with the bagpipes and then say the 'Selkirk Grace' attributed to Burns: 'Some hae meat and canna eat,/ And some wad eat that want it; / But we hae meat, and we can eat / Sae let the Lord be thankit.' Then there's the food, followed by speeches, and then people perform works by Burns, before it all ends with everyone singing 'Auld Lang Syne', which may not have been written by Burns at all!

It's a great evening and a great celebration. It's a celebration of Scottishness. It's a celebration of traditions, including food. And it makes people feel good about themselves, mostly Scots, though others are often invited to join in. Its strongest attraction is that it binds people with a sense of community, not exclusive but warm and welcoming, and allows them to do more than just have a meal together – important though that is. There's much to be said for celebratory dinners, and even more if they draw in people who are often forgotten. So let's celebrate more often, invite more people for dinner and give them a chance to eat, drink and be merry – and be part of something that makes them proud of who they are, whether they be Scots, Irish, English, Welsh, Jewish, Christian, Muslim or whoever …

May we use the example of Burns Night to reach out, proud of our identity, to others who are proud of theirs, and share some traditions with each other in our busy lives. Amen.

BROADCAST MONDAY 25 JANUARY 2016

January 26

Edward Kessler

Confucius told his disciple that three things are needed for government: weapons, food and trust. If a ruler can't hold on to all three, he should give up the weapons first and the food next. Trust should be guarded to the end, as 'without trust, we cannot stand'. Politicians, economists, philosophers and sociologists have all recently commented on the decline of trust. It is time to add a religious voice to the conversation.

There is a general perception that trust has declined, which particularly gathered momentum after the 2007 financial crisis and the (near) collapse of the banking sector. Some would say the financial markets lost sight of their moral duty and bad conduct (such as financial deception), and the failure of the banks to stay within the social (and moral) consensus have contributed to the decline in trust.

Although 'trust' is widely used in economics and finance, it is not primarily an economic or financial term. The key words in the markets are spiritual: 'credit' (from the Latin *credo* meaning 'I believe') and 'confidence' (meaning 'shared faith'). Indeed, United States coins bear the motto 'In God We Trust'.

Trust is relational: it cannot be commanded but needs to be given freely. And rebuilding a culture of trust requires good conduct.

This is the virtue of religion and is fulfilled by proper religious practice, which frees us from the tyranny of false gods — and there are many, including Mammon — that claim our attention. GK Chesterton famously said: 'When people stop believing in God, they don't believe in nothing, they believe in anything.'

Lord, help us strive to rebuild the trust our society so urgently needs. Amen.

BROADCAST MONDAY 26 JANUARY 2015

January 27

Leon Litvack

A story is told of how, after World War II, relief agencies scoured Europe in search of Jewish children who had been hidden by their parents with gentiles. In one case, an American rabbi called Eliezer Silver learned of a convent in Alsace-Lorraine in which a number of Jewish children were meant to be found. He approached the Mother Superior with his claim, and was told that there were only Christian orphans, all baptized, in her care.

Nevertheless, he insisted on seeing the children, who in some cases had been separated from their parents for more than five years, and would have had no opportunity to practise their Jewish faith. He was granted five minutes, just before bedtime. He entered the dormitory, and whispered softly in Hebrew 'Shema Yisrael' ('Hear O Israel'). At first he heard nothing, and so he whispered again, 'Shema Yisrael'. Suddenly he heard a child whimpering; he went over to the little bed, and said a third time, 'Hear O Israel', and a small, broken voice answered 'Adonai Eloheinu, Adonai Echad' ('The Lord is our God, the Lord is one'). He heard the same response from across the room, and so confirmed that some of these children were in fact Jewish. He was allowed to leave with these child victims of the Holocaust, who eventually made their way to Israel.

Today is Holocaust Memorial Day, which commemorates, among the many who died, one and a half million children of many faiths. We give thanks that in our day, in many parts of the world, children can live their lives without fear of being harmed for who they are, and are able to express themselves and their faiths in a free and open fashion.

Lord God of all, on this most solemn of days, hold dearly to Yourself the children, for in them is our brightest hope for a better future. Amen.

BROADCAST FRIDAY 27 JANUARY 2012

January 28

Edward Kessler

Bertrand Russell once said that if God exists, then He has written a detective story with all the clues pointing the wrong way.

I understand what he means.

Somehow you feel that the biggest thing there is ought to be visible in some way. Why, if God is there, is He so elusive?

Judaism is a religion of questions. The greatest prophets asked questions of God, and famously Job asked the most searching questions and God replied with a few questions of His own.

Abraham Twerski, the Harvard scholar, tells the story of his Polish teacher being delighted when he asked a good question. 'You are right,' he would be told, 'you are 100 per cent right and now I will tell you where you have gone wrong.'

Religious faith can be portrayed as naïve, blind and unquestioning. The philosopher asks but the believer just believes. Religious belief is too often seen as the suspension of critical intelligence. But few believers come to the position of faith without having asked the enduring questions of humanity. After all, what is the asking of a question if not itself a profound expression of faith in the meaning of human life? To ask is to believe there is an answer. Far from faith excluding questions, questions testify to faith.

When faith suppresses questions, it dies; when it accepts superficial answers, it begins to whither. Our faith is not opposed to questioning; what it is opposed to is the shallow certainty that we understand all there is.

By asking questions, we serve God. May a question asked in reverence be the start of a journey toward God. Kein Yehi Ratzon *— may this be God's will. Amen.*

BROADCAST FRIDAY 28 JANUARY 2011

January 29

Jonathan Wittenberg

In Jewish practice, one of the first blessings one says in the morning is for one's health: 'God, You formed the human being with wisdom, creating many passages. … If one is closed which should be open, or open which should be closed, it's impossible to rise and stand before You …'

I remember experiencing that impossibility. I was in a flower shop and bent down to pick up a rose. I simply couldn't straighten up again. For days I could scarcely walk. Whenever I needed the bathroom, I would wonder, 'How am I going to pull up my trousers?'

I'd always known that for millions of people such disabilities are a daily reality. But it was then that I began to think about it.

I admire the hourly courage and determination of those for whom getting up isn't rolling out of bed, but a whole sequence of actions which must be carefully thought through.

I respect those who support such people through attentive but not overbearing kindness. I honour those who care for them, and who uphold human dignity even when circumstances are trying.

If we're privileged to be healthy, we're liable to treat our bodies like familiar tools, taken for granted unless they go wrong, taken as a given until we grow old.

I remember the sadness of watching my first dog, once swift as the rabbits, grow too old to run. The truth is that life and health are wonderful but also fragile, temporary gifts.

God, teach us to use life and health well, for kindness and goodness, while we are privileged to have them.

BROADCAST TUESDAY 29 JANUARY 2013

January 30

Mark Beach

On this day in 1649, King Charles I was executed at the end of the Civil War. His belief in the divine right of kings had brought him into conflict with the emerging strength of Parliament. Perhaps he is best remembered in the van Dyck portrait which shows him as a flamboyant man, but he was also a man of deep faith whose convictions about the nature of monarchy were derived from his Christianity.

The conflict with Parliament was not his only disagreement. On his accession to the throne, Charles sided with those who wished the Church in England to revert to its more traditional, Catholic form in place of the Calvinist influence that had held sway for the previous century. The appointment of William Laud, a high churchman, as Archbishop of Canterbury was one mark of this.

The Civil War was only in part caused by Charles's ecclesiastical policies, but they certainly did not help. In end, however, it was his insistence on episcopacy which led to his death. Offered a deal by which he would allow the Church to lose its bishops, he refused. It is for this reason that some believe Charles to have been martyred for his faith.

Behind all this turmoil in public life, there lies a man of great personal faith whose actions, although they may not always have worked out as he intended, were nonetheless based on that faith.

Almighty God, we pray for those whose good intentions do not always result in good actions; and we pray that the choices we make today may be good in both intention and reality. Through Jesus Christ our Lord, Amen.

BROADCAST MONDAY 30 JANUARY 2012

January 31

YY Rubinstein

One of my favourite photographs was taken in this very BBC building in Media City, Salford. Downstairs in the foyer sits a blue police telephone box or, as you probably know it, a 'tardis'. In case you ever wondered what that stands for, by the way, the answer is: 'Time And Relative Dimension In Space'. You know, Dr Who's time machine!

This summer I spent two weeks speaking at synagogues all over London, in my capacity as the official Jewish students Chaplain for the North West of England, serving 14 universities. It was a very tardis-like experience. As I moved from synagogue to synagogue, ex-students appeared in front of me as though they had just stepped out from that famous blue police phone box.

And it's a funny thing, but over 22 years I discovered that no matter what course my students undertook or qualification they achieved, whenever I met them ten years or so later, very few had actually forged a career relating to their subject.

A mathematician had become a stand-up comedian; a musician ran a charity to lend medical equipment to sick people. I even had one student with a PhD in philosophy who became a police sergeant!

Life likes to have its little joke: 'If you want to make God laugh ... tell Him your plans!'

One of my great teachers once told me something his father, who was a rabbi, used to say, which I have tried my best to make a part of who and what I am. 'It doesn't matter what anyone else says or does. As long as I can look at myself in the mirror and say I am a decent person, I did the right thing.'

Almighty, as life likes to have its little joke and things rarely turn out the way we thought they would, help us to be able to say those words and know that they are true, so whatever happens or comes along, it's we who will have the last laugh.

BROADCAST FRIDAY 31 JANUARY 2014

February 1

Simon Doogan

Happy St Brigid's Day.

Some say that Brigid's father was a chieftain, that her ancestry was princely; others that she received several good offers of marriage before taking the habit and becoming a nun.

But what seems indisputable is that when she renounced whatever pleasures were on offer in her 5th-century Irish world, Brigid embraced in their place a life of tireless and boundless charity

I'm old enough to remember the demise of the halfpenny copper coin. Its withdrawal was announced on this day in 1984 and there was widespread anxiety over whether prices would be rounded up or rounded down. It seems aeons ago now but concerns were very real at the time, especially over any effect on the retail price index and living standards for the poorest people in the country.

And if those concerns from 1984 sound familiar to you, it's probably because you heard them again when VAT went up at the start of January.

At any time of economic stringency, the first question for people of a moral and spiritual outlook is: 'Will this have a disproportionate effect on those who can least afford it?' 'If it will, then what can we do to help them?' becomes the second question, and the one answered so inspirationally by Brigid and those in every age who try to give and not to count the cost.

God of all grace, by Your Spirit You trouble us with the thought that holiness and sacrifice might be directly proportional: grant us opportunities this new day to discover that in giving away what we have, we learn something fundamental about Your love for us in Christ. Amen.

February 2

Mark Beach

Today is the feast of the Presentation of Christ in the Temple, and officially marks the end of Christmas, although I know that you packed away your decorations weeks ago in the fear of bad luck after Twelfth Night.

The Presentation marks the day on which Jesus was taken, by his parents, to the Temple in Jerusalem to be 'designated as holy before the Lord', as St Luke puts it in his Gospel.

In medieval Christianity, today was primarily regarded as a feast day of Mary, marking her purification after childbirth, and indeed the Book of Common Prayer commemorates it in this way.

More recent liturgical scholarship and practice have turned the focus, rightly in my view, to Jesus and to the words of Simeon, an old man who had waited in the Temple 'looking forward to the consolation of Israel' – again Luke's words.

Simeon took Jesus in his arms and praised God, asking to be allowed to 'depart in peace, for my eyes have seen your salvation'. Describing Jesus as a light to lighten the gentiles, he then turned to Mary and in an instant moved from incarnation to crucifixion – 'and a sword will pierce your own soul too'. And so not only does today mark the conclusion of our celebrations of Christmas, but it also points prophetically to Good Friday, to the cross and to Mary weeping as she watched her son die in agony and cruel torture.

Lord God, You are the source of everlasting light. Your Son Jesus was recognized by Simeon in the Temple and welcomed as the promised Messiah. May we see the glory of the Lord Jesus and shine with His light in the dark places of Your world. Amen.

BROADCAST THURSDAY 2 FEBRUARY 2012

February 3

Edwin Counsell

It's perhaps a basic human need to feel the touch of another person, whether that's an embrace or just a consoling arm around the shoulder. On this day in 1986, Pope John Paul II visited the refuge in Calcutta run by Mother Teresa and her nuns caring for some of the poorest of that city who were sick and dying. John Paul fed the hungry, consoled the sick and prayed over the dying, leading Mother Teresa to describe his actions as 'the touch of Christ'.

The care we extend to those in greatest need is both the most basic response and the highest calling of humanity, because it reflects the values we model as individuals and as a society. Caring for others can be a career choice for some or it can be a necessary task when a loved one is left vulnerable by disability, age or infirmity. It seems to me that caring for the poor, hungry and dispossessed is different, not because it requires any more or less generosity of body, mind or spirit, but because it can reflect the shortcomings of the world, with its cause so often rooted in inequality, injustice or inhumanity.

Mother Teresa made the service of the poor in Calcutta her life's work, while raising the profile of that work on the world's stage along with an expectation that the causes of poverty should be addressed by a global audience of wealthy nations. For those who were starving or near to death in her refuge 30 years ago, I doubt it mattered too much that they had a high-profile visitor on that day. It was the simple act of someone reaching out to hold, feed or comfort them that made a difference.

So, in our lives today, may we know the power of an act of generous kindness, in the embrace of a loved one, in a hand extended to a stranger or in the ongoing work to lift those most in need out of their poverty. Amen.

BROADCAST WEDNESDAY 3 FEBRUARY 2016

February 4

Edward Mason

I don't think I can recall another time in my life when money has been in the news so much. Throughout the day we're told about the FTSE and late at night, I'm reassured – or worried – to hear how Wall Street closed.

Now, I know these days of biting recession are tough. Many will feel vulnerable to redundancy, homes are under threat and income from savings is perilously low. It's tough out there – especially for someone whose source of income has actually dried up.

But, if we're not careful, money can dominate every moment and make us lesser human beings.

I once knew someone who would say, 'It's only money.' This usually came up when something important and costly had to be bought or paid for. We all know it can be hard – even for those of us that have enough – to write the cheques for kids' university fees, pay for a holiday or buy that birthday present. We can become quite stingy and only hand over the money grudgingly. So it's helpful to remind ourselves that 'it's only money' and that there are far more valuable things around.

In the Bible, there's a letter that St Paul wrote to people who were experiencing tough times. He says, 'Be joyful always, pray continually; give thanks in all circumstances.' He knew that being grateful – even in the tough times – puts us in touch with God and a better life.

So, Lord God, I thank You for giving me life today. Help me to foster good and loving relationships in my community and, if I start to let money become more important than people, help me to remember, 'It's only money.' Amen.

BROADCAST WEDNESDAY 4 FEBRUARY 2009

February 5

Sharon Grenham-Thompson

Today is my grown-up daughter's birthday, so she's very much on my mind this morning. Later this week she leaves for Beijing on a three-month secondment for work. When she was much younger, and away from me for any reason, we used to joke about the 'stretchy glue' that bound us together, however far apart we might be. I think the next few months will test the elasticity of that bond!

I have several friends whose children live on the other side of the world. And many of us know what it's like to be separated from our kids as a result of divorce. It's nearly always hard, for parents and offspring, but I'll never forget what my then mother-in-law said to me on the day my daughter was born. 'Remember,' she said, 'that this child doesn't belong to you – she's an individual in her own right. Your job is to love her and care for her, but it's also to help her to separate from you one day.'

The greatest gifts we can give our children are the ability to look after themselves, to negotiate the world with confidence, and to teach them that successful relationships are about helping one another and interdependence rather than expecting someone else to meet our every need.

Gradually learning to step back is a vital part of loving parenthood, whether it involves waving our child off at the airport, cooperating with the ex over contact arrangements, or maybe letting our kids make their own mistakes without immediately rushing in.

And so God who is Mother and Father to us all, we entrust our children to You. May we also understand that, even when we fear You are far away, Your bond with us, Your children, is never broken. Amen.

BROADCAST WEDNESDAY 5 FEBRUARY 2014

February 6

Clair Jaquiss

It took me a little while to get up to speed on how to behave at a football match. Where we sit, there's plenty of choice language, a great deal of advice shouted to various players and to the referee, and the occasional 'Well done, son!' We're not in the singing part of the ground, but it seems to be OK to join in some of the chants even if you're the only one on the row doing so.

When any group of people get together, there's custom and ritual — and football's no different. It takes you a while to learn the hymns, and then even I blush when I realize what the words are. We are supporters of a team but also have to learn who we 'hate'. There are historic reasons which go back into the mists of time. Of course, most people don't actually hate certain opposing teams, we only hate them in a football sense.

But there's another powerful collective memory which unites people, and today Manchester United supporters remember particularly the Munich air crash of 6 February 1958 when 21 people died including seven promising players on their way home from a European cup match. Among the banners spread out at the Stretford end is one that reads 'Flowers of Manchester. We will not forget.' It hangs there among the chants, the roars, the whistles and the groans. Loss is something we live with one way or another. Perhaps the raw nature of grief mellows, but not always; and remembering with others has some measure of reassurance and comfort. Football tragedies have their own particular poignancy, and football fans and their families grieve together and alone. In the midst of the questioning and bewilderment of grief, a prayer for today:

God who loves us, send down into our hearts that peace which the world cannot give, and keep us in love and charity. Amen.

BROADCAST FRIDAY 6 FEBRUARY 2015

February 7

Leslie Griffiths

On this day in 1964, the Beatles arrived in New York to scenes of indescribable excitement. Thousands of screaming teenagers were waiting for them. The security measures put in place were normally brought out when kings or presidents were in town. No kings in America, of course, but there was always Ed Sullivan holding court. The mop-headed Beatles appeared on his show not once but twice and hauled in the largest audiences ever. 'Beatlemania' was the word coined to describe all this – and that's exactly what it was. Just two years after this triumphal entry, John Lennon claimed the Beatles to be more popular than Jesus, a remark that caused uproar and gave the Ku Klux Klan an excuse to put on their witches' hats and come out hunting.

I'd only recently become a Christian at this time and I simply couldn't work out what all the fuss was about. It seemed obvious to me that, at least during his lifetime, Jesus couldn't hold a candle to the Beatles as far as popular support was concerned. Large numbers came to hear him from time to time but they soon melted away once they'd worked out what he was asking of them. He died with just a handful of his friends around him.

The crowds came later. Millions and millions of them. And his popularity has lasted not just centuries but millennia. That's the proper measure of his success. Looked at this way, even the most ardent Beatles' fan would surely want to qualify the comparison made by John Lennon all those years ago.

Dear Lord, help us to enjoy the accomplishments of contemporary culture and yet cling to the truths that have for so long upheld us through times of change and challenge. In the name of Jesus. Amen.

BROADCAST TUESDAY 7 FEBRUARY 2012

February 8

Richard Littledale

I can still remember the moment as if it were yesterday. My father came home from work, and as he turned to hang up his coat he had a big smile on his face. 'We're getting a new car,' he said. Now, we had replaced the car many times before, as us children had got bigger and bigger. We had never had a brand new car, though. The excitement was palpable as the smart new car in British racing green pulled onto the driveway.

We really long for truly new starts, don't we? The calendar year is barely 40 days old, yet resolutions are creaking under the onslaught of reality and it would be nice to wipe the slate clean. Or maybe we could be like the snake – shedding a skin every time it gets too tatty and sporting a shiny new one instead?

For some, today is the day to start again. It marks the start of the Chinese New Year – and this year is the Year of the Monkey. According to tradition, monkeys are witty, intelligent and have a magnetic personality – so this new year might suit some down to the ground. Many who will watch the traditional Chinese New Year celebrations may envy the prospect of beginning 2016 all over again.

The Christian faith is shot through with the idea of new beginnings, whether it is Noah stepping from the ark onto fresh soil, Saul blinking in the light and leaving his murderous past behind … or Jesus telling a puzzled cleric that he 'must be born again'. Always, always, the possibility of new beginnings is held out.

Dear God, let today be a day for new beginnings – be they great or small. Today, let the prospect of new possibilities outshine old regrets. Amen .

BROADCAST MONDAY 8 FEBRUARY 2016

February 9

Mark Coffey

'Fatigue,' said Benjamin Franklin, 'is the best pillow.' Apparently rats sleep for up to 14 hours a day, while elephants and giraffes need only three to four hours a night – that's an hour's less kip than Winston Churchill's reported average, though he was an advocate of the afternoon nap.

Aware that, by definition, one cannot consciously enjoy the sensation of sleeping, the philosopher Montaigne had his servant wake him in his chateau so that he could have a good go at it as he fell asleep all over again. Marcel Proust had the first part of his classic work *In Search of Lost Time* rejected by publishers for taking 30 pages to describe the observations of an insomniac trying to get to sleep. And the Bible even records one Eutychus falling out of a window as he dozed off during a sermon of St Paul. Fortunately, the apostolic prayers were heard and he recovered.

Neurological studies have observed volunteer sleepers in brain scanners, and there is some evidence to suggest that as the mind relaxes, a process of clearing up the clutter of our emotions from the previous day goes on. So there's every reason to cut the caffeine intake, get right away from the PC and relax with a good read, or even Radio 4, before you hit the hay. In our hectic world of apparently ever-increasing productivity, there's a wisdom in the words of Jesus who said 'Do not worry about tomorrow, for tomorrow will worry about itself. Each day has enough trouble of its own.'

Eternally watchful God who never sleeps or slumbers, we thank You for the gift of sleep; for its renewal and the reminder that, mercifully, there are limitations on the demands of each day. Amen.

BROADCAST TUESDAY 9 FEBRUARY 2010

February 10

Leslie Griffiths

When I first met Omar, he was a widower bringing up a teenage son all on his own. He felt the lack of a partner keenly and eventually wrote to his family in Pakistan to ask them to find him a wife. Soon he brought Mary, his new wife, back to London, and it was wonderful to see their happiness as they began this new and demanding chapter in their lives.

As Mary didn't speak a word of English, it was tough for both of them, though, and also for us as we tried to welcome her and make her feel at home. Within a year or so, Mary became a mother and it was the birth of little Sharon that marked a turning point in her life. She brought her child to our mums and toddlers group and she was able to relate to other young mothers. But it was when Sharon began to speak that we noticed a little miracle happening under our eyes. Almost from the beginning Sharon set her mind on helping her mother develop her language skills, first as her interpreter but then as her instructor. Sharon is now 12 and has younger siblings. She's interested in all the things children of that age like to do. But she's never lost her vocation to be her mother's teacher. And English is now no longer a problem for Mary. Brilliant. As Jesus reminded us, sometimes we learn the deepest things out of the mouths of babes and sucklings.

Dear Lord, open our eyes and our ears to sense the little miracles happening around us. Inspire us so that we may ourselves perform such deeds and bring happiness and gladness into the lives of the people we meet. We ask this in the name of Jesus, our Lord. Amen.

BROADCAST FRIDAY 10 FEBRUARY 2012

February 11

Mark Langham

The small hamlet of Lourdes lies in the foothills of the Pyrenees in southwestern France. Over the centuries it was much fought over – more than its size would warrant. But its real fame dates from 11 February 1858 when a 14-year-old girl claimed that a beautiful lady had appeared to her in a grotto near the town. That girl was Bernadette Soubirous, and today we celebrate the 150th anniversary of the apparitions of Mary that have made Lourdes one of the largest Catholic shrines in the world.

Whatever your thoughts about apparitions, there can be no doubt that Lourdes is a remarkable place. The numbers of sick who come to pray, and to bathe in what's traditionally regarded as the miraculous stream that rises near the grotto, make it a unique and moving experience. Some hope for physical healing; more desire *spiritual* health – healing of their spirit, a sense of closeness to God. And the presence of so many sick people makes Lourdes a powerful sign. As a healthy adult, I find myself on the outskirts at Lourdes, relatively unimportant. It is the sick, the frail, those who usually stand on the margins, who here are the most important and remain the centre of attention.

It's a wonderful vision of priorities turned upside down; perhaps a lesson in how the world should be.

Lord, may we stand aside to allow those who usually stand on the outskirts to be at the centre. Through their example, may we recognize Your blessings to us. Amen.

BROADCAST MONDAY 11 FEBRUARY 2008

February 12

Richard Littledale

By the time that many people hear this, they will have been woken by all manner of extraneous noises. It might have been a feline dispute in the road outside, a plane flying overhead or even the noise of the radio itself. Of all the sounds in the world, the hardest to ignore is a baby's cry. The survival of our species depends, quite literally, upon our inability to ignore it … we are hard-wired in such a way that we cannot let it go unchecked.

I want to spare a thought right now for those who would love to be woken by that sound. They are the people who long for their nights to be interrupted by a baby's cry or their days by the rhythm of a baby's life – feeding and changing and caring. Right now one in four pregnancies in the United Kingdom ends in early miscarriage or stillbirth. One quarter of those who long for the sound of their baby's cry do not get to hear it.

Last year, people started using the word 'miscourage' when talking about miscarriage – and I applaud the initiative. For too long the stigma of something unmentionable has been added to the considerable heartache of failing to carry a pregnancy full term. This should not be so, surely? And if talking about it helps, then the least the rest of us can do is listen.

There's a touching verse in the Psalms where David says that God has 'kept his tears in a bottle'. In other words, none of them have gone unnoticed. Could you let somebody talk who needs to today?

Dear God, we pray today for those who long to hear their baby's first cry, and those who are working to ensure that they can. Amen.

February 13

Mark Langham

There is nothing quite so frightening as an interview. I've done my fair share, and although most went well, no interview is ever anything less than terrifying. Some interviewers seem to take pleasure in watching you squirm, showing not a scintilla of emotion. You'd almost think they were enjoying it.

It's astonishing how easily a word, a gesture, can make the candidate feel either at ease or unsettled. A good interviewer will tell you that sometimes a candidate needs to be encouraged and sometimes challenged.

We've got to ask the same question of ourselves, in all honesty, as we stand before God. Does our faith encourage us or challenge us? Religion is sometimes portrayed as being afraid to confront, only a bland set of feel-good suggestions. At other times religion seems an unyielding set of demands that terrorize the faithful.

In this season of Lent, we experience in Jesus the true nature of our faith. Through his 40 days in the wilderness and his temptations, Jesus encourages us by being one of us; in his suffering, he walks with us in our troubles.

But then Jesus marches out of the wilderness and challenges his hearers, 'Repent! Do things differently!' Followers of Christ can never be content to remain where they are. There's work to be done.

God accompanies us in our weakness and challenges us in our sinfulness. If our faith is all concession, we don't do justice to Christ's call to repentance. But if faith is all condemnation, we do violence to God's compassion.

Lord, help us in this season of Lent to accept the challenge of the Gospel, knowing that, as we struggle, Christ struggles at our side. Amen.

BROADCAST WEDNESDAY 13 FEBRUARY 2008

February 14

Tina Beattie

Thomas Aquinas, the great medieval philosopher, wrote that 'the poverty of our language forces us to overload the word "love".' That's certainly true of our modern culture, but I think Aquinas would have seen something of truth and meaning in Valentine's Day, because it's not about loving possessions or objects. It's a celebration of that most fundamental human desire – to love and be loved. All those red roses and hearts and anonymous cards express that desire, and that's why today is about the true meaning of love, for all its follies and frivolities.

But Aquinas would also have cautioned that our desire for love can't be fully satisfied by any other human being. It's God's call to us from beyond the horizon of death and, like those Valentine cards, it sometimes comes to us from an anonymous sender, as a tantalizing mystery. To be human is to be created by and for love, but to look to another human for the perfection of love is to condemn ourselves to a lifetime of failure and frustration. Only when we understand the eternal nature of love itself are we able to love abundantly and generously in the here and now.

So let's enjoy the exuberance of those hearts and flowers, and celebrate the desire for love that they represent. But let's also recognize that they are garlands on the face of eternity. In the light of eternal love, we learn to give and receive the kind of love that makes us human and satisfies our heart's desire.

'Love bears all things, believes all things, hopes all things, endures all things. Love never fails.' Today, Lord, may we enjoy the celebration of love and discover anew the enduring power of love that never fails. Amen.

BROADCAST SATURDAY 14 FEBRUARY 2009

February 15

Alison Murdoch

The American psychologist Dr Kristin Neff is an expert in self-compassion, which she describes as 'giving yourself the same kindness and care that you'd give to a good friend'. She encourages us to imagine that a close friend feels really upset about something. How would you respond to them, especially when you're at your best? Next, how do you respond to yourself when you're feeling upset? What tone of voice do you use? Is there a difference, and if so, why? What factors or fears lead you to treat yourself and others so differently? And how might things change if you responded to yourself with the same love and warmth that you choose to offer your friend?

I'm a latecomer to the idea of self-compassion. Growing up, I was told to pull myself together, stop brooding and put the other person first. Yet the Buddha said there is nobody in the world more deserving of our kindness and love than ourselves. Simply, from a practical point of view, if we're not in touch with our own pain and suffering, how can we reach out with empathy and understanding to others? If we can't forgive ourselves, how can we forgive anyone else? And if we don't know what it is to be peaceful and at ease, what effect does that have on the people around us?

Whereas self-esteem is invariably linked to feeling 'good' or 'successful', self-compassion is about relating to ourselves positively, warts and all, whatever's happening. It's about attending to our feelings and nurturing our sense of confidence and self-worth. And in this frantic world we live in, it often starts with finding just five minutes when we can be alone and offline.

Let's pray that all of us can find ways to show ourselves more kindness during the week ahead.

BROADCAST MONDAY 15 FEBRUARY 2016

February 16

Peter Whittaker

I held the baby while her mother settled the older brother at the table in the coffee shop. I looked at the face of the sleeping child. Her small hands were opening and closing as she slept. I was genuinely filled with awe and wonder — something I've always felt powerfully when I've held babies. We're incredibly and beautifully made, so clever, so complex, so well adapted to our surroundings. Each one of us is unique.

We're the product of that incredible human journey that began eons ago in Africa. Gradually our ancestors travelled, colonized and inhabited the whole earth. They wandered the planet, thrived, and now we are billions. But still each person is unique. We're also part of an incredible human journey made by each one of us. A journey that begins inside the womb and for most of us goes through childhood into the many phases of adulthood, and on to the end of our individual life on earth. The Psalmist says of God: 'You created every part of me, you put me together in my mother's womb.'

I want to learn to value the uniqueness in the other person. Too often I'm self-centred — I'm uniquely made, I'm special. But I forget that in God's eyes the same is true of all the people I meet. The same is true even if they get in my way when I'm rushing around or if they insist on me producing identification when I *know* who I am! The 'other' person is also special and unique. Let me treat them that way, at least today.

Parent God, for the way we're so wonderfully made, we give You thanks. May we treat with respect all the people we meet today. And may each of us rest in Your love throughout the incredible journey of life. Amen.

BROADCAST THURSDAY 16 FEBRUARY 2012

February 17

Alison Murdoch

'Didn't you hear me say that I've already fed the cat?' I say, as I watch it crawl upstairs to sleep off a second supper. 'I warned you yesterday that we were about to run out of tea!' Or, with a sense of sadness rather than frustration, 'That was our song on the radio ... but I guess you didn't hear it.'

Does someone you love suffer from deafness? My husband doesn't hear as well as he used to. Parties are now a struggle, and we avoid pubs with background music. Back home, I can never call to him from another room or when he has his back turned and can't read my lips. And since he understandably doesn't like reminding me of this, he's become very good at bluffing, which can lead to some interesting misunderstandings.

If I was hearing this about someone else's partner, I'd be full of concern and compassion. What must it be like to struggle with such a key aspect of human interaction, to miss out on former pleasures, and to frequently find yourself isolated in a silent world of your own? Yet sadly my experience is that, however much I want to be kind to the person I love the most, it doesn't come easy. I miss being able to whisper together, and find it hard to repeat myself without sounding irritated. His struggle becomes ours, and even mine.

'We learn to be loving by watching how unloving we can be,' says the Buddhist teacher Ondrea Levine. Kindness is like a muscle that we all possess but that doesn't always get the workout that it needs.

Let's pray that we can all strengthen our kindness muscle and learn to be kinder to the people we feel close to.

BROADCAST WEDNESDAY 17 FEBRUARY 2016

February 18

Tina Beattie

Faith, hope and love, but the greatest of these is love. St Paul wrote those words at the dawn of the Christian era, but they've lost none of their relevance today. Love may indeed be the greatest, but hope is what we're left with, when our dreams come to nothing and neither faith nor love can sustain us. Hope holds us when we have nothing to believe in and nothing to look forward to beyond the small and patient endeavours of everyday life.

Hope is not the same as optimism. Optimism neglects the present to invest in the future. Hope is a quality of the here and now, a sustaining way of being in the world, come what may. Optimism is easily destroyed by failure, and the cynic is perhaps only the disappointed optimist. But hope is our defence against cynicism. There is, as Barack Obama recognizes, an audacity to hope, for it is the shining spirit of life which refuses to give up, even when the odds are stacked against us. He writes of a low point in his career, when he was 'freed from worry by low expectations', and he tells of how his passion for politics was rekindled by his encounters with ordinary families, and his discovery of 'just how modest people's hopes were, and how much of what they believed seemed to hold constant across race, region, religion, and class'.

Optimism can lead us to trample on other people's dreams in the pursuit of our own ambitions. Hope binds us together and invites us to believe in a common destiny made possible through our daily commitments, values and decisions.

Lord, help us to rediscover in the modest audacity of hope and the sharing of visions, a sustaining energy for the work we do today. Amen.

BROADCAST WEDNESDAY 18 FEBRUARY 2009

February 19

Tony Rogers

When people really listen to what you say, there's a fair chance feedback will follow. Recently I suggested that the expression 'Cleanliness is next to godliness' was a rather bizarre statement. The Bible alludes to pots being pristine on the outside and filthy within, and I remarked that I had no idea who was foolish enough to have coined the phrase. Soon afterwards, someone came back to me with a self-satisfied grin. 'Bet you can't guess who said it!' she said rather smugly. Well, I knew it wasn't Jesus, but beyond that I was clueless. 'Let me read what was said,' she continued — determined to milk every last drop of her knowledge. Although the expression is rooted in ancient history, it seems that the first person to latch on to it was none other than John Wesley. He used it in a sermon when he was speaking about good clothes and neat appearances being a sign of respect for others. Fair point, Mr Wesley, but I'd just like to say that when outer cleanliness is deemed essential, but inner godliness is neglected, how can the one be next to the other?

We may be passionate about our daily shower, but we need to remember that man does not live on soap alone. Certainly well-scrubbed and sweet-smelling, but often different inside. I was berated by a sixth-former who appeared to hold me personally responsible for global warming. Though I was a bit taken aback by her remark, she made a valid point. Perhaps the modern equivalent of inspecting the inside of a pot is to look at my carbon footprint?

This prayer of St Brendan may help us see the perspective of our place in the world:

'Lord, help me, for Your sea is so big and my boat is so small.' Amen.

BROADCAST MONDAY 19 FEBRUARY 2007

February 20

Anna Magnusson

There's a Gerard Manley Hopkins poem called 'The Starlight Night' that begins: 'Look at the stars! look, look up at the skies!'

It always pops into my head on cold, black nights when the stars are glittering, or when there's an impossibly bright moon hanging above the houses. The words are perfect: they capture how it *feels* – that rush of wonder and excitement – when you look up into the vastness, and are caught between worlds: the earth under your feet, the infinite universe beyond.

No doubt that's a bit purple for astronauts and astronomers, but the fact is, it's the looking up and beyond the here and now that drew us into space in the first place. It's what took us to the moon, built the space shuttles and – on this day in 1986 – launched the Mir space station. For 15 years, Mir orbited the Earth more than 86,000 times. Russian, and later American, astronauts lived on board for months on end. They even raised the first crop of wheat to be grown from seed in outer space.

That compulsion to venture into the unknown – it came out of confidence and energy and vision. Today it sometimes feels as if our heads are bowed, and we don't look up so much. It's hard to see past what's right in front of us in *this* world: economic turmoil, people and countries struggling to pay their way and survive. Travelling to Mars seems a bit irrelevant when people can't borrow money to buy a house down the road.

And yet, we *still* feel the tug of the infinite, we still need to look up and be awed by the created universe.

And as we look, may we know the presence of God, who is beyond us and within us, now and forever. Amen.

BROADCAST MONDAY 20 FEBRUARY 2012

February 21

Janet Wootton

I wonder, as you wake on this February morning, whether you're yearning for the past, contemplating the day ahead or worrying about the future. It's going to depend partly on the circumstances you're facing. But it's also in our natures to be dwellers in the past, the present or the future.

A book by Graham Adams has incidentally (because that is not what the book is about) helped me to understand that it is not so much about which time-frame we live in as how honest we are about it.

Someone who lives in the past can tend to see it as a golden era, forgetting or ignoring any wrong that was suffered and done. Living in the present can often mean drifting along in a daily routine, unthinkingly shut off from a world of diversity and change. People like me, who are constantly driving into the future, are in danger of trying to force the world to conform to our ideals, never mind anyone else.

Into such diverse lives and temperaments, God comes to confront our natural dishonesty and transform us. With God's help, we dare to see the past with clear eyes, and seek reconciliation and forgiveness. In God's love, we allow ourselves to be shaken out of complacency. And under God's gentle guidance, we can take a rest from changing the world whether it likes it or not, and work with others and with God.

Timely and eternal God, we thank You for all the times of our lives. Recollect to us the good we have known and done; forgive us for our wrongs; help us to walk with You into bright futures; and give us the hours of this day to treasure and enjoy. Amen.

BROADCAST SATURDAY 21 FEBRUARY 2015

February 22

Johnston McKay

After a television programme exploring faith, an old lady wrote to my first boss in the BBC, Ian Mackenzie, to say how disappointed she was that the eminent theologian on the programme had, in her words, 'dodged the question of the Resurrection'. Ian wrote back saying maybe there are various ways of looking at the Resurrection, and she wrote back asking bluntly, 'Do you believe in the Resurrection?' Ian wrote back briefly saying, 'Yes.' The old lady replied that she now felt free to go on searching.

In other words, a positive answer at that moment liberated her.

As a result of that correspondence, the television company Ian worked for in London began a long-running series called 'Looking for an Answer', in which viewers sent in questions. On one programme, a bishop answered questions about life after death. One of the questions was from the old lady whose letter had inspired the programme. She asked: 'Will I see my husband again?' The Bishop said 'Yes.' Never was there a less evasive reply.

Shortly afterwards a letter arrived from the old lady, who felt her question had not been taken seriously and she was very disappointed. In fact she had been given a totally unqualified answer, but at that moment, a simple answer did not liberate her. Mysteriously, a simple 'yes' had meaning for her on one occasion, but not on the other.

Which is why I am glad the poet TS Eliot wrote that Christianity is always evolving into something that can be believed: not because the faith changes but because we do and see things differently at different times.

Loving God, speak to us the word we need to hear, when we need to hear it. Amen.

BROADCAST FRIDAY 22 FEBRUARY 2013

February 23

Janet Wootton

Four weeks ago today, on Republic Day, the Government of India announced the annual Padma Shri awards for distinguished service by civilians. Among the awards for Science, Literature, Art and Sport was one given under the category 'Other' to Jadav Payeng, a forestry worker, who had spent his life planting trees.

In an interview for the BBC World Service, he described how he started. It was a particularly hot year in the 1970s, when as a teenager he noticed that snakes were dying from exposure under the relentless sun. He went to the community elders to ask if anything could be done. Their response was to give him a bamboo sapling to plant — one single tree.

From that time onward, Jadav Payeng planted more trees, and there is now a dense forest of about 1,300 acres. In his interview he recorded that there were not only snakes in the forest but elephants, deer, tigers and a variety of birds. In addition, the erosion of the land has been halted.

This one-man environmental campaign is based not on a desire for money, honour or fame, but, in his own words, for the pleasure of seeing the animals and birds in the forest.

Recently, he said he had dreamed that the animals were joining him in planting trees. Clearly, the forest has taken on its own life, and is creating its own ecosystem. If poachers and loggers can be kept at bay, it will thrive now in its own right.

God of creation, we give You thanks for the resilience and diversity of the natural world. Forgive us when our greed and indifference contribute to devastation. Thank You for the courage and tenacity of all those who work to restore what has been lost. Amen.

February 24

Sharon Grenham-Thompson

Today is the feast day of St Matthias, the man who replaced Judas Iscariot as one of the Twelve Apostles after Judas died. He was chosen by casting lots — not unusual in the ancient world, and a way of allowing God to have the final say.

It would be interesting, wouldn't it, if our MPs were chosen like this! But the modern world, of course, does things rather differently. In commerce, look at how a whole industry has grown up around the task of recruitment. Matching the right person to the right job is big business, and a lot of time, money and effort's invested in making the right choice.

Generally, we like to have a lot more control over our choices, and would rather not leave things to chance. Chance is risky, and leaves us vulnerable — who knows what might happen? The more we can control, the safer we are.

So our children rarely go out to play, we spend years of our lives longing for something different, we keep our assets and our hearts safely locked away. The more we try to control, the sadder we are.

Choices must, of course, be made responsibly, with others in mind. But allowing ourselves and those others a little slack, taking a step beyond the margins of our self-imposed restraints, could do wonders for our relationships, our work and our inner selves.

After all, it was chance that discovered penicillin, chance that revealed Australia to Captain Cook, chance that you are you and I am me.

Or perhaps it was not simply blind chance …

There's always room for You, Lord God, to have the final say. Help us to loosen our grip a little, to take a risk and discover ourselves, and maybe You, in the process. Amen.

BROADCAST THURSDAY 24 FEBRUARY 2011

February 25

Janet Wootton

Any devotee of the cryptic crossword will have come across the near-anagrams around the words *anger, angered, enraged* and *danger*. And know that the same letters can spell *endanger* and *end anger*. All very useful to the crossword compilers.

These words resonate in the English language because of their closeness in spelling and sound. We can see the danger that anger causes: road rage, violence in the home, street fights fuelled by alcohol and drugs. And we also see the fractures in human society along whose edges we rage against one another's moral values, race or religion.

So could we end anger? It is the seductive message in the lyrics of John Lennon's song 'Imagine'. Nothing to kill or die for, and – for good measure in today's violence-torn world – no religion too.

But perhaps to end anger might endanger something about our humanity. I am quick to become angry – I wish I was not, as I end up upsetting people and having to apologize. But I am also grateful for slow-burning anger against poverty and injustice and abuse, because it provides the impulse and the energy to do something about them.

There are things in this world to which the only rational response is powerful anger: not a thirst for revenge, nor the desire to harm the perpetrators, but the power to speak out against wrong and put things right.

This is recognized in a surprising verse from a hymn about Jesus by John Bell and Graham Maule, in which Jesus is described as 'raging' against injustice, and the singer is invited to rage with him in the cause of good.

God, may our anger never endanger our relationships or the lives of others. But may steadfast rage right wrong, in Your power and Your love. Amen.

BROADCAST WEDNESDAY 25 FEBRUARY 2015

February 26

Anna Magnusson

My father had a little 'Words' book in which he jotted down good lines he'd read, or quotations he liked. There's one I remember particularly because I stuck it on the wall beside my desk. It's from the 17th-century scholar Robert Burton and it says: 'There is no greater cause of melancholy than idleness; no better cure than busyness.'

My father was one of the few people I ever heard use the word 'idle' rather than 'lazy'. It was one of his words. He said it held the added sense of a *pleasure* and *delight* in not having anything to do. Those moments were rare for him. He was always working. For him, a moment of idleness was to get up from the typewriter, sit in his chair by the window and take a few puffs of his pipe. Then, back to the desk, back to the work he delighted in.

There's a great creative energy in doing what you love. I met a fifth-year vet student called Ruby who had set up a clinic in Glasgow where homeless people could bring their dogs. They get free basic vet care, and people donate food, and things like toys and collars for the dogs. Ruby's passionate about the human—animal bond, particularly for homeless people who've lost so much. She wants them to be able to hold on to that relationship — which is often the only stable thing in their lives.

Ruby saw the need, so she started the work. No melancholy, no idleness, just busyness and the enthusiasm to create something better. She and my father would have got on like a house on fire.

For the people who look around them and see how to make life better, for their energy and commitment, thank You, Lord. Amen.

BROADCAST FRIDAY 26 FEBRUARY 2016

February 27

Sarah Rowland Jones

Good morning. Today Anglicans commemorate George Herbert – a parliamentarian, priest and poet for whom I have a particular fondness.

He was born in 1593 in Mid Wales, a few miles from where I grew up. (By coincidence, he also has relatives buried in my church in Cardiff.) George Herbert's gift with language and rhetoric swept him into politics. He was briefly a Member of Parliament, and it seemed a career at court awaited him. But then he unexpectedly turned to the Anglican Church and spent the last three years of his life as a parish priest, dying of consumption aged only 39.

Throughout his adult life Herbert was a prolific writer of religious verse, though it was only published after his death, to immediate acclaim. Such was his fluency and lyricism, he was described as 'a soul composed of harmonies'. Much of Herbert's poetry enjoys lasting popularity in the words of well-known hymns. For example we still sing, 'Teach me, my God and King, in all things thee to see.' It's this capacity to avoid dividing the world into sacred and secular that is particularly engaging.

Herbert reminds us that, wherever life takes us, God reigns over it all. 'Let all the world in every corner sing, my God and King!' he wrote. It's no platitude. His writings tell us he often wrestled long and hard with the God he came to know. As one poem puts it, 'Love bade me welcome. Yet my soul drew back.'

Herbert encourages us to keep on striving after God and his redeeming love, in action, not only in church, and not only on Sundays.

So in the words of George Herbert ...

King of glory, king of peace, help us to see You in all situations,
and seven whole days, not one in seven, let us praise You. Amen.

BROADCAST SATURDAY 27 FEBRUARY 2016

February 28

Mary Stallard

One week into Lent and my resolve to keep the season holy is already crumbling. My birthday falls in Lent so I've rarely succeeded in avoiding rich food and drink for the whole 40 days, but this year I've been trying to live a Christian lifestyle with regard to my impact upon the environment. For the first week of Lent, I've been concentrating on recycling. But the boxes for paper and tins are now overflowing on my kitchen floor and I've already made one trip to the supermarket when I forgot to take my own bags. The main temptation I habitually face in Lent is to give up trying because I fail so easily.

But if only I can hold fast to its teachings, my faith ought to help me with this. Christianity has much more to say about failure than it does about success. It teaches that we are loved for being the people who we are, rather than for what we might become. Jesus made this plain in his choice of friends: he didn't choose people with powerful connections, wealth or great education. He chose Peter who constantly got things wrong, who denied him and ran away, and Mary whose life had previously been a mess and who didn't recognize him in the garden after the Resurrection. Jesus was able to see people with the eyes of God, showing them the faithful love that is constantly forgiving. Through the power of this love, Peter went on to become the rock upon which the Church was built and Mary became the first person to tell the good news of the Resurrection.

When we feel we are constantly letting God and others down, we need to remember to forgive ourselves and to carry on. The whole point of learning to live the Gospel in small ways is so that we can be building blocks in the far more important work of making God's loving concern for all known to others.

Creator God, give us the will and the humility to seek to live in harmony with ourselves and Your whole creation. Help us to recognize and honour the connectedness of all things and never to be discouraged by our failures. Amen.

BROADCAST WEDNESDAY 28 FEBRUARY 2007

March 1

Sarah Rowland Jones

Happy St David's Day! On his deathbed, St David, the patron saint of Wales, commended his followers to 'be faithful in the little things'. Jesus said something similar in his parable about a man who, before going on a journey, entrusted varying amounts of money to three servants. On his return, the two who had received larger sums reported how they had put the money to work and increased his investment. To each the master responded, 'Well done! You've been faithful when trusted with small things — now I'll trust you with much greater responsibilities!'

But then there's the third servant. He had merely dug a hole in the ground to keep the money safe. He returns it to his master saying 'Sir, I knew you were a harsh man, reaping where you did not sow, and so I was afraid and hid your money — here it is — take what is yours.'

Not surprisingly, he's condemned. At the very least, he could have deposited the money with bankers.

Jesus tells parables to get us thinking on many levels, and so I'm prompted to reflect more deeply on why the third servant got it so wrong.

I see that we should invest and grow what God entrusts to us — whether wealth, abilities, experience or anything else. And, as St David taught, nothing is too small to begin with.

I'm also reminded we shouldn't be motivated by misplaced fear about God. The God of love is not a small-minded and vindictive master. God's desire and delight is for us to make the most of our lives, as flourishing, contributing members of our communities and the wider world.

Lord God, may we know Your joyful encouragement to be faithful in the small things that today brings, so that we may be faithful too in the big questions that come our way. Amen.

BROADCAST SATURDAY 1 MARCH 2008

March 2

Rosa Hunt

From the two-year-old, who is absolutely determined to dismantle the stair gate, to Captain Kirk exploring 'space, the final frontier', we humans love to push against limits. When the Concorde aircraft flew for the first time in 1969, the noise of the engines completely drowned out the barrage of applause from the watching crowd. The aim, of course, was to build a commercial aircraft which could break the sound barrier, and Concorde did achieve its first supersonic flight in October that same year.

If there's a barrier there, humans like to try to go beyond it, but I wonder whether there are some barriers which we shouldn't seek to cross? In the 4th century, the Roman Emperor Constantine convened a council to try to assure peace in his territories. For once, the issue causing widescale dissent was not merely political but rather philosophical — are there things that the human mind cannot grasp and define? Can we speak of God in the same language that we use to describe everything else; can we understand Him in the same way as we understand the created universe?

Constantine's peer Ephrem believed that to attempt to analyse God and fit Him neatly into categories of thought and language was blasphemy. Thus, he wrote his theology as poetry, believing that it was through the symbolic language of poems that the paradoxical presence *and* absence of God in our lives could best be approached. A poem is not a logical argument leading inexorably to a single conclusion; instead, it allows us to hold multiple images in tension.

Father God, You have revealed Yourself through Your Son Jesus Christ, and yet sometimes when we need You most, You seem to hide Your face. We pray for all who seek You, who long for Your healing and loving presence in their lives, for those to whom You seem very far away. May they experience a touch of Your love and joy as they go about their lives this day. Amen.

BROADCAST MONDAY 2 MARCH 2015

March 3

Jenny Wigley

In recent years, scholars have been rediscovering the Jewishness of Jesus — there's been a recent television programme and endless books. But for me, Jesus is still the man who fits no categories. He transcends all boundaries, which is how his followers came to be not just a reform movement within Judaism, but a worldwide Church with many millions of members.

It all began with that young rabbi travelling round the villages of Galilee, gathering disciples to help spread the good news of the kingdom. People tend to think of that first community of Jesus's followers as very small indeed — the 12 disciples. Yet the Gospels tell us that there was a much bigger group — 70 were sent out on a preaching mission.

And they describe a pretty varied bunch: Galilean fishermen, men and women of wealth and high social standing, radical nationalists and those who collaborated with the Romans. Truth be told, if we try to see what they all had in common, there is only one thing, or rather, one person — Jesus.

St Paul, reflecting on all this some 20 or 30 years later, described the Christian community as a 'new creation'. He wrote of how God was remaking people in his image, no longer divided and competitive but as united and cooperative as if they were all parts of one body working together.

It doesn't sound much like today's world — or today's Church, more often than not. But for Christians, the 'new creation' reminds us that God sees us not simply as we are, or as we have been, but as we *can* be, full of the potential that comes from Spirit-filled relationships with Him and with one another.

God of community, You make us one in Christ so that we may reveal the transforming power of Your love. Help us to discern in one another the gifts with which You bless us, and to use them in the service of others. Amen.

BROADCAST TUESDAY 3 MARCH 2009

March 4

Rosa Hunt

I was speaking to someone last week who has a little granddaughter aged two. He described to me how life in his quiet, orderly household changed instantly as soon as the child arrived at their front door. When the doorbell heralded the entrance of Lucy and her retinue, whatever task he or his wife happened to be engaged in at the moment was immediately abandoned, with no hope of resumption until she had returned home.

But without knowing it, the child gave her grandparents the gift of her presence. It was a gift which couldn't be ignored, and one which demanded not only an acknowledgment on their part that she existed, but also that they in turn gave her the gift of their entire presence. Lucy, like every other two-year-old, quite naturally demanded the whole of her grandparents' love and attention for the few hours they shared. And they were delighted to give it.

In this sense, a relationship with the God of the Bible is far more like a relationship with a two-year-old toddler than one with a teenager. God isn't content to spend hours on His own in His room while you and I are busy working, and for us to just pop in to see how He's doing on a Sunday morning. God makes Himself fully present in our lives through His Spirit, and in return He demands our entire presence, indeed our whole lives. Oddly, practising being present to God seems to help us be more present to other people too. In this digital age, when various devices claim and fracture our attention, to give another human our whole attention can be a rare and precious gift.

Father God, forgive us for the times when we've listened with only half our attention, when we've bought items without noticing the salesperson, when we've spoken when we should have listened, or rushed on instead of pausing. Help us in our busy, distracted world to be people of integrity who have the capacity to give our whole presence to those we encounter, and especially to those we love. Amen.

BROADCAST WEDNESDAY 4 MARCH 2015

March 5

Jenny Wigley

When I got married, my friend Emma gave me a cookbook. Inside was a message about how 'Abraham and Sarah entertained angels unawares'. In the story in the Book of Genesis, three strangers appear from nowhere. Abraham invites them into his tent, and he and his wife Sarah present them with a generous — if hurriedly prepared — meal.

That ministry of hospitality has always been important in lots of faith traditions. It was taken up by many of the monasteries, who offered a meal and a bed for the night to travellers. And it was developed further as the religious communities invited people to share their way of life for a brief time on retreat.

Retreats offer the opportunity to take time out to rest, reflect and pray as a way of recharging your spiritual batteries, so that you're ready to re-engage with the world you've left behind. There's a chance to 'touch base' with God in a different way, because the community will have its own particular rhythms of prayer and work and worship.

I remember once going on a retreat that required me to spend eight days in silence. The not-talking didn't worry me as much as the not-doing-anything. I was used to being occupied. But really I'd just been preoccupied. The discipline of silence helped me discover the wonder of just walking and sitting, reading and daydreaming.

And it only happened because that little community had welcomed me, and for that brief time, allowed me to share their life. To invite another to step over the threshold opens up so many possibilities: a stranger may become a friend — and the unexpected guest makes possible an encounter with God Himself.

God of community, You come to us in the form of friend and stranger. Help us to welcome You into our communities, our homes and our hearts, so that in giving and receiving, we may entertain angels unawares. Amen.

BROADCAST THURSDAY 5 MARCH 2009

March 6

Mary Stallard

Sometimes it's the words that are never said that have the greatest power to influence our lives or change us. The worst telling off I ever received as a child was utterly silent. Just remembering it makes me shiver. My friend's mother caught me out doing something we both knew was definitely not allowed, but she said nothing. She looked at me, took my hand, and walked me home. All the way there I thought about what she'd do; I was sure she'd go and speak to my parents. But she didn't: she left me at our front door. For the next few days I waited, in some panic, for my punishment: it never came. I don't believe she ever told anyone. It was a clever response on her part. Nothing else could have made me think so seriously about my behaviour as her silence.

One of the most interesting stories about Jesus tells of his refusal to speak in the face of wrongdoing. A woman accused of adultery was brought to him and the teachers of the law wanted Jesus to sanction her stoning. Jesus gave them no answer. He kept them waiting while he bent down and drew in the dust. Eventually he said, 'Let the one who is without sin throw the first stone,' and resumed his silence. The people all drifted away, the elders first, and Jesus and the woman were left alone. He famously told her that he did not condemn her and that she should 'go and sin no more'.

Perhaps more significant than Jesus's interaction with this woman is his encounter with the angry crowd. He prompted those who felt heated to reflect on their own actions and he did this without attacking or accusing them. The greatest repentance in this story belongs to the crowd who put down their stones and walked away from violence.

Spirit of integrity, may we find you in the silence we encounter today. If we are tempted to words or actions which may hurt others, guide us instead toward that which builds up and heals. Amen.

BROADCAST THURSDAY 6 MARCH 2008

March 7

Edward Mason

Today I'm thinking about Aashira. I met her just outside the doctor's. That wasn't where I'd first seen her, though.

I'd seen her dance! Aashira had been abandoned as a baby, literally left by the side of the road, as many girls are in that part of the world [India]. I sometimes wonder about her mother. She must have been so desperate!

By a miracle, Aashira was swept up by a project that takes in the discarded and provides foster mothers in little family communities. It began when one young man, far from his own land, was confronted by a small group of homeless children. He heard the call of God on his life to 'look after orphans in their distress' and to provide a home for them. With little money and no support, he took them in. Now, 50 years later, the project houses 900 children at any one time, and it's one of the most beautiful, peaceful and wholesome places I know.

It's where I saw Aashira dance. Aged about ten, she could perform highly technical, traditional dance with the energy and controlled passion that made the audience hold its breath on that festival day.

Aashira was born HIV positive. That's why I met her outside the doctor's. She'd been in for a check-up. She'll need both anti-retro viral drugs *and* a loving home to keep her jumping and spinning, learning and living.

So, Lord God, we pray today for all who work on the frontiers of science, determined to understand disease and overcome it. We thank You for that young man, now old and coming to the end of his life, who responded to Your call. Help us to do the same. Amen.

BROADCAST SATURDAY 7 MARCH 2015

March 8

Shaunaka Rishi Das

'The youth of today, that's the problem. They have no respect, not like we had in our day. Not for the old, the law, our leaders, religion, anyone.' How many times have we heard or even spoken words like that?

The unfortunate reality is that for some young people they're true, but they're also true for people of older generations.

Recently a good friend of mine shared an experience he had had — and a lesson learned. He was visiting his parents for a family reunion. All was well until his father started to do one of those things that always got his back up. As was his usual habit, he became intolerant of what he saw was his father's intolerance, and made an issue of it. The exchange became vocal and loud. No one backed down and his father left the room. It was only then that he became aware that his four- and six-year-old boys had also left the room.

My friend's wife sympathized with him, but reminded him that his father was older now and may be finding it difficult to see his role in the family. This could excuse his father's insistence on respect. She also observed that the boys were upset by the conflict and that they may grow up to treat him as he treated his father, if that's their example.

My friend was appalled at his behaviour and apologized to both his father and to his boys for the incident. So I pray:

Please Lord, help me to cultivate respect. When I meet those who have more than me, let me be very happy; when I am with those who have less, let me help them achieve more; and with my peers, let me praise them and not have to compete. Hare Krishna.

BROADCAST THURSDAY 8 MARCH 2007

March 9

Sharon Grenham-Thompson

We normally expect spies to influence politics, national security and secret wars. We don't usually hear of their reports having a theological effect. But when Moses sent 12 spies into Canaan after the Exodus from Egypt, they came back to tell him that the land was fertile but the enemy strong. Ten of them were all for turning back from the border. Only two urged Moses to trust God and press on. The people wanted to retreat, and the story goes that God was so angered by their lack of trust that only those two were allowed into the land – the rest of the tribes of Israel were made to wander in the wilderness for a generation.

In the 4th century, when writing his great work *The Life of Moses*, Bishop Gregory of Nyssa commented that the Israelites had done a lot to upset God after the Exodus by their dissent, their idolatry and their various misdemeanours, but that it was their turning away from the Promised Land that proved their undoing. So Gregory, using the Promised Land as an allegory for heaven, suggested that it's not necessarily our human failings that anger God, so much as our refusal to believe in his power to redeem and our unwillingness to trust God for our salvation.

For many people, this still rings true today. Caught in the headlights of ecological and financial disaster, we, the frightened rabbits, wish we could just run away.

In our Lenten penitence, merciful Lord, may we turn our gaze from the devices and desires of our own hearts. Instead, we pray, help us to fix our eyes on You, and the hope of salvation. May we remember that Lent always turns into Easter. Amen.

BROADCAST TUESDAY 9 MARCH 2010

March 10

Roger Hutchings

I'd like to reflect briefly on words. Anyone who broadcasts on radio probably enjoys words. Certainly I do. I don't go quite as far as someone I know, who is delighted to have a new, rather obscure word appear each day on the screen in her pocket. But still, I like words, and they are for me, as a Christian minister, the vehicle through which I seek to express and encourage faith, and to lead others in prayer.

So, what about leaving words behind altogether? For a parson, that's a challenge! Well, last weekend, I shared in a service of Holy Communion which, from beginning to end, included no spoken words. If you're familiar with such a service, you'll know that there are usually pages and pages of spoken words, only a few of which would be regarded as absolutely vital. Instead, on this occasion, the minister silently conveyed the content purely by gesture, action and symbol, inviting us to respond in movement and contemplation. Of course, words went on being formed in my mind — though not as continually as I expected. The pure emotional response didn't need words, and we served and were served by our neighbours with bread and wine. As everyone present left and greeted each other, still in silence, the power of the shared experience was reflected in the warmth and peace of our acknowledgment of each other. These were precious moments.

God, whose Word formed us from nothing, and whose Word lived among us in Jesus, we give thanks for language and all that we can express. We give thanks also for silence, and ask that we may know moments of quiet peace this day. Amen.

BROADCAST SATURDAY 10 MARCH 2012

March 11

George Stack

With its music, culture and extraordinary history, I've long been fascinated by Spain. The fortress town of Ávila in Castile is quite spectacular. It was there that the great St Teresa persuaded St John of the Cross to become her spiritual director. Together they followed the mystical path called the 'Ascent to Nothingness'. This teaches that God is all, and a life which is already overcrowded cannot receive the fullness of God's gift. So the challenge of this teaching is to empty ourselves of those things we think give identity, security and meaning to our lives. In that emptiness, we'll discover the things of God. St John of the Cross described this as *nada*, nothing. Let nothing come between yourself and the ground of your being — God Himself.

The greatness of John's mystical path lies in his objective, heroic, analytical and rational approach to the subject. He avoids the extremes of emotion which promise heaven or threaten hell. He invites Teresa and those who follow him to realize that nothing is lost and all is gained in opening the depth of our being to the presence and the love of God.

So, a prayer of St Teresa:

Let nothing disturb thee,
Let nothing dismay thee.
All things pass.
God never changes.
Patience attains
All that it strives for.
He who has God
Lacks for nothing.
God alone suffices.
Amen.

BROADCAST TUESDAY 11 MARCH 2008

March 12

Sharon Grenham-Thompson

'By the strength of our common endeavour we achieve more than we achieve alone.' These words come at the beginning of the updated Clause Four of the Labour Party constitution, and could be seen as a foundational principle of the parliamentary party.

Away from parliamentary politics, it's also a phrase that echoes St Paul when he refers to the Church as a body made up of many parts needing to cooperate. That's a useful image in my everyday work as a prison chaplain. In that role I see the results of individualistic thinking day after day. I try to encourage the prisoners to see themselves as part of something bigger than themselves. That might be their family, it might be the group they meet with for education, it might be the prison chapel congregation. It might even eventually turn their gaze to society as a whole, and bring about a realization that with rights come responsibilities, and that little is achieved unless we cooperate with one another.

But in any area, relationships and cooperation are key. Managers worry about staff engagement, workers grumble about low morale, families lament their loss of communication. No policy, incentive or therapy is likely to work as thoroughly as renewing our sense of relatedness and interdependence – our need for one another.

And so, Lord, we pray for a fresh sense of respect for one another. Help us to try to bring out the best in our colleagues and relations, to acknowledge efforts made, even in the absence of success. Amen.

BROADCAST TUESDAY 12 MARCH 2013

March 13

Calvin Samuel

'Bow down and worship me' was the last of the three temptations Jesus faced in the wilderness. Unlike the temptations to turn stone to bread or leap from the Temple, which employ a subtle approach, this is a full-frontal assault.

The temptation of idolatry is perhaps the most common of all. It is the temptation to put something in the place of God, an attempt to replace a God who demands too much with an alternative that demands comparatively little but offers in return precisely what we desire. 'I will give you the world if only you worship me.'

The temptation of idolatry is attractive, at least in part because it is based on transactional terms that are simple to understand and to control. We perform certain services and in return receive certain benefits.

Such transactional terms are perhaps sufficient when outlining a contract but they are insufficient and indeed inappropriate when dealing with personal relationships, which are far more complex.

Modern-day idols include money, fame, power, success or even work. None of these are negative; in fact, precisely the opposite. This is what makes idolatry such a seductive form of temptation and provides justification for sacrificing vital human relationships on the altar of achievement.

The end might be positive, but often the means of achieving that end is less so. That, in a nutshell, is the temptation of idolatry; the temptation to remove God from the equation to enable unfettered pursuit of our ambition.

Jesus resisted that temptation. So should we.

Merciful God, forgive us when we place too high a value on the things we desire and too low a value on the relationships through which our humanity is both experienced and expressed. Amen.

BROADCAST THURSDAY 13 MARCH 2014

March 14

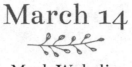

Mark Wakelin

You often hear people say, 'It's only human nature,' and you get the impression that human nature isn't such a good thing to have. Certainly there's enough in the daily news to make us think there's much room in our species for improvement. And an honest reflection on some of my own inner thoughts and desires makes me realize I too have much to learn!

I fear sometimes that the messier reality beneath my acceptable public face is the real me. Where's God in what's supposedly God's greatest creation: human beings? One of the struggles that people seem to have with God in the Bible is, surprisingly, that God believes in their potential far more than they do. He wants Moses to sort out Pharaoh; Isaiah to prophesize; Jeremiah, as a very young person, to take on the old guard; and Gideon, who really feels totally inadequate, to defeat the invading hoards of the Midianites. The New Testament is also full of stories of people whose encounter with Jesus is one in which God's faith in them exceeds their own self-belief.

The challenge is that, beneath our fairly smooth and presentable surface impression, there may indeed lie a rather messier and more complex reality, but beneath that, deeper down than even the best therapists can dig, is the most fundamental reality of what it is to be human: that we are 'created in the image of God'. This is the ultimate of 'designer labels' — we're quality goods. We may think human nature is a poor thing, but that isn't the truth at all.

Help me today, creator God, to find You in myself and other people, to discover the deepest reality of my own worth and the worth of others. Amen.

BROADCAST WEDNESDAY 14 MARCH 2007

March 15

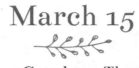

Sharon Grenham-Thompson

'Beware the Ides of March.' A phrase full of foreboding, forever linked with the day in March 44 BCE when Julius Caesar was assassinated. Some dates go down in history as days to send a shiver down our spine. Who doesn't remember the terrible events of 9/11? Then there's the resonance of the 11th day of the 11th month, marking Armistice Day at the end of World War I. Less solemn perhaps, but many will remember the barely suppressed panic as the year 2000 approached, and again at the end of 2012, with the hype about the end of the world supposedly predicted by the Mayan calendar. On a much more personal and individual level, we all have days that hold a particular meaning for us — anniversaries of meetings, partings, births and deaths, first and lasts.

If the day holds an especially negative memory for a family or a nation, it tends to overshadow everything else that happens on that day in the future, and can even interfere with the very necessary process of moving on from grief or anger. But when Gordon Wilson publicly forgave his daughter's killers after the Enniskillen bomb in 1987, he not only decided that the terrible events of the day would not hold him forever in the past, but he was also key to the change of mindset that eventually led to the Northern Ireland peace process.

And so, Lord of time and eternity, we ask for grace to accept each new day as a chance for peace and loving our fellows. We pray for the strength to acknowledge great sorrow and yet also move into a hopeful future. Amen.

BROADCAST FRIDAY 15 MARCH 2013

March 16

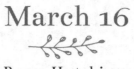

Roger Hutchings

Recently I was invited – not, I hasten to add, by the famous Radio 4 programme – to choose what music I might take to keep me company as an island castaway. Now, music plays an important part in my life. I play the piano and organ, and sing in a choir. And over the years, I've listened to recorded music from pop to jazz to classical. Picking just a small selection didn't come easy.

There was never any doubt, though, whose music would be the absolute essential. Like millions before me, I'm captivated, inspired, excited, rendered speechless in amazement by the music of Bach. A year or two ago, I visited his tomb. He was originally buried in a very ordinary grave and forgotten. Now, when later generations have come to recognize his genius, his remains lie in the chancel of the church where he worked for so long as organist and choirmaster: St Thomas's, in Leipzig. There, today as every day, admirers will place roses and other flowers on the grave, in a simple act of thanksgiving. And in a few days' time, when his birthday is celebrated, a friend tells me that balloons may well decorate the statue of the great man which stands outside the church. Music poured out of Bach – week after week, year after year, for entertainment and delight, yes, but also, profoundly, as an expression of Christian faith. He gave back to God what he believed he had received as a gift.

Praise God this morning for all that music can express of our deepest human feelings and thoughts. Thank God this morning for those who dedicate their skill as composers and musicians to inspire us. In the name of Christ. Amen.

BROADCAST FRIDAY 16 MARCH 2012

March 17

Glenn Jordan

Beannachtaí na Féile Pádraig oraibh!

The blessings of St Patrick on you all.

Today, people all over the world, those who are Christians and those who aren't, will be celebrating the feast day of St Patrick. Although he is mostly associated with Ireland, he is also patron saint of Nigeria. And the parade with unofficially the biggest attendance today will be in Savannah in Georgia, USA.

My childhood memories from the '70s are dominated by wind, rain and cold standing on the main street in my home town of Bray watching a pitiful parade slink by. I remember my dad pointing out to me an almost-blind Éamon de Valera, Irish civil war leader and early Prime Minister of the Irish Republic, while we huddled for shelter in a shop front.

Much has changed since those days, not least through the effects of the fabled Celtic tiger, which now has lost most of its bite. Today the celebration is less a religious event and more a huge tourist trap – just our luck that it all happens in March and not the height of summer.

That said, despite the cheesiness and the crass commercialism that often dominates the day, it is worth remembering the saint and some of his words and prayers, so …

This day I call for you: God's strength to direct you, God's power to sustain you, God's wisdom to guide you, God's vision to light you, God's ear to your hearing, God's word to your speaking, God's hand to uphold you, God's pathway before you, God's shield to protect you, God's legions to save you. Amen.

BROADCAST TUESDAY 17 MARCH 2009

March 18

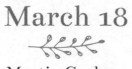

Martin Graham

Yesterday the Irish and all those who have a touch of Irishness in them celebrated St Patrick's Day, a feast celebrated like no other in cities and countries across the world where Irish men and women have made their homes in the past two centuries.

The story of Patrick is shrouded in myth and legend, and his mission to Ireland can seem a little romantic: he preached and converted a nation. But the reality was quite different. From the little he wrote he gives us an idea of just how difficult it was and, most importantly, how the only reason he came to Ireland was because he believed God called him to be there. Clearly, it wasn't his own idea, as he wrote: 'Daily I expect to be slaughtered, or defrauded, or reduced to slavery or to any condition that time and surprise may bring.' God asked Patrick to undertake a mission, a very definite one, which meant a lot of personal sacrifice on his part.

God is also calling us to mission, which we will accomplish largely through the way we live, not simply by what we say. And perhaps we will only get to plant seeds of faith, just as Patrick did, by praying for those who will come after us and witnessing to what we believe in as well as we can.

Most Holy Trinity, may we, like St Patrick, respond to Your call and bring Your good news to those we meet. Amen.

BROADCAST MONDAY 18 MARCH 2013

March 19

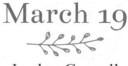

Lesley Carroll

This time of day is a little early for my breakfast, but I'm already looking forward to some scrambled eggs and maybe smoked salmon. Will it be a bagel or toast? Too many choices. I hope there will be no bits of eggshell in the scrambled egg – there's nothing worse, guaranteed to spoil a good breakfast!

On this day in 1994, one of the largest omelettes ever made was cooked in Yokohama, Japan. It took 160,000 eggs. I can imagine there were a few shells cooked into the omelette, but the chefs could surely have been excused on that occasion, given the cracking enormity of the task.

For after all, you can't make an omelette without breaking eggs. The inference is that in doing something good there will always be negative implications. I would like to think that that isn't always the case, that negative implications can at least be minimized, if not eradicated. Minimizing negative implications is about mindfulness of others and mindfulness in how we go about things.

You can't make an omelette without breaking eggs, but then eggs are only useful when they are broken. It isn't the same for people. A broken egg provides a great breakfast, but breaking people is quite another thing. We can damage other people very easily and without thought, and it matters. So the Bible (Philippians 2:3) urges us to think differently: 'And you should not do anything with contention or empty glory, but in humility of mind, let every person esteem his neighbour as better than himself.'

So today, Lord, we pray for those who have been intentionally or unintentionally broken by others and we ask for their healing and help. Amen.

BROADCAST THURSDAY 19 MARCH 2015

March 20

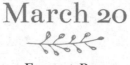

Ernest Rea

Last Saturday marked the feast day of Joseph of Arimathea. The Gospel accounts tell us that he was an open-minded man who was searching for the kingdom of God. He was a witness to the events of Jesus's trial and death, and he must have felt that an injustice had been done. Because when he realized that there was no tomb in which to bury the body of Jesus, he approached the disciples and offered to give his own specially prepared tomb in the Garden of Gethsemane. And it was there that the climatic events of the Easter story, the resurrection of Jesus, took place.

Joseph has exercised a strange fascination for people down through the ages. Later legends told strange tales about the Holy Grail visits to Britain and King Arthur and the Round Table – none of them based on any factual evidence. It's what he did for Jesus and his motivation that have significance. John's Gospel tells us he was a secret believer, scared to confess his faith openly for fear of what might happen to him. But Matthew, Mark and Luke contented themselves with saying he was a searcher. And the weight of evidence is on their side, which puts him in the same category as most of us who live in Britain today.

We're searchers. The majority of us sit lightly in relation to Christian doctrine. And for that reason many are shy of calling themselves in any way Christians. But here at the heart of the Christian story stands a man who is honoured for the fact that, at a crucial moment in history, confused and uncertain as he was, he did a noble act.

Lord, strengthen the faith of those who believe, and give us grace, when in doubt, to act in love. Amen.

BROADCAST TUESDAY 20 MARCH 2007

March 21

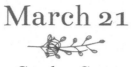

Gordon Gray

On this day in 1999 we lost one of our best-loved comedians, Ernest Wiseman, stage name Ernie Wise, of that unique duo Morecambe and Wise. Together, they were as much part of our Christmas fare as turkey and Brussels sprouts. When many of us feel overwhelmed with life's problems, laughter is indeed the best medicine. This includes the ability to laugh at ourselves, our mistakes and foibles, the predicaments we get ourselves into. Laughter helps us not to take ourselves too seriously

As the straight man of the pair, Ernie Wise filled his role admirably. We could identify with him and his treatment at the hands of the ebullient, self-confident Morecambe, who, let it be said, was never cruel in his put-downs. And Ernie Wise also played to perfection the role of 'second fiddle', who nevertheless had his own unique contribution to make.

Sometimes we have to be content to play that secondary role, supportive when someone we feel is less capable than we are is stealing the limelight, receiving the accolades, doing the honours. This can be a challenge to self-esteem. But if we can retain a sense of humour we will survive. Far from being 'killjoy', the Bible is, in fact, full of references to joy — 'the joy of the Gospel', as Pope Francis has put it. And that's not far from laughter.

Lord God, thank You for those who bring laughter into our lives. Thank You for humour, banter, fun. Thank You for the innocent cheerfulness of children, who can make us smile even through our tears. May we bring joy into the lives of those around us today. Amen.

BROADCAST FRIDAY 21 MARCH 2014

March 22

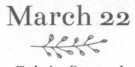

Calvin Samuel

If I am ever listening to the radio at this time of the morning, the chances are that it will be to the sound of a kettle boiling in the background. Other people have probably had a shower already, let alone turning on the tap to fill up a kettle. The thing is, they can. This year we might have had our fill of excess water with all the storms and flooding recently, but at least we *have* water to drink. In this country we see fresh water from the tap as one of life's givens. If ever there is the prospect of running out of water, we fall into a blind panic — buying up the bottled stuff with apocalyptic zeal. I know, because I have done it.

A few years ago there was a problem with our local pumping station, and within hours of the announcement every supermarket shelf for miles around was swept clean of bottled water. Today is World Water Day, which draws our attention to the billion people in the world without access to clean water for drinking, washing, cooking or sanitation. A billion is such a huge number — more than any of us has ever seen gathered in one place. Scattered across the world, they will wake this morning in places where the quest for water will occupy their every waking hour until the sun sets tonight. We remember them today, along with the policy-formers and decision-makers who affect their lives.

O God who made the oceans and the rivers which feed them, yours was the hand which bored the tiniest hole for the tiniest spring to bubble from the hill. Yours was the hand which bent the majestic rivers on their course. Today we cry out to You for the thirsty and for those who will bring them fresh water to drink. Amen.

BROADCAST SATURDAY 22 MARCH 2014

March 23

Ann Holt

The advertisement for a headteacher read: 'Wanted — someone who can walk on water!' Clearly they needed someone quite extraordinary!

The idea of walking on water comes from Matthew's Gospel in the King James Bible — of which we are celebrating the 400th anniversary. Jesus had sent the disciples to sail out to sea while he went off to pray. A gale blew and the disciples were afraid when they saw Jesus walking toward them on the water. Ever impetuous, Peter tried to do the same, but after a few steps in a raging sea, fear got the better of him and he took his eyes off Jesus. He started to drown. But Jesus took him by the hand and brought him to safety.

The advertisement for the school may have been designed to attract attention rather than describing a literal need, but the truth is that anything demanding will probably take us all out of our comfort zone. The American author John Ortberg has written a book called *If You Want to Walk on Water, You've Got to Get Out of the Boat*. Many of us have discovered that trusting Jesus to be with us in such situations makes all the difference and enables us to do more than we ever imagined. It really does feel extraordinary, if not miraculous.

Before he walked out onto the water and defied the elements, Jesus prayed to his father.

For strength and power to face the challenges of the day ahead, Good Lord be our provider. From fear and adversity, good Lord be our deliverer. Amen.

BROADCAST WEDNESDAY 23 MARCH 2011

March 24

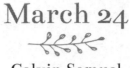

Calvin Samuel

Wherever you live in the northern hemisphere, it is now officially spring. It's a moveable feast, of course, coming in at different times in different places — but by now we have all caught up. There's a tradition associated with the spring in Siberia which is called 'the whispering of the stars', and it has caught my imagination since the day I first heard it.

In the very coldest parts of Siberia the air is so cold in winter, they say that people's breath freezes as they speak. According to legend their very words freeze there and then, falling to the snow below with a 'plop' as they land. If you walk past the place where the words were spoken just as spring comes and the snow melts, the words can be heard all over again. Exclamations, questions and snatches of conversation all come back to life with the warmth of the spring sunshine. This is the 'whispering of the stars'.

I have to confess that I find the prospect slightly alarming. What if the words I had spoken in the depths of winter really could come back to haunt me in the warmth of spring? What if a throwaway comment or an ill-tempered rant really could be heard again by a stranger passing by? It's only a legend, of course, but it's a reminder that words, once spoken, have a life of their own. Where they are heard, and how they are heard thereafter, are not necessarily in our control. Like cats let out of the proverbial bag, they have a habit of running amok if we don't choose them carefully.

O God, who spoke the universe into life, we thank You today for the gift of speech. May our words be wholesome and positive, however long they might be remembered. Amen.

BROADCAST MONDAY 24 MARCH 2014

March 25

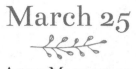

Anna Magnusson

Just about this time in 2003, a woman called Vicky Jack started on a journey. The day was sunny and the snowdrops were nestling in a corner of the back garden. She took a last look across the River Balvaig, glittering in the sunshine, and locked up the house, which lies on a narrow track in the Stirlingshire village of Balquhidder. Three weeks later she was at Base Camp on Mount Everest.

People say Vicky looks as if a puff of wind would blow her away. She's wiry and slight, and has a softly-spoken, almost shy manner that masks an iron will. A will that made her the first Scot to climb the seven highest summits on the seven continents — and which got her to the top of Mount Everest. She's not a professional climber, and that journey took her seven years of climbing in her holidays, training on the hills after work, and using her savings to travel all over the globe. It was a huge undertaking — but its beginnings were small. She simply decided, one day, to get to know Scotland better by climbing the Munroes — and she just went on climbing higher and higher.

I asked Vicky once if she found it hard, looking up at Everest, to begin the climb, when she knew all the danger and hardship that lay ahead. 'Well,' she said, 'I called it a hill, not a mountain, because that's not so scary. And I never look too far ahead.' In her mind's eye, she saw her destination. But when she started, she looked down — down at her boots — and climbed one step at a time.

Lord, help us to begin whatever our journey is today. Wherever our first step takes us —
may You also be there. Amen.

BROADCAST WEDNESDAY 25 MARCH 2009

March 26

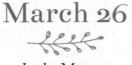

Judy Merry

A couple of weeks ago, a Jewish friend invited my husband and me to join her family for a Sabbath meal. After the blessing and the shared cup of wine we sat down to eat and, over the chicken soup, my friend said, 'It's a great feeling to know that this evening — all over the world — Jewish people will be saying the same prayer and sitting down to share the same meal with family and friends.'

Tradition is one of the things that binds together people of the same faith, but if traditions are changed or adapted some will argue that is 'watering down' the faith, while others will say it's simply reinterpreting it to make it relevant in today's society.

This tension is reflected in the secular world. There's been a great deal of discussion recently about whether tradition is a good or a bad thing in education. Michael Gove calls himself 'an unashamed traditionalist' and he's been arguing for a return to an education system in which children sit in rows and learn about kings and queens and how to do mental arithmetic.

I certainly do wish some of my students had been taught formal grammar in the way I was — then I wouldn't have to explain how a well-placed comma can help you make your point more clearly. On the other hand, I wish I'd done less algebra at school and learned more about things like early day motions and which layer of local government is responsible for emptying the bins.

Maybe we need to ask whether we're clinging to traditions — secular or sacred — out of nostalgia and habit, or because they have real value. The value of the Jewish Sabbath is that it's a pause in your week in which you can reflect on what is really important. And it's also an opportunity to show the warmth of your hospitality to people both inside and outside your community.

We pray that we may hold to those traditions that have true value — those that enhance our lives and draw us closer together. Amen.

BROADCAST FRIDAY 26 MARCH 2010

March 27

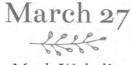

Mark Wakelin

Sometimes you only realize what really matters when you hit a significant bump in life's road! Priorities can change when, for example, you get poorly — with worry, hospital visits, medications and what are euphemistically called 'procedures' that leave you anxious and wary of any one wearing rubber gloves. In the quieter moments you may wonder at how much energy you've put into some things that seemed so important to you, and regret far more important things that somehow just passed away.

Immediately after Jesus's baptism, he goes into the wilderness for a long time. All his priorities are questioned here, all his hopes and dreams, his longings for what might be and what part he might play in that. It's not difficult to imagine the anguish and the heartache of such a difficult time, and to notice, as we approach Holy Week, the similarity with the painful struggle in the Garden of Gethsemane. Jesus stands for all of us who have ever been in that lonely place of worry and fear.

None of us welcomes the wilderness or the hard times, and yet sometimes it's only through struggle that we find ourselves and also find God, bringing us strength and hope. I know at other times suffering seems to be nothing but a negative thing, grinding us down and apparently defeating our hope with generous amounts of despair — but not always. And perhaps surprisingly often, it is in the 'garden of tears' or the 'wilderness place' that, despite and through our struggle, we find clarity about what matters.

Lord Jesus, you know what true temptation means and, like us, you struggled with doubts and fear. Help us at such times to notice the things that really matter and give us hope for the future. Amen.

BROADCAST TUESDAY 27 MARCH 2012

March 28

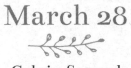

Calvin Samuel

On this day in 1965, Dr Martin Luther King stood on the steps of the state capitol in Montgomery, Alabama, and addressed the weary crowd before him. They had walked some 54 miles, and many were footsore and sunburnt. He said, 'We have walked through desolate valleys and across trying hills. We have walked on meandering highways and rested our bodies on rocky byways.' He went on to talk about the length of the struggle for civil rights, anticipating the question forming in many minds: 'How long is this going to take?'

Whenever we take on a struggle, be it a personal one, a moral one with injustice or a political one, we are inclined to ask the same question. Once the first flush of enthusiastic energy is over, the reality of the situation dawns upon us. The obstacles in our way look bigger than they did before, and we doubt our ability to see it through. Looking ahead, the road seems to stretch up and up toward the all but invisible brow of the hill.

Looking out at the crowd before him, Martin Luther King reassured his audience that 'the arc of the moral universe is long, but it bends toward justice'. Those words have been a comfort ever since to those caught up in a struggle for their cause. When the odds seem stacked against them, they look up and try to pick out the arc of the moral universe stretching high above them and bending toward justice on the horizon.

O God, we thank You today for those voices that inspire us to persist in the quest for justice on this earth. When the road seems long and steep, help us to persist, we pray. Amen.

BROADCAST FRIDAY 28 MARCH 2014

March 29

Edward Mason

I have in my hand a small newspaper cutting. It's about Japanese firefighters preparing to go to the stricken nuclear power plant at Fukushima, a place name unknown to most of us just a week or so ago but which now will never be forgotten.

It joins the growing list of nuclear accidents: Windscale, Three Mile Island and, of course, Chernobyl.

Amidst all the speculation about Fukushima, we might take a moment to give wondering respect to the rescue services as they volunteered to go into mortal danger for the sake of others.

The earthquake and tsunami in Japan have brought terror and desolation to this now stricken country. Our ears still ring from the cry of those whose families, homes, livelihoods and whole communities have been literally swept away. Yet, in it all, we hear of self-sacrificing love – men and women giving all for the sake of others; risking the jaws of death. For me, these acts of love and duty echo the words of another who, on the night that he was to do the same, said, 'No one has greater love than this, to lay down one's life for one's friends' (John 15:13).

A more modern translation puts it like this: 'This is the very best way to love. Put your life on the line for your friends.'

So, Lord God, we give thanks for the courage of all who face danger on behalf of others today. Help us let go of self-interest and, in pursuit of love, be ready to put our life on the line. Amen.

BROADCAST TUESDAY 29 MARCH 2011

March 30

Mark Wakelin

An undercurrent in the biblical motif of the 'wilderness' is the extraordinary image of the promise of the desert that will flower. It is precisely where you see only dryness, dullness and emptiness that refreshing water, bright colour and fullness will be found. This is the often-repeated story of hope.

Hope is a very particular thing in scripture. It is most emphatically not optimism. Optimism might look at the desert and point out its many glorious features, wax lyrical about the dunes, the primitive simplicity of the colour scheme and the glory of being alone and away from the noise of the city. Hope is different, it is evoked when God promises and the promise of God is trusted. Both matter: God who promises and we who trust. God doesn't see only the good in what is, but the good that will be. God's promise is to be trusted because God is able and God is willing. We are invited to trust not because of what we can see, but because imagination, quickened by God's word, sees what one day will be.

Such hope is hard to live with, because it is not instantly comforting. There is, in a sad sort of way, more comfort and ease in despair and cynicism. The hope of what might be, of God's coming kingdom, awakes in us a longing that is hard to bear, hard to live with. For the future demands our obedience in the present. A kingdom comes of love, so we must love now. A kingdom comes of justice, so we must be just now.

God of the future, awaken in our present such longing for Your kingdom, that Your will may be done on earth as it is in heaven. Amen.

BROADCAST FRIDAY 30 MARCH 2012

March 31

George Stack

In the world of politics and in the history of religion, the city of Jerusalem has always been a place of ambiguity and even conflict. Jerusalem is the city of three great world religions: Judaism, Christianity and Islam. The remains of the Western Wall of the Temple, the Dome of the Rock and the Church of the Holy Sepulchre are just three of the 220 sacred monuments in the city. No wonder Jerusalem is recognized by UNESCO as a World Heritage Site.

The ambiguity which is at the heart of Jerusalem will be soon played out in a particular way. On Palm Sunday, Christians remember the triumphant entry of Jesus into Jerusalem. He entered a city excited at the celebrations of the great feast of Passover. He stepped into the revolutionary fervour of a city which wanted to overthrow the Roman occupation. Some thought that he would be the fulfilment of the longed-for Messiah who would complete all Jewish hope.

Public opinion is fickle. Triumph turns to tragedy. The great hymn 'My Song is Love Unknown' spells it out clearly, drawing us in as it tells the story:

Sometimes they strew his way,
And his sweet praises sing;
Resounding all the day
Hosannas to their King.
Then 'Crucify!'
Is all their breath,
And for his death
They thirst and cry.

Lord, when the journey is long and hard, and the direction is confusing, help us not to be distracted by contradictory voices, but guide us to follow the path of justice, integrity and truth, no matter where it leads. Amen.

BROADCAST SATURDAY 31 MARCH 2012

April 1

Sheila Watson

Mark Twain tells us that today is the day which reminds us of what we are on the other 364. The April Fools' Day festival dates back to Roman times. It is a bit of fun — a reminder not to take ourselves too seriously. Sometimes we need drawing out of ourselves, our preoccupations and preconceived ideas. We need to remember how to play.

One person who embodies this *joie de vivre* is Jean Vanier, recent winner of the Templeton Prize for his outstanding contribution to life's spiritual dimension. In 1964 he began L'Arche, now a worldwide network of communities where able-bodied and those with disabilities, mental or physical, live together in mutual dependency. At its heart is the discovery of what the seemingly weak can teach the seemingly strong — that each of us needs to know that we are a source of joy; that we are loved.

Play is key. When there are oranges for desert at L'Arche, he tells us, there's a tradition of throwing the peel. Everyone, even visitors — once they have lost their inhibitions — throws themselves into it. People come out of their isolated worlds. Those who cannot communicate in conversation join in through play.

Lord, help us not to take ourselves too seriously today. Help us to regain that inner sense of play which helps us see that we are not called by You to do extraordinary things, but to do ordinary things with extraordinary love and tenderness. Amen.

BROADCAST WEDNESDAY 1 APRIL 2015

April 2

Tom Wright

Down and down we went, into an old dungeon. It was underneath the house of the 1st-century Jewish High Priest. At the very bottom our guide explained that, though you can never be sure, it's likely that Jesus spent the night there after his arrest and the preliminary hearing which had declared him worthy of death. We stood there and felt the horror and desolation. And we read Psalm 8 – one of the ancient Jewish laments:

My soul is full of troubles, my life draws near to the grave;
I am shut in so that I cannot escape; my eye grows dim through sorrow.

Down and down goes the poem, into the depths of despair. And even God, it seems, is part of the problem. '*You* have caused friend and neighbour to shun me,' we read, and the poem ends with the sodden weight of despair: 'darkness is my only companion.' On that day, in that place, I found my thoughts and prayers stretching out to all the people who cry out in that way from their own misery, who have lost everything that makes life good, not least hope itself: the poor and unemployed in my own region, the multiple continuing sorrows of the Middle East. And I thought of Jesus going down into that same place of darkness and suffering.

God's answer is not to dispense remedies from a great height but to take the pain into his own hands, his own heart. On Good Friday God himself entered our god-forsaken darkness. As another ancient Jewish poet put it: on him fell the punishment that makes us whole, and with his wounds we are healed.

Lord Jesus Christ, as you went into the darkness and horror on our behalf, we pray for all those who cry out of their own misery and sin; that your suffering will bring them healing, forgiveness and hope. Amen.

BROADCAST FRIDAY 2 APRIL 2010

April 3

Janet Wootton

A week ago today, one of this country's great figures was laid to rest. Many words have been written and spoken in the last couple of weeks about Tony Benn: a man who became avowedly more socialist as he got older, not less; a brilliant orator and debater, razor-sharp mind, tireless campaigner for many causes.

Although a convinced atheist, he was brought up as a religious nonconformist in that fiercely independent Christian tradition, congregationalism. His mother, Margaret, Lady Stansgate, was the first President of the Congregational Federation when it was formed in 1972, and was herself a great social campaigner, with a sharp political mind.

Tony Benn continued to speak at and attend events organized by congregational churches. He would say that his political ideals were shaped by this upbringing in a non-hierarchical structure in which decisions are taken locally by the membership of each church.

Nonconformity and dissent, both religious and political, are right at the heart of our national heritage, though we tend not to celebrate them as much as we do those closer to the heart of the establishment.

The church I attend honours the heritage of John Bunyan, imprisoned for his nonconformist beliefs, and writer of the amazing allegory of the Christian life, *Pilgrim's Progress*. Along the road is what used to be another church, named after John Howard, the prison reformer, who was stirred to action by the terrible conditions in the gaol where Bunyan had been held a century earlier.

We thank God for nonconformists, who challenge the status quo by their words and actions. Forgive us for comfortable conformity and give us the strength to dissent from all that is partial and unjust. Amen.

BROADCAST THURSDAY 3 APRIL 2014

April 4

Barry Morgan

Some people sincerely believe that everything in their lives was decided for them beforehand by God. The decisions they make have all been mapped out – all they have to do is to follow the plan, to live out what they regard as their destiny.

Others of us see no such clarity in the pattern of our lives. While we may still believe in God and seek His guidance to make the best choices we can, we hope that things will work out as we choose one particular course of action rather than another.

Tomorrow is Palm Sunday, the beginning of the week the Church regards as the most holy in its year as it tries to recall the events of the last week of Jesus's life, when we are told 'he set his face toward Jerusalem'.

I wonder how he felt. Did he know what was going to befall him because it had all been pre-destined by God – and all he was doing was acting out the divine plan? Or was he like some of us? Not knowing any precise details of what lay ahead that week, but knowing from the example of the prophets who had gone before him that if you challenge authorities, religious or secular, you are not likely to end your life in comfortable old age.

Jesus certainly knew the risks he was running as he rode into Jerusalem. He challenged the Temple authorities and refused to defend himself properly against the accusations levelled against him. But things could have turned out differently had he backed down, left Jerusalem, kept a lower profile. He chose not to do so because at every stage during this last week of his life, he felt he was being true to his own values and to what God wanted him to do – true, in fact, to his own destiny.

Lord, help us to realize that wherever we are and whatever we do, You are also there. Give us grace to trust Your loving purposes and keep us faithful to You. Amen.

BROADCAST SATURDAY 4 APRIL 2009

April 5

Richard Chartres

'I do wish I had a faith,' someone said to me this week. They were polite and wistful, but further conversation revealed that they thought that believing in the Resurrection was really just floating off into some never-never land of wishful thinking.

Actually the message of the risen Jesus was very different. He told his friends to go back to their homes; to go back to Galilee where they had first met. They were to re-immerse themselves in ordinary life but to live their lives in the light of Jesus's way of dying and living.

Jesus did not point the way to dropping out into another world. He immersed himself in this world with all its beauty and tragedy. He took flesh and lived among us, but by doing so did not leave this world as he found it. He was not 'otherworldly' or 'this-worldly', but instead taught his friends how to live in a *next*-worldly way.

So the 11 remaining disciples went to Galilee and met with the risen Christ in a mountainous place, and there, as St Matthew says, they worshipped him but some doubted.

Doubt is not the opposite of faith. We should respect our honest doubts which often serve to move us forward from an immature, self-serving understanding to a deeper trust in the self-sacrificing love of God.

The opposite of faith is a life locked up in itself, the disengaged and risk-averse life which is in reality a living death.

Father, deepen our hunger to see Your plan fulfilled for the spiritual evolution of the whole human race and for a world at peace in which there is justice for all humankind and care for the whole of creation. Teach us the imperfections of our understanding and lead us in the way of Your Son Jesus to worship You in spirit and in truth. Amen.

BROADCAST FRIDAY 5 APRIL 2013

April 6

Anna Magnusson

There's a scene in Alan Bennett's play *The History Boys*, when one of the boys complains bitterly during a poetry class that he can't understand poetry – meaning, also, that he can't see the point of it. The teacher tells him that *he* never understood it either; but, he says, looking at the boy: 'Learn it now, know it now, and you *will* understand. … whenever.'

'Whenever' – this is the heart of it. Poetry is like air, and love, and suffering: it enters you and becomes part of you. It shapes you, marks you and schools you. Not in a momentarily dramatic way, but gradually, quietly, over a lifetime. The words and the meaning – they return when you need them, when you thought you'd forgotten them. Whenever.

My mother's generation was probably the last one to learn poetry thoroughly and relentlessly at school: it was still an era of recitation and party pieces. All their lives, my mother and aunts could remember the poems they'd chanted as schoolgirls. But it wasn't just the *words* that had settled inside them: when my mother was in her '80s, and was still able to speak it out loud, Milton's 'On His Blindness' could reduce her to tears: 'When I consider how my light is spent,' she would begin, sitting in her chair by the window, looking out to the garden, 'Ere half my days in this dark world and wide' – and all the hurt and loss and *hope* of the poem would brim up from her own life and experience. From the understanding of the years.

This morning, may the poetry of God's love and spirit settle within us, and bring light and understanding. Amen.

BROADCAST SATURDAY 6 APRIL 2013

April 7

Ian Bradley

Mindfulness is one of the great mantras of our time. Bestselling books, CDs, apps and courses present it as a technique which will relieve anxiety, stress, irritation and tiredness.

At its heart is an emphasis on resting in clear awareness of the present moment and allowing yourself to be just as you are. Mindfulness meditation focuses on breathing and on recognizing when the mind has wandered. When this happens, there's no recrimination or rebuke but the mind is led gently back to the breath. Thoughts, especially those that dwell on regrets about the past or fears about the future, are treated as clouds passing across the sky.

Something close to mindfulness is at the heart of Christianity. In his Sermon on the Mount, Jesus told the crowds who'd gathered to hear him not to worry about their lives. He commended the birds of the air and the flowers of the fields for not fretting about what they are going to eat or wear. This isn't the only time that he urged his followers to live in the present and not dwell in the past or worry about the future. When one of his disciples asked to be allowed to go off and bury his father before following him, Jesus famously retorted, 'Follow me, and leave the dead to bury the dead.'

Many great Christian mystics over the ages have developed techniques of meditation similarly aimed at freeing their minds from distraction.

Merciful God, You understand all, forgive all, absorb and encompass all. Teach us not to dwell on the past or be filled with fear for the future but rather to live fully in the present, breathing in time with Your divine breath and spirit. Amen.

BROADCAST TUESDAY 7 APRIL 2015

April 8

Leslie Griffiths

A few years ago, I visited Florence. It's the only time I've ever been there, but I felt as if I knew it like the back of my hand. I seem to have spent my life learning about people and ideas connected with the place, and being there was just like wearing my favourite old jumper — it seemed to fit me perfectly and I felt so much at home in it.

We stayed in the hotel that had served as the parliament for those fighting for a united Italy in the late 19th century. Everywhere we found statues or plaques for Garibaldi, Mazzini and so many other architects of that struggle. The *Risorgimento*, it was called, the drive to give birth to a nation.

Everywhere we went in Florence, we seemed to find evidence of the cultural giants who brought Europe back to life after the so-called Dark Ages. In one single church, the church of Santa Croce, I found tombs for Michelangelo, Dante and Machiavelli. The *Renaissance*, we call it, the re-awakening of culture and rebirth of a continent.

I was in Florence in the week after Easter. All the churches still bore ample evidence of the celebrations that had taken place the previous Sunday — every one of them was still bedecked with huge arrangements of white flowers. This marked the *Resurrection*, an event that redefined the horizons of human hope and gave birth to a worldwide and life-changing faith.

Risorgimento, a national movement; *Renaissance*, the awakening of a continent; *Resurrection*, a message for the whole of humankind. There's a new definition of the three 'R's for you!

Dear Lord, in the light of the resurrection of Jesus, help us to live with hope in our hearts and to know that we'll never walk alone. Amen.

BROADCAST TUESDAY 8 APRIL 2010

April 9

Barry Morgan

We once owned a dog who always knew when we were going on holiday. As soon as the tailgate of the car was open, he used to leap in and curl himself into a ball in the corner while the luggage was loaded around him, even though it might take us a couple of hours to actually get going. He had the unerring knack of remembering the family routine for going away on holiday and was just terrified of being forgotten.

Humans also have a fear of being forgotten by their friends or families, or by their work colleagues once they have retired. The dying thief on the cross asked Jesus to remember him when he came into his kingdom, in spite of all the crimes that he had committed. He did not want to be consigned to oblivion.

On the night before he died, Jesus took bread and wine and, after blessing them and giving them to his disciples, he asked them to do the same in the future to remember him. I do not think he did so because he was afraid of being forgotten, rather it was something he did for their sakes. When we dis-member something, we break it apart.

Re-membering by contrast is an act of putting things back together again or making whole. As Jesus approached his death, his disciples would all flee and be separated one from another — be dis-membered. Re-membering what Jesus did the night before he died would have the effect of reconstituting them as a group, of reminding them that they were all members of his community and so belonged both to one another and to him and that this act of remembrance would fill them with hope.

Lord, help us to join You in your work of healing and of breaking down barriers of division and hostility. Amen.

BROADCAST THURSDAY 9 APRIL 2009

April 10

David Chillingworth

I was an 18-year-old living in Belfast when The Troubles began in Northern Ireland. When the Belfast Agreement of 1998 marked the beginning of the end – on Good Friday 15 years ago today – I was 46. It was half a lifetime. And the Agreement could only be the beginning of the end – conflict that has built up over generations takes generations to heal.

Sometimes – not often – people would say, 'I wonder if we shall ever see an end of this.' In the apparently unending succession of violence, murder, intimidation and fear, that seemed unlikely. People didn't look too far ahead. Today was enough to be dealing with.

But a time came when it did begin to change. Old enemies began to talk. Uneasy deals were done. The tide of violence began to retreat.

Conflict seems to go on and on. It embeds itself in family, community, faith community or workplace. It seems to acquire the ability to feed on itself and to sustain itself indefinitely. Each hurt, insult or injury becomes the seedbed for the next and the one after that. In Northern Ireland, we used to talk about the 'politics of the last atrocity'. It becomes difficult to see how the cycle can ever be broken.

So this day of the memory of a conflict which lasted half a lifetime is also a day of hope. It stands for the possibility that there comes a time in every conflict when it's time to settle. It's for all those conflicts which, however we try to resolve them, continue to destroy the present and damage the future.

Father, in every situation of conflict that seems unresolvable, bring Your healing peace and love and, above all, bring hope. Amen.

BROADCAST THURSDAY 10 APRIL 2014

April 11

Anna Magnusson

This is a story of meeting someone from the past.

In a street in Budapest, there's a statue of a thin man in a long coat, his hands in his pockets, his shoulders hunched and head slightly bowed. He's leaning back against a sort of fence post. When I first saw him from the end of the street, I wondered why someone was standing so still and quiet in the rain. I went closer and saw how delicate and vulnerable the back of his neck was like a small boy's.

His face was thin and drawn, his eyes closed, the water trickling down his cheeks. Standing beside this stone man in the rain, I absolutely wanted to know who he was. Etched into the fence post were the words: 'Miklós Radnóti'.

Afterwards I looked for his story, with that feeling of having met someone for the first time and wanting to know more. Miklós Radnóti was a poet, one of the finest in Hungary. He was born a Jew but converted to Catholicism to escape the anti-semitism raging through the country. Neither his conversion nor his poetry saved him: during the war he was conscripted into labour camps, and then to a copper mine in Serbia. He died, along with thousands of others, sometime in November 1944 on a forced march back to Hungary.

After the war, his body was found in a mass grave in the Hungarian village of Abda. In his coat pocket was a tiny notebook, soaked and battered. They dried it in the sunlight, and discovered his last poems – telling his story after death.

Let this be a prayer for all those who died unknown, for those who survived evil, and for the ones who wrote it down. Amen.

BROADCAST THURSDAY 11 APRIL 2013

April 12

Gopinder Kaur

Since the days he first started strumming a guitar, my husband's been a huge fan of Paul Weller, following with devotion all the songs he's written and sung with bands like The Style Council and The Jam. As for myself, I'd never really stopped to listen to Weller's lyrics, letting them pass me by as they were carried along with the music. But I've come to see him as a poet who can paint the simplest picture of the human condition with real depth and poignancy.

In Sikh tradition, it's through lyrical poetry that our spiritual teachings are expressed and shared. Guru Nanak is the faith's founder and in many of the paintings and accounts of his life he's pictured sitting in the shade of a tree, poised to sing to the accompaniment of the *rabab*, a string instrument played by Bhai Mardana, his childhood friend and travelling companion. In moments of inspiration, Guru Nanak would say, 'Bhai Mardana, pick up your *rabab*. I hear the *bani*, the heavenly teachings, descending.' Then *Gurbani*, the sacred verse that flowed from the Guru's lips, would unfold as the melody of Mardana's *rabab* filled the air and words would blend with music to awaken the heart as well as the mind.

The singing of *Gurbani* to music is still part and parcel of Sikh life but sometimes the actual meaning of the words passes me by. But every now and then, something unlocks the lyrics and releases their richness of meaning. It's then that the spiritual message becomes compelling and life-changing.

Creator God, help us to learn the art of listening to the words of your song. So may we discover your pathway to a more uplifting and enriching way of living.

BROADCAST SATURDAY 12 APRIL 2008

April 13

Gordon Gray

Easter is at once the most sacred and the most secular Christian festival. From that moment in the Mass at midnight on Saturday when the priest announces '*Christos Aneste*' — 'Christ is risen' — and the congregation responds 'He is risen indeed', and the darkened church is flooded with light, Christians proceed to celebrate in praise and prayer, in word and sacrament, the astonishing, incredible, delirious event of Christ's resurrection. Easter Sunday is the culmination of the Christian year.

But Easter is also the first major secular holiday of the year, arriving in this part of the world as spring is shaking off the cloudy clasp of winter. Time for important sporting events, such as the US Masters on Augusta's azalea-flanked greens and fairways.

Today, on Easter Monday, that note of festivity continues. While for some it has to be 'business as usual', for many Easter Monday is the day for the first family outing of the year, for getting out into the garden, for a walk in the park — a day to lay aside the depressing issues that threaten us, to be light-hearted in the face of adversity. And all this against a backdrop of that culture-shaping story that tells of the triumph of hope over despair, of wholeness over brokenness, of love over conflict, of life over death.

Help us, Spirit of the Living God, to perceive You in the new life of nature's springtime as in the story of Christ's rising from the dead, so that we may escape, for a moment, the weight of our worries and the world's woes. Amen.

BROADCAST MONDAY 13 APRIL 2009

April 14

Roger Hutchings

Like, I guess, the majority of people, I drive a car. I also ride a bike. Living as I do in a busy city, and increasingly conscious of what our behaviour does to the planet, I'm doing my best to do less driving and more riding. But whether on the streets or in the local park, it often seems as though there's a simmering battle between pedestrians, cyclists and drivers. Sometimes that battle comes to the boil, and one local cyclist was physically attacked last week.

Which is why we have the Highway Code, of course. I was amused, in a diary full of such snippets, to read that today's the day the first Highway Code came in – in 1931 apparently. It makes you wonder what sort of chaos there was before that. Far fewer vehicles, no doubt, but plenty of bikes and people. I expect most of the time there was sensible give and take, and it worked. But there's always someone who thinks he or she is invulnerable, and doesn't give a damn about anyone else. A bit of Highway Code and traffic law seems a proper precaution, to say the least.

Codes and laws are part of religion too. If you look in the Bible, and the Old Testament in particular, not only do you find the familiar Ten Commandments about basic stuff, but you find lots of detail about bits of social behaviour. They didn't have a traffic problem in those days, but they had plenty of need for agreed ways of living in a community. God may not have a view about driving on the left, but the testimony of centuries of believers is that just and peaceful communities are very much God's concern.

May God help us today to avoid ill-temper and selfish behaviour, to live with respect and care for our fellows, and to travel safely. Amen.

BROADCAST SATURDAY 14 APRIL 2007

April 15

David Walker

Perhaps the strangest story of all during Holy Week is Jesus cursing a fig tree. We're told that he was hungry one morning on his way into the city and found it bore no fruit. Passing by the tree on the same journey the next day, the disciples see that it's completely dead and withered. While tales of Jesus using divine power in pursuit of selfish ends are common in some of the apocryphal accounts of his life, they strike a discordant note in the canonical Gospels.

The events of the first Easter have always been seen by Christians as connected to the fall in the garden of Eden. 'As in Adam all die, so also in Christ shall all be made alive,' says St Paul, writing to Corinth. Adam and Eve, ashamed of their nakedness, make themselves coverings of fig leaves, hiding their bodies from each other even as they prepare to hide themselves from God. So maybe as well as the obvious point about fruitless trees, the curious incident of the fig tree in the morning is about the undoing of the shame of Adam — original shame if you want to call it so. It is this shame that prevents women and men being fully present both to one another and to the One who can pardon the sin that leads to shame. God is always far more ready to forgive than you and I are to ask for forgiveness.

Lord Jesus, in your love you crumble to dust the fig leaves with which we cover our shame. Help us to stand before you, not seeking to hide our sin, but to see your smile and to hear your words of forgiveness. Amen.

BROADCAST TUESDAY 15 APRIL 2014

April 16

Gopinder Kaur

When I was young and needed to translate between English and Punjabi, the word for 'name' was easy: 'name' in English and '*nãm*' in Punjabi. As well as meaning 'name' in the everyday sense, *nãm* is a word that goes back thousands of years to the scriptures of ancient India. It appears verse after verse in Sikh teaching to evoke the all-pervading presence of the creator in creation, the essence that holds all existence together. As Sikhs, we are told to remember *nãm*, in the sense of 'Name of the Divine', by chanting and meditating on it and making it part of the fabric of our being.

Nãm is also part of the threefold motto given to us by Guru Nanak, the founder of the Sikh faith: *Nãm Japo, Kirat Karo, Wand Chhako* – remember the Divine Name, work hard and share with others, so that everyday life revolving around work, family and society isn't separated from a focus on the sacred.

Whenever we make someone's name a part of our lives, we enter into a deeper relationship with that person and things no longer remain impersonal. Even the sound of a name, particularly of someone dear to us, can bring the essence of that person's presence to our hearts.

So *nãm* is a reminder to me that, whether it's the Divine Name, or that of someone or something we cherish, a name can make a deep impression on the way we see and go about living our lives.

Nanak nãm milai tã jeevãn, tan man theevai hariã …

Oh my Creator, may I be blessed with the gift of nãm, *your Divine Name, which makes the mind, body and all one's being blossom forth in radiant joy.*

BROADCAST WEDNESDAY 16 APRIL 2008

April 17

Tony Rogers

'The whole community of believers was united, heart and soul; no one claimed for his own use anything that he had, as everything they owned was held in common.'

Those words from the Acts of the Apostles are one of the hallmarks of the early Christian Church, and however far from that ideal we may have moved, there have always been movements that have tried to return to those roots. The early followers of St Francis wanted to live in such a way that they would not only share a communal life, but would also be untrammelled by property and possessions, and live like the disciples of Jesus who went about their business travelling light, without haversacks or purses, and relying on the hospitality of others. But even those idealistic Franciscans couldn't quite agree as to whether this was the right way forward, so within a few years of their foundation, they split into those who continued to move from place to place, and those who believed that they needed roots and a home base.

In one way or another, those traditions within the Franciscan family have lasted, though with modifications. But it's just one important dimension of Christian living. We can live in a community without any personal possessions, or we can own our own property, have our own things and still be generous, outgoing and inclusive. The statutory and voluntary agencies of care try to do what they can to alleviate poverty, loneliness and illness. And while all human organizations have their shortcomings, it's important for us to recognize the good that's done.

Lord, we thank you this morning for those who bear witness to the Gospel in different ways; and for the gifts of churches, religious communities and new movements which express Your love in prayer and action. Amen.

BROADCAST TUESDAY 17 APRIL 2012

April 18

Martyn Atkins

The Diet of Worms reached a critical point this week in 1521. This is not the latest fad in weight loss, but refers to the questioning of a young monk. A Diet was a formal gathering to deliberate and pronounce upon matters relating to the Holy Roman Empire; Worms was the place in Germany where this took place, and the monk in question was called Martin Luther.

Luther's various publications, including the famous *95 Theses*, were placed on a table and he was asked to revoke the heresies they were said to contain. He asked for time to reflect and on 18 April reappeared before the court where the same question was put to him: will you recant?

His response — sometimes rendered 'Here I stand, I can do no other' — is one of the great speeches of history. 'Unless I am convinced by the testimony of the Scriptures or by clear reason,' he said, 'I am bound by the Scriptures I have quoted and my conscience is captive to the Word of God. I cannot and will not recant anything, since it is neither safe nor right to go against conscience. May God help me.' Yet Luther was, for all his courage and greatness, one who suffered from mental illnesses, clinging to God and to faith in the depths and darkness. Here is one of his prayers:

Behold, Lord, an empty vessel that needs to be filled.
My Lord, fill it.
I am weak in the faith; strengthen me.
I am cold in love; warm me and make me fervent,
* that my love may go out to my neighbour.*
I do not have a strong faith; at times I doubt.
O Lord, help me. Strengthen my faith and trust in You.
With me, there is an abundance of sin; in You is the fullness of righteousness.
Therefore I will strive to remain with You. Amen.

BROADCAST SATURDAY 18 APRIL 2015

April 19

Roger Hutchings

The other Saturday, I was standing behind a large gravestone to keep out of the wind as I sketched a lovely church nestling beneath a circle of sheltering trees. A sign on the door suggested the church was built in the 7th century, but I suspect that may have been romantic exaggeration. Perhaps there's been a church on that site in the Menai Straits for that long, but the stones that make up the present building don't look that old to me. Over the years, stones *do* crumble and fall away, and new ones have to replace them if a church is not to fall into ruin. There were too many individual stones to draw them all, but I hope I suggested the strength of that place of worship, with its thick walls and deep doorway, in my drawing.

Tomorrow, in many churches, including mine, we'll be opening our Bibles to read a bit of the first letter of Peter, which speaks about Christians as 'living stones' in the 'temple' which is the company of all the followers of Jesus. I guess such metaphors can be pushed too far, but the idea that we who worship are a living temple serves to remind me that large and small stones, rough-hewn and smooth stones, moss-covered and even crumbling stones are *all* part of the building's strength. We can say, then, that each Christian, each worshipper, is making a living contribution to the whole company of faithful people.

Lord Jesus Christ, the sure foundation of our faith, you have called many different people to follow you. In whatever style we are built, whatever role we have in your living temple, may we stand together to strengthen your kingdom on earth. Amen.

BROADCAST SATURDAY 19 APRIL 2008

April 20

Tony Rogers

We all know people who are so used to having unexpected guests drop in at meal times that they work on the principle of ensuring that there's always enough in the pot to go round. When Jesus fed a crowd of people on the hillside, it had been a long day. The people were hungry, and the apostles were all for sending them home. But a boy was spotted with a couple of fish and a few loaves, hardly enough to feed a multitude. However, the food went round and there was some to spare.

This was one of the miracles described in the Gospels, but there's another dimension to this story, which impacts on the whole world every day. And that's the question of food shortages and food mountains. I'm sure that you can remember that inbuilt sense of justice that comes to the fore whenever sweets are being handed out. Children are quick to say, 'He's got one more piece of chocolate than me.' We're more likely to spot the inequalities when we're the victim. But we also learn that when we try to eke out our rations, then the results easily outweigh the smaller portions. Jesus came to show us that the apparently impossible dream can be achieved; that, if we set out with a goal in mind, that goal can be reached. Our life of prayer teaches us to put behind our human limitations, and live under the wider vision of God.

O God, You open wide Your hand, giving us food in due season. Out of Your never-failing abundance, satisfy the hungers of body and soul and lead all peoples of the earth to the feast of the world to come. This prayer we make in the name and power of Christ our Lord. Amen.

BROADCAST FRIDAY 20 APRIL 2012

April 21

Martyn Atkins

I was privileged to attend the Royal Maundy at Sheffield Cathedral, at which Her Majesty the Queen, whose actual birthday it is today, distributed Maundy money – or, as it's now described, 'Maundy gifts'.

The practice of giving alms and foot-washing on Maundy Thursday, the day when we remember that Jesus Christ washed the feet of his disciples, goes back at least to the 13th century. Foot-washing at the Royal Maundy itself was discontinued in the 1730s, though there are symbolic reminders in the modern service. Some assisting the Queen are girded with linen towels, and carry nosegays of pungent herbs as a quaint reminder that going near dirty feet was not without its consequences!

In the 15th century, it was decided that the number of recipients should be related to the age of the Sovereign: one for each year. At that time Maundy money was given only to those of the same sex as the Sovereign, but that changed in the 18th century, and today as many men and women as the age of the Sovereign receive the Royal Maundy. So in Sheffield, Her Majesty distributed 89 pence in beautiful little purses of red and white to 89 men and 89 women.

It was enormously moving to watch ordinary men and women, some very fragile, some in wheelchairs, receiving their gifts from a smiling, gracious Queen: ordinary men and women who, it became clear as I spoke to some of them afterwards, had done extraordinary things for good and for others.

Lord Jesus, servant king, we thank you today for all those whose humble service has enriched our lives and the lives of our communities; those who in modest but real ways emulate your own generous, life-changing self-giving. Amen.

BROADCAST TUESDAY 21 APRIL 2015

April 22

George Stack

Early in the 20th century, the psychologist Carl Jung developed a theory of dreams and dream analysis, and a way of bringing dreams to the conscious surface of a person's mind.

But dreams and dreamers are not always popular. The dreams of Joseph, recorded in the Book of Genesis, made his brothers jealous of him. They hatched a plot to dispose of him. 'Here comes the man of dreams,' they said. 'Come, let us kill him.' Fate intervened, and they decided to sell him as a slave. They eventually paid the price for their treachery.

And when dreams become prophetic visions, they often cause controversy and violence. This is what Martin Luther King experienced as a result of his 'I have a dream' speech, made in Washington, DC, in August 1963. For many, he became the prophet of the 20th century and the voice of the Civil Rights movement. But many did not want to hear him speak. 'Kill the messenger and we don't have to listen to the message' is the story of Easter. It's the story of martyrs who have given their lives down the ages for integrity. And it's the story of the assassination of Martin Luther King in 1968. Yet without a vision, the people perish. Where would we be if there weren't people who dreamed dreams and had visions to inspire and challenge and give leadership and hope?

O Christ, our morning star,
Splendour of light eternal,
Shining with the glory of the rainbow;
Come and waken us from the greyness of our apathy
And renew in us your gift of hope.
Amen.

BROADCAST WEDNESDAY 22 APRIL 2009

April 23

Martyn Atkins

On the same date that St George of England is said to have slain his mythical dragon, the virus causing HIV/AIDS was discovered in 1984, paving the way for a long and continuing production of anti-AIDS and retroviral drug regimes.

In spite of these advances, HIV/AIDS remains a major health risk for the population of the world today, particularly, but not only, in parts of Africa.

In the 30 or so years since AIDS entered public consciousness, attitudes toward it – and those who contract it – have changed enormously and very largely for the good. Thankfully gone are the days when it was considered simply a gay disease, resulting in the further discrimination of victims, when – abominably – even some Christian ministers, refusing to enter the hospital rooms in which dying victims lay, shouted condemnatory prayers that God would yet save 'prodigal sinners'.

Yet the situation today remains tragic in some parts of the world. So many HIV/AIDS victims are children, infected from birth: children of parents who themselves have the virus, children almost alone in the world because of the ravages of the disease, whole communities misshapen from generation to generation.

St George's dragon was mythical: this enemy remains horribly real, and lurks beneath and beyond a whole host of other pandemics that come and then go. So the fight must continue.

God of compassion, so many of Your children are worn down by sickness, suffering and stigma. Help us to make real the vision that Jesus spoke of as 'the kingdom of God', where justice reigns and tears are wiped from every eye. Amen.

BROADCAST THURSDAY 23 APRIL 2015

April 24

Jeremy Morris

Recently I had a family holiday on the west coast of Scotland. Unfortunately we had one of those washed-out weeks when it seemed never to stop raining, and everyone was grumpy and wanted to go home. But there was one highlight, a daytrip to the abbey on Iona, when, just as the ferry across to the island got under way, the sun came out and we had three hours of glorious weather.

In those three hours the world, and our week, were transformed. The sea was a glorious, deep blue. And life was good after all.

Since then, I've thought much about the suddenness of beauty, how it catches us off-guard sometimes, as if we're suddenly shown something in a new light. Those monks must have worked or prayed through the long, wet, dark hours of winter, only to look up sometimes and see, with new eyes, the radiance with which God had clothed the world around them.

I've often heard people say that Iona is a special place. And yet most of us are stuck with city life, with traffic jams, delayed trains, overdue bills, the school run or the pressing deadline. We're like the monks, face down, jaws set, pressing on with what we must do.

It's hard sometimes to see the beauty around us, not only in places and buildings and nature, but in people and the things they do and say. Perhaps we could hold up our heads a bit more often and look more closely. Perhaps we could allow ourselves to be surprised by our world.

Help us to see our world with Your eyes, Lord, so that we may learn the pattern of Your love, and knowing it, we may be strengthened to follow it, all our days. Amen.

BROADCAST TUESDAY 24 APRIL 2012

April 25

Cathy Le Feuvre

The countdown has begun.

For many thousands of people, the preparation is over. The long winter months of training are behind them.

Tomorrow they will line up for the London Marathon.

I'm always amazed by this spectacular event. The sheer determination of the runners is astonishing. Of course, the elite athletes — the top marathon runners in the world — will be there, and we expect to see them at their best. But lining up for the same event will be many more for whom this activity is not a full-time career. Those running for fun, for charity, to beat their own best times.

I'm informed by friends braver than me who have completed the London Marathon that for many runners there's a moment in the race when they 'hit the wall'. This is the point when it's tempting to look back at the vast distance already travelled and think 'I've had enough!'

But it's then, I'm told, when it's important not to think of the miles already completed but to look ahead and anticipate the end of the journey. To plough on, break through the pain and complete the race.

St Paul, writing to early Christians in Philippi, used the analogy of a race to encourage them not to give up on their faith. 'I've got my eye on the goal, where God is beckoning us onward — to Jesus,' he says. 'I'm off and running and I'm not turning back!'

Lord, at times it's tempting to give up on life, especially when things are getting tough. Help us not to dwell on past mistakes or setbacks but to start again today to look forward with optimism into the future with You. Amen.

BROADCAST SATURDAY 25 APRIL 2009

April 26

Andrew Martlew

Like every day of the year, today has its own crop of significant anniversaries. But at least one event didn't make the news headlines on this day. Not because it wasn't significant, but because the people who knew about it didn't want to make it public. It was only because the news was literally carried on the wind that the Soviet Union had to announce the catastrophic failure of the nuclear reactor at Chernobyl. To say that the engineers in charge had behaved irresponsibly would be a truly awful understatement. A *discussion* about how the cooling system would cope with a loss of external power might have been a sensible thing to do, but to actually try it, well, the results speak for themselves – the cooling system didn't work, and the reactor exploded and the effects spread for hundreds of miles and lasted for years. But on the day of the meltdown, they said … nothing.

That desire to hide bad news isn't confined to the old Soviet Union. None of us like to own up to mistakes. I know I find it easier to keep quiet when I've got something wrong rather than own up and face criticism – no matter how justified.

Wouldn't the world be a better, more open, more honest place if we all made it a little easier for people to admit their mistakes? If you and I were a little more willing to forgive the faults of others, a little less censorious. Even, perhaps, ready to help people put things right rather than stand on the sidelines and criticize?

Lord, give us the strength to bear one another's burdens, not least the burden of failure and error. Give us the depth of charity that makes it easier for others to admit their mistakes, that forgives in gentleness without sacrificing our own integrity. Amen.

BROADCAST SATURDAY 26 APRIL 2014

April 27

Jeremy Morris

Today the Church of England celebrates the life of Christina Rossetti, the Victorian poet who is best known today for the words of the popular carol 'In the Bleak Midwinter', which we seem to sing at King's every year. Rossetti was a highly talented writer, whose poetry was inspired by her intense religious faith.

With a poet's skill, she took images from our northern European winters, and turned them into a parable of the spiritual wasteland into which Christ's coming is a ray of light and hope – 'earth stood hard as iron, water like a stone'.

It isn't really to the point that Christ was born in a Middle Eastern context – one of dry heat, not frozen winters. Rossetti saw that we have to interpret the truth and beauty of God's world through the things with which we are familiar. Faith talks to us and connects with us, in and through the world we know.

Poetry can help us to see the eternal in the particular, the richness and depth of meaning in specific, ordinary things. And religious faith is, in that sense, like poetry. It's not that it lacks truth – far from it – but its truth is not the same in kind as that of physics or mathematics – it always suggests more than can actually be expressed in the very limited capacity of human language.

Faith, at its best, helps us to see the way in which those we meet, and the things we experience, are part of a larger and wider view, with a horizon stretching into the distance, at the edge of which – so many of us believe – we may find God himself.

Lord of all, help us to see in the many particular people and things we encounter today the greater beauty of Your world, that our hearts be made alive to Your truth. Amen.

BROADCAST FRIDAY 27 APRIL 2012

April 28

Mary Stallard

Words about peace commending 'brotherly love' usually make me smile. Remembering the tussles I've had with my brothers, I'm not sure this image is always helpful.

While we often prize our relationships with our parents and siblings, and may have found much love and support from them, family life can also be the arena for our deepest wounds and worst behaviour.

The Bible seems to endorse the experience of those of us who have known squabbles at home and have sometimes struggled to be generous and forgiving with relatives. It's hard to think of a single Biblical story about a family where everyone gets on well — from the first child Cain, who murdered his brother Abel, to Joseph whose 11 siblings schemed against him, through to the prodigal son and his mealy-mouthed older brother: relationships within the families in scripture are usually complicated.

There are only very brief mentions of Jesus's family in the Gospels. These reveal the worries and pressures that many of us can recognize. There's the story of Jesus wandering off to the Temple as a young boy, going missing for three days and being told off by his mother. We also get a glimpse of his family's continuing anxieties when, as an adult, Jesus leaves home and seems preoccupied with his work. Instead of offering an escape from these gritty complications of humanity, the Bible tells of a God who wants to be involved in our conflicted relationships and to redeem them. Jesus encouraged people to do this by relating to God in a personal way as 'Abba', meaning 'Dad', and to others as members of the greater family of humankind, where everyone's valued and where the glue that holds us together is forgiving love.

Patient God, in all the struggles and conflicts of our lives, help us to be as generous and forgiving to each other as You are with us. Amen.

BROADCAST WEDNESDAY 28 APRIL 2010

April 29

Cathy Le Feuvre

Long walks on a beach – it's my idea of heaven!

So, when I visit my family home in Jersey in the Channel Islands, I do try to take advantage of some of the wonderful beaches that the island has to offer.

At low tide, particularly, many of the beaches just stretch out for miles – sandy and clean.

Walking one afternoon recently, I was aware that I wasn't the first person to be on the beach that day. The evidence of others was everywhere. Tiny bird and other animal tracks. Large, medium-sized and small human footprints. There were wheel tracks – one looked like a bicycle and another indicated that a pram had been that way before me. There were several areas where the sand was quite stirred up – an impromptu football game or cricket match, perhaps? And, of course, this being a beach, there were sand castles!

The following morning I was there again – the exercise does me good – but I arrived on the beach just as the tide was going down.

There were no footprints, no tracks. Overnight the sea had washed away all the evidence of the previous day's activity. Here it was – a wide expanse of beach, a clean canvas awaiting the new day.

Sometimes our lives get so messed up, it's hard for us to see where our journey is taking us. But Jesus promised that when we believe and put our trust in him, all the things we have done wrong in the past are literally washed away.

Lord, today, some of us need a fresh start in life. Others of us could do with a bit of a freshen-up. Fill us with Your spirit and start us on the journey to a better future. Amen.

BROADCAST WEDNESDAY 29 APRIL 2009

April 30

Craig Gardiner

The other day I had my check-up at the dentist. Normally our conversation is predictable: 'How often do you floss?' and 'Any trouble with your gums?'

But this time I was asked: 'On a scale of 1–10, how happy are you with the appearance of your teeth?'

It kind of threw me. If I answered less than an average 5, there might be work to be done. My approach to dentistry is, if it ain't broke, then don't poke about. But I wanted to be truthful and my pearly whites aren't that wonderful – maybe they'd score 5 or 6.

In the end, I fudged the issue, saying something like: 'Once upon a time, appearance might have been important, but I'm married to someone who loves me, even with gnashers that are less than perfect.'

But no sooner had I spoken than I began to ponder if a little work done could do wonders for my passport photo and my self-esteem. Could we raise my dental scorecard to a 7 or an 8?

For some people, essential dental surgery can totally transform their lives, but for many more of us, cosmetic work is more of a luxury option in a society that insists that the prettier we are, the more we'll be liked. Lying in the dentist chair, I pondered that what we're worth isn't down to the whiteness of our teeth or a body that's toned. Neither is it about the money in our bank account or the heights of our IQ.

Instead, each of us is beautiful because we're created by God – made in His image. Each one of us is priceless, simply because we're loved by Jesus Christ and filled with His Spirit. For all that heaven longs for us to change, God accepts us just the way we are … and for me, at least, that's just as well.

Lord, today we thank You for loving us as we are and for promising that the best is yet to come. Amen.

BROADCAST THURSDAY 30 APRIL 2015

May 1

Peter Baker

Some days and dates seem to have more power than others in popular consciousness. Today, 1 May, is one of those. There's something imperceptibly real that recognizes, in the advent of this month, that summer is on the way, that nature is doing its job.

Traditionally for some, the day is celebrated with maypoles and Morris dancing. But my first encounter was in the late 1970s, up at Oxford, among those students who would wake with the dawn on May Day to join hundreds on Magdalen Bridge. The ritual always began in those years with organized chaos and noisy silence. Few if any cars were on the road at that time of the morning, so we spilled across Magdalen Bridge and waited below the Great Tower. The sign was the red-robed choristers from the college and school appearing behind the high parapet. From there at 6am precisely, in beautiful harmonies, they would break out into the most glorious sound. It was magical. Human voices rending the still air. One felt alive even after so little sleep. Alive to the gift of existence and the wonder of creation.

The thing that struck me then and since was how this essentially pagan festival, rather like Christmas, had been absorbed by the Church and made somehow part of the Christian tradition, invested with a wider meaning as a result. For the songs the choir sang were hymns to God the creator, pieces of religious worship defining reality as the expression of a Personal Presence whose voice gave order to the world and whose hands shaped the design of nature.

Not that belief in such a God is essential to an appreciation of life or the rhythms of the seasons. For me, though, it's good to know to whom I can say thank you for the sheer wonder of existence.

Creator God, Lord of sun and moon, day and night, spring and summer, thank You that You awaken the dawn, calling everything into being and upholding it. Amen.

BROADCAST WEDNESDAY 1 MAY 2013

May 2

Michael Ford

Today, along the muddy Bagmati River flowing through the Kathmandu Valley in Nepal, the quiet chants of the Hindu priests and the chimes of temple bells are broken intermittently by the piercing sound of wailing grief. Many of the religious monuments in Nepal no longer provide a traditional place of spiritual solace. Tall towers and pagodas were reduced to rubble. People perished as they prayed.

A week after the earthquake, the death toll is still rising. The staggering statistics are hard to take in, the extent of the destruction difficult to believe. Funeral pyres burn night and day. Images of tragedy abound – children wrapped in orange and gold cloth, draped with marigold garlands, their families weeping beside them. But along with the cries of anguish, there are also prayers of thanksgiving to Lord Shiva for survival – even if life now means the misery of squalid conditions without food, water or tents, and the real risk of disease. Hospitals are running out of medicines and need fuel to operate.

Tension is rising over the slow pace of aid deliveries, and there's raw frustration over the coordination mechanisms involved. While angry and frightened people flee on overcrowded buses, aftershocks and landslides hamper the rescue workers who must stay.

This is not the time for geological or theological discussion, only for deep human compassion and an immediate humanitarian response. So we pray:

Creator God, Lord of the universe, we bring before You the displaced people of Nepal, all who have lost their lives and all involved in coordinating and carrying out the relief operation. Amen.

BROADCAST SATURDAY 2 MAY 2015

May 3

Andrea Rea

It is the time of year when many towns and cities hold music festivals, with competitions for solo singing, instrumental music, orchestras, choirs and so on. Recently, I was adjudicating at a festival in a small town in Northern Ireland. Whenever I have to 'sit in judgment', as it were, over children who come to play or sing in these events, I'm reminded of my days as a music teacher in another town. The festival programme there always had a quote on the front cover by the musician and broadcaster Sir Henry Walford Davies. It read, 'At a festival, competitors do not set out to beat each other, they set out to pace each other on the road to perfection.'

I used this at the time to instruct my own pupils about the way to look at their own participation in festivals and competitions, and I think about it now when awarding prizes one musician or another. That very useful quote helped my students to be less nervous when competing onstage at a festival, and it helps me now to see my role not in terms of making final judgments, but of marking progress on that elusive, imaginary road to perfection.

The best result, I think, is when a young musician plays from the heart and somehow conveys part of themselves in the music – unique and joyous. I think I'm with the artist Salvador Dalí on this. He said, 'Have no fear of perfection: you'll never reach it.' To that I would add, 'but you can have a lot of fun trying'. And that goes a long way.

Lord God of our imperfect world, help us to see perfection in the irregular and chaotic details of our everyday lives, and let our striving be toward grace in both triumph and defeat, in whatever we do. Amen.

BROADCAST SATURDAY 3 MAY 2014

May 4

Michael Ford

More than ever before, life is a race against time. A Japanese magnetic levitation train has broken the world speed record, reaching a top speed of 374 miles an hour. China has the fastest computer, operating at 33.86 petaflops. The world's largest fast-food chain has expanded to over 41,000 branches across the globe.

If we let ourselves, each of us can fall prey to this way of living. As a journalist, I remember racing back to Broadcasting House to meet a deadline, only to be brought to a halt in Covent Garden by a guy who held out his arms as a barrier and said: 'Slow down, man, it ain't worth it.' And he was right.

Society has an obsessive compulsive issue with speed. The spiritual life, on the other hand, doesn't operate in top gear. It's not about instant results through the latest apps but, in the words of the Benedictine writer Sister Joan Chittister, a 'slow, slow uncovering of the mechanics of the soul'.

The journey from winter into spring is a marvellous lesson in unfolding and learning to wait. Patience is how we learn to grow. Love between two people that's rushed is often only infatuation; and grief is a process that can't be hurried, despite modern trends to fast-forward rather than pause.

I remember being in a monastery, talking to one of the older sisters about her long life as a cloistered nun. What spiritual insights, I wondered, had she discovered in all those years. 'I've been here since 1955,' she replied. 'And I'm still waiting for something to happen.'

So this morning we ask You, Lord, to slow us down so that we can begin to see Your goodness in others — and in ourselves. Amen.

BROADCAST MONDAY 4 MAY 2015

May 5

Chris Edmondson

Responding to a mocking comment that answered prayer was mere coincidence, the former Archbishop of Canterbury William Temple replied: 'That may be true, but I've noticed that when I pray, coincidences happen, and when I don't, they stop.' Or as a friend of mine used to say: 'If you think it's a coincidence, have a dull day!'

The collapse and cardiac arrest of Bolton Wanderers footballer Fabrice Muamba on the pitch in March has led to what one newspaper called 'a widespread prayer campaign'. As Bishop of Bolton, I, along with so many others locally, have been deeply moved by this outpouring of love and concern, and of course share the joy of what even the most cynical commentators are calling Fabrice's miraculous recovery.

So was it coincidence that, as well as the club doctor, there was a Tottenham fan in the crowd who was a cardiologist? Or that Fabrice was able to be taken quickly to a hospital close by that could offer the best possible specialist care? Given what happened, it's hard to argue with Fabrice's own words: 'I am walking proof of the power of prayer.'

Prayer is essentially about relationships, and what the world has also learned over the weeks the Muamba story has been around is that he and his family are devout Christians; they have spoken openly about their relationship with God, including his dad praying with him before the game for protection.

Prayer or coincidence? Even when we pray fervently, we have to acknowledge things don't always work out as we'd like them to. But in this instance I'll settle for the words of one of the other players on the pitch that day: 'We are very happy the medics did a great job — and we have to thank Almighty God as well.'

Lord, thank You for the gift of prayer. Today, please increase my confidence that You both hear and answer the cries of our hearts. Amen.

BROADCAST SATURDAY 5 MAY 2012

May 6

Michael Ford

It could have been a case for Edward Marston's railway detective. Two black
trolley bags, identical in design, shape and weight, are travelling close to their
passengers on the 8.50am train from Cardiff Central to Manchester Piccadilly.
Somewhere along the line the cases are mistaken. Opening mine an hour or
so later, I find myself staring in disbelief at layers of women's attire and shiny
patent shoes. Then I blush even more. If the lady's taken mine, she'll be in
for an even greater surprise – a black cassock, white collar and a number of
devotional accoutrements.

The experience set me thinking that discovering our true path in life can
be equally baffling. While some people never doubt the route mapped out
for them, others aren't so sure that God has blueprints. They're convinced at
first they're following the right path and couldn't possibly misread it. But then
they turn out to be wrong. The psychological can so easily masquerade as the
spiritual when we're learning the ways of God – and of ourselves.

I once set out hesitantly on a course of action that many believed was my true
vocation, and they persuaded me so for a while. But it was only by experiencing
what I *wasn't* called to that I realized my real calling was actually what I'd been
doing all along. I just needed, as it were, a new set of clothes. Like the black case
on the 8.50 to Manchester, I was convinced the vocation was mine for a while
but then I realized I was in fact mistaken.

So this morning we bring before God all our errors of judgment, and ask for the
confidence to use our mistakes to deepen our relationship with Him. Amen.

BROADCAST WEDNESDAY 6 MAY 2015

May 7

Andrew Graystone

In a televised interview, David Frost once asked Archbishop Desmond Tutu how – in the face of all the suffering he had seen in the world – he managed to remain so optimistic. The Archbishop – echoing some words of Martin Luther King – said, 'I've never been an optimist. I am a prisoner of hope – which is different.'

I guess that optimism is really just a personality trait – a tendency to look on the bright side of life, to believe that things will turn out for the best. To be a prisoner of hope is a different thing. It doesn't come from personality. In fact, it may run entirely counter to your personality. For those who believe, hope is a stark, sometimes even painful, fact of life. 'I have no doubt,' Archbishop Tutu said to David Frost by way of explanation, 'that this is a moral universe and goodness and love and caring are ultimately what will prevail.'

The 1st-century Church in Rome was suffering severe persecution when Paul wrote to them:

> We rejoice in the hope of the glory of God. Not only so, but we also rejoice in our sufferings, because we know that suffering produces perseverance; perseverance, character; and character, hope. And hope does not disappoint us, because God has poured out His love into our hearts by the Holy Spirit, whom He has given us.

Living Lord Jesus, thank you that in a world of despair, you are our hope. In a world of darkness, you are our light. In a world of sorrow, you are our joy. Hold us captive to this hope until it blossoms into the joy of heaven. For Jesus's sake, Amen.

BROADCAST WEDNESDAY 7 MAY 2008

May 8

Andrea Rea

Today's date, 8 May, has special significance because of its association with the end of World War II. 'VE Day', as it's known, is important all over Europe, and has been since 8 May 1945 – the very first VE Day. This year, its arrival is set against commemorations of the beginning of World War I – 100 years ago. It is a bleak convergence, a stark reminder of the terrible recurrence of wars in the 20th century – wars that claimed countless lives, not only of soldiers, but of civilians, ordinary people, in deadly, terrible times.

The numbers of those who died in the wars are staggering – and while we may try to understand why these wars, and others since, happened, we can never fully comprehend the consequence of the loss of so many millions of lives. Men and women who would have met and married but never had the chance, and the children who might have been born to those couples – lost. Musicians and poets who did not compose their best works – lost. Intelligent, intuitive leaders, compassionate thinkers who might have changed the course of human history, but did not survive to have their chance to make a difference – lost.

When we remember victory, we are also commemorating defeat – and as the date of each battle's anniversary comes and goes, so too the roll-call of those who never came home from those battles. This year, on VE Day, when we think about the end of World War II, we are also a little bit haunted by the fact that less than 21 years – barely a single generation – separated that war's start from the end of World War I.

Lord of life, be in our thoughts now and in the time to come, as we remember our wars and pray for peace. Amen.

BROADCAST THURSDAY 8 MAY 2014

May 9

Maggi Dawn

Fifteen years ago this weekend, Nelson Mandela became South Africa's first black president. He called apartheid a 'human disaster'.

'We saw our country tear itself apart in terrible conflict,' said Mandela. 'The time for healing of wounds has come. ... Never, never again will this beautiful land experience the oppression of one by another.'

It takes enormous determination to see peace and justice restored when a country has been torn apart by inner conflict and enmity. But it's not just a modern problem. Justice for the oppressed is a cry that has been heard in every culture, right back through history. Centuries before Christ was born, it was a theme that ran through the ancient writings of the Old Testament.

The prophet Micah asked, 'What shall I bring when I come to worship God? What sacrifice shall I make? Shall I bring lambs as an offering, or rivers of oil?'

Micah answered his own question, saying that God had already shown us the right way to worship. We don't need to make a great display of religious devotion through ritual sacrifice. What's required of us is much simpler but much more demanding, and it's this: to do justice, to love mercy and to walk in humility before God.

Religious rituals have no meaning in themselves if they're not bound up with a change of heart. The sacrifices God looks for are justice and mercy – even toward those we consider our enemies.

Loving God, we give You thanks that You gave Yourself for us. Fill us with a longing for justice, and make us able to show mercy to those who have wounded us in the past. Amen.

BROADCAST SATURDAY 9 MAY 2009

May 10

Clair Jaquiss

Today is Monday — washday. Now that dates me. Actually, the tradition was
beginning to wane as I grew up. My granny had a fearsome mangle that was
manhandled out of the garage on Monday washdays. We would watch her
feed through the steaming washing and the suds would swish into a grey zinc
tub below — blotched white with years of use. Granny's mangle squeezed that
laundry within an inch of its life. There was no 'delicates' setting in her book.

There was a physicality about those washdays which we've lost with the luxury
of automation: putting in a load to wash overnight when the electricity's
cheaper — saving water, washing cooler.

We take it for granted that the silicon-chipped setting will do the business
and at the end of the cycle all we need to do is hang it up or transfer it to the
dryer. Even those stray coins and buttons are presented neatly for us to retrieve
at the edge of the machine's porthole.

Plunging hands into soapy water for washing up or cupping clean water from
the washbasin to rinse your face is pleasingly physical — and a reminder of our
dependence on the skills and expertise of suppliers and scientists to pipe that
delicious resource directly into our homes to wash and to cleanse.

The power of water as an agent of cleansing flows through prayer and liturgy
as well. It becomes a metaphor for renewal — washing away what separates us
from God and offering a new start. So let our experience of water this morning
and through the day give us opportunity to pray.

*Almighty and merciful God, the fountain of all goodness, who knows the thoughts of
our hearts, wash from us the stains of our past and clothe us with Christ so, as God's
children, all may find a new dignity and live a refreshed life in all its fullness. Amen.*

BROADCAST MONDAY 10 MAY 2010

May 11

Eugene O'Neill

A Premiership football manager was asked about the pressure on him after a run of bad results.

'Pressure?' he answered, 'Football's not pressure. Pressure is millions of parents around the world with no money to feed their children.'

His words have come back to me thinking about the poor souls adrift or drowned in the Mediterranean in these last weeks – provoking a response of shock that the Pope has called 'days of tears'.

Perhaps all the more so because I live beside the sea, I have found the images haunting and the human desperation and suffering almost unbearable.

One BBC correspondent illuminated the reality of those who drowned by giving them names and telling their stories.

In almost every case, they were the pride of their African villages, despatched with their communities' blessings and prayers; their passage paid for by collections of scarce money scraped together.

They represent each village's sacrifice so that a few can carry the aspirations of all to a better life and dignity through hard work.

They were people seeking hope.

Among them, I'm sure, were fathers and mothers looking for ways to feed their children. In their number, certainly, were offspring encouraged by their parents to pursue something better.

They stir up echoes of my emigrating Irish ancestors setting out for England or America – travelling on foot to harbours to embark on a new life.

Father, often the pressures of life tempt one to pull the duvet over one's head and wish it would all go away. May the struggles of others help keep our own in perspective. May empathy with those afflicted by such tragic events be a summons to social justice and care.

BROADCAST MONDAY 11 MAY 2015

May 12

Maggi Dawn

We're thinking this week about the idea of giving. But is there any such thing as genuine altruism? Many philosophers believe there isn't. If we give our time, energy and resources to helping others and building a better world, then although that involves material and personal sacrifice, there are rewards for us, too. After all, if we build a better world, then we ourselves will live in it. So when we engage in volunteer work, give to charity or campaign for justice, maybe we're not being as selfless as we'd like to think.

But whether or not it's possible to be genuinely selfless, I think the more important issue is to recognize that we can't have a passive relationship with the world we live in. The choices we make about where we put our time and energy – however small those choices may seem – really do make a difference to the state of the whole world.

Jesus said to his followers, 'Love your neighbour as you love yourself.' But I don't think his words were meant as a test to prove a philosophical point as to whether or not we could be selfless. Rather, he was calling people to realize that every action, however small, has an impact on everyone else. The way we act toward our families, in the workplace and in our everyday lives is every bit as important as campaigning for justice at a national or international level. Every person, every day, has the potential to help build a just society.

Loving God, we thank You that You gave Yourself for us. May we never underestimate the impact of our own actions on the world around us. Amen.

BROADCAST TUESDAY 12 MAY 2009

May 13

Andrew Graystone

Laughter is infectious. However bad the joke, if someone is really creased up, it's almost impossible not to laugh with them.

At this time of year the Church remembers Julian of Norwich, the 14th-century mystic who was, as far as we know, the first woman to write a book in English. Julian was an anchoress, meaning that she spent her life alone, voluntarily walled up in a cell. When she was extremely sick and expecting to die, she had a vision of the love of God. It hardly sounds like comedy gold. But in her vision, she says:

> I laughed mightily, and that made all those who were with me laugh also, and their laughing made me happy. I wanted all of my fellow Christians to see what I had seen, so they could all laugh with me. But I did not see Christ laugh, for I saw that our laughter is for our own comfort, rejoicing in God that the devil is overcome.

What seems to have set Julian of Norwich off here is a radical optimism that in the end good will overcome evil. It's a theme repeated in her writing, and it goes well beyond mere hope. This isn't the hollow cackle of an empty universe but the joyous belly laugh of someone who's just worked out how the world's joke ends.

Loving God, through Your Son Jesus Christ You have won a victory over sin and death. Give us an infectious joy in our salvation, so that others will wonder what's come over us and join in the celebration of Your love. Amen.

BROADCAST TUESDAY 13 MAY 2014

May 14

Andrea Rea

There are days — and we all have them — when you just don't feel like doing anything, and even getting out of bed seems like way too much bother. The French have a word for it, and the English-speaking world has borrowed it: *ennui*. In fact, the English-speaking world has positively embraced it: Sylvia Plath, Langston Hughes and Lord Alfred Douglas have all written poems with 'Ennui' as the title. Never mind the poetry or the etymology, it isn't a particularly nice feeling or concept — it suggests boredom, and possibly laziness.

Recently my attention has been drawn to stories about remarkable people who are perfect, shining examples of what must surely be the absolute opposite of ennui. The BBC Young Musician of the Year competition was broadcast just this past weekend. Every one of the competitors seemed to be a fantastic example of dedication to their musical instrument, their studies and their friends and family, all while managing to practise amazing numbers of hours every day. No ennui there!

And just last week, paralyzed former horse rider Claire Lomas finished the London Marathon after 16 days of walking with a pair of bionic legs. Again, I can't imagine anyone with her stamina and determination ever being bored or wanting to stay in bed.

Remarkable, inspiring people and their achievements come in many forms, and set against their strength of character and dedication, my own small goals seem very achievable indeed — and ennui has no part in any of them.

God who set the stars in motion and has blessed us with tasks to perform and gifts to nurture, help us to keep going and to make the most of every single hour. Amen.

BROADCAST MONDAY 14 MAY 2012

May 15

Peter Baker

The genius of the Psalms, according to Athanasius, the early Church Father, is that they don't simply speak *to* us, they speak *for* us. They describe how we feel. One minute there's delight as we ride high, enjoying the experience of a clear faith, while the next we spiral down into anxiety, confusion and despair.

It's the issue of integrity that surfaces toward the end of Psalm 19, with the recognition of the two halves of our life. 'May the words of my mouth and the meditation of my heart be acceptable in your sight, O Lord my Rock and my Redeemer.'

The awareness of that space between mouth and heart – the outer and inner life – is often a challenge. We become painfully conscious of feeling one way but acting or speaking another. We're pulled apart, the self is split. Of course, some deny any sort of necessary relationship between the private and the public identity of an individual. Or at least, they argue, one's personal life should not be confused with any social or professional role we might perform. What we are and do behind closed doors is irrelevant to the rest of our lives. But I have sat with too many people in my work as a pastor to know that this separation is neither emotionally healthy nor practically possible in the long run.

And so the Psalmist longs to close that integrity gap in his own life. The key, he acknowledges, is his heart. This is the place where values are formed, motives fashioned and words have their source. So as we move into a new day, it is crucial that we pay attention to the interior life and what feeds it. We are influenced perhaps more than we realize by the environments we inhabit, the images upon which we focus and the messages we download.

Lord, may we be sensitive to our environments of choice today, may we be mindful of the gap that can exist between attitudes and actions. We pray through Christ our Rock and Redeemer. Amen.

BROADCAST SATURDAY 15 MAY 2010

May 16

Gemma Simmonds

On this day in 2001, John Prescott, the Deputy Prime Minister, punched a protester who threw an egg at him during a visit to North Wales. Public opinion at the time was divided. Some people complained that a political figure should show more restraint and dignity than to get into a brawl by fighting aggression with aggression. Others said it was only an instinctive reaction to being assaulted, and any other red-blooded male would have done the same.

The idea of 'turning the other cheek' is not one that generally caught on among the followers of Christ. Christians have done their fair share of slaughtering their enemies down the ages, and Christian theology has shown itself ambivalent about the morality or otherwise of war. But there's no doubt that the forgiveness of enemies and peaceful resistance to violence are some of the strongest hallmarks of Christian belief and behaviour.

Forgiveness of others when they have hurt or angered us can demand immense strength of character. It's hard to forgive. We can pardon injuries when we're able to find excuses for them, but forgiving others from the heart is another matter entirely. Embedded in the one prayer that Jesus taught us is the petition that God should forgive us as we forgive others. This seems to leave us little choice if we want our own sins to be forgiven. The promise is that God will give us the courage and generosity to forgive. The challenge is that we have to ask for it.

Lord Jesus, You taught us to forgive all injuries. Widen our hearts and minds so that we can make room in our lives for the seeds of Your forgiving love to grow and bear fruit. Amen.

BROADCAST SATURDAY 16 MAY 2015

May 17

Andrea Rea

I was at a baptism this week in the church where I play the organ, and it was a thought-provoking morning for a number of reasons. The church, like many, has an ageing congregation, so we don't see too many baptisms, and it was lovely to have children and babies there, as well as the child's parents and their friends and other family members. There was a real sense of occasion and everyone was wonderfully well dressed.

Most of the baptism party hadn't been in the church before. In fact, it seems that most of them hadn't been in any church for quite some time. But the baptism clearly was important, and even if it meant something different to each one of us there, it gathered us together. Talking with friends after, I wondered about the notion of having your baby baptized when you weren't particularly religious or even necessarily a believer yourself. Someone suggested that, as a sacrament, baptism has a sort of life of its own in the way it works, both in what it symbolizes in terms of the Church and what it represents in the life of a child.

I'm reminded of a folk song called 'Going Down to the Well with Maggie' by a local singer-songwriter. It describes a child spending time with an aunt and learning about the world through simple chores like fetching water, which is, of course, a powerful symbol in the sacrament of baptism. The song talks about the profound impact those simple lessons can have, and says: 'She knows what she is giving me, but not what I receive.' And I think baptism, or prayer, or anything else that we might not fully understand or even believe in, still has the power to reach us and give us what we need, whether we realize it at the time or not.

Dear Lord, thank you for the water of life and the many ways in which we receive it. Amen.

BROADCAST THURSDAY 17 MAY 2012

May 18

Becky Harris

How often when we wake do even the most vivid dreams of our sleep vanish, leaving us with tantalizing, half-remembered fragments? Dreams that seemed to carry such significance and meaning, if only we could remember them. But as we give ourselves to another day, so the dreams fade and are gone. Have they left us any richer? — shaped our thinking while we slept? Or are they just a valve through which our subconscious deals with the events and emotions of the previous day?

'All men dream: but not equally,' said TE Lawrence — or Lawrence of Arabia, as he's remembered, and the anniversary of whose death it is today. 'Those who dream by night in the dusty recesses of their minds wake in the day to find that it was vanity: but the dreamers of the day are dangerous men, for they may act their dream with open eyes, to make it possible.'

While Sir Christopher Wren was supervising the construction of St Paul's Cathedral, it's said that a journalist interviewed some of the workers, asking the question, 'What are you doing?' The first worker replied, 'I'm cutting stone for ten shillings a day.' The next answered, 'I'm putting in ten hours a day on this job.' But the third said, 'I'm helping Sir Christopher Wren construct one of London's greatest cathedrals.'

Each day is a gift from God that offers the opportunity to make a difference. But, to make a difference, we need a clear sense of vision and the ability to make intentional choices that will bring our dreams to reality.

St Paul reminded Christians in the early Church, 'Be very careful how you live — not as unwise but as wise, making the most of every opportunity.'

So Lord, at the start of this day, implant the seed of Your vision within us and give us wisdom to bring it to fruition. Amen.

BROADCAST WEDNESDAY 18 MAY 2011

May 19

Peter Smith

The two great commandments that Jesus gave to his followers were that we must love the Lord our God with all our heart, mind and strength, and that we should love our neighbours as ourselves. That second commandment is often the one that gives us the greatest difficulty. If we're honest, we know that we can sometimes be very self-centred and that makes us suspicious about loving ourselves. We tend to get caught up in feelings of guilt because we think that self-love must necessarily be selfish. We feel that we must always give and give to others without any regard for our own wellbeing. But I think that to take that attitude can lead to a pretty miserable life, which, taken to extremes, can lead to deep anxiety and even mental breakdown. We have to learn that we need time for ourselves. That is a basic human need and we ignore it at our peril.

The noisy and frenetic culture in which we live can delude us into believing that our fulfilment and happiness lie in the instant gratification of our desires and wants. But when we reflect on our experience, we discover that we can't find our true selves simply in material and sensual gratification, or in the chattering world of mobile phones and the constant lure of our digital audio players.

Beyond all that, there is a deeper place, a deeper life that is part of our nature. In silent reflection we can rediscover the wonder we have in enjoying the simple pleasures of life – a stunning sunset, a wonderful poem or a picture by a superb artist. In meditating on such beauty, we can begin to discover our own God-given beauty, which He wants us to love and enjoy as He does.

Lord, help us today to find time to rediscover the silent rhythm of the nature You have given us, so that we may be refreshed by the beauty of ourselves and Your creation. Amen.

BROADCAST TUESDAY 19 MAY 2009

May 20

Gemma Simmonds

The Buckinghamshire market town of High Wycombe has a custom dating back to medieval times of weighing the new mayor in full public view in order to see whether he or she has been getting fat at the taxpayers' expense. The mayor and corporation are traditionally required to sit on a specially erected scale to have their weight recorded and compared with the previous year's. If their weight is steady, the mace-bearer calls out the weight, adding the words, 'And no more!' This means that they're judged to have worked hard for the local community, who cheer and clap to show their appreciation. But if the mace-bearer finds that the mayor's weight has crept up, he adds the words, 'and some more!' This means that the mayor is judged to have lived a year of indulgence at the ratepayers' expense, so the crowd jeers and boos. In the past they would also throw rotten tomatoes and fruit.

In other parts of the world there are less colourful ways of trying to assess whether or not public servants have done a good job on behalf of those they represent. We say of people who are arrogant and over-bearing that they 'throw their weight around'. We also say of people whom we treasure and value that they're 'worth their weight in gold'. The doors of many medieval cathedrals show the devil and St Michael weighing up each soul to find out its worth. Often St Michael is seen leaning on the scales to make them come down in his favour. God is willing to put his weight behind us in order to save us.

Merciful God, You know our every thought and deed. Judge us not by what we deserve, but by the measure of Your love. Amen.

BROADCAST WEDNESDAY 20 MAY 2015

May 21

Lindsay Allen

I'm looking at a photograph of a garden path.

It's broad and straight, and runs from the front door of the house, down the well-kept garden and to the street. There's nothing remarkable about it, except that just outside the gate, where the path runs through a security wall, is a memorial plaque. It marks the spot where the owner of the house fell, killed by an assassin's bullet.

I'm in Delhi and the house belonged to Indira Gandhi, the then Prime Minister of India.

Within hours of her death, her son Rajiv was sworn in as her successor. Six-and-a-half years later, on this day in 1991, he too was assassinated.

It's a sobering reminder of the risks taken by political leaders all over the world, and a timely warning that politics has a higher purpose than providing material for current-affairs programmes.

Despite the high profile it gets in the media and the ill-advised behaviour of some politicians themselves, politics is not part of the entertainment industry; and while, thank God, we live in a democracy where those who lead us may be held to account, they are not there to be the butt of relentless criticism, abuse and humiliation for the entertainment of a cynical public.

The Apostle Paul, in his letter to Timothy, urges him 'that requests, prayers, intercession and thanksgiving be made for everyone, for kings and all those in authority, that we may live peaceful and quiet lives in all godliness and holiness.'

Heavenly Father, we pray for all those who have the responsibility of leadership. We pray especially for our Queen as Head of State, for the Prime Minister and the Deputy Prime Minister and for all those leading devolved assemblies. We pray that You will give them wisdom and insight and diligence in government. And we pray for their protection. Amen.

BROADCAST SATURDAY 21 MAY 2011

May 22

Mark Wakelin

Tomorrow is the feast of Pentecost, celebrating the disciples' experience of the Holy Spirit. A lot of people describe that moment as the birth of the Church. It's a strange story full of images that are hard to imagine and ideas that are even harder to grasp. I wonder, sometimes, if we don't over-complicate it, though, and if a normal use of the word 'spirit' wouldn't cover what we mean. The Bible says that God 'is love', and perhaps that's all we need to know about this awesome moment. God pours out the essence or spirit of himself upon a group of very unhappy men and women, and that changes everything for them.

One of the Resurrection stories tells of Jesus breathing on his disciples so that they can receive the Holy Spirit. You have to get pretty close to someone to feel their breath, as close as a mother to her child or perhaps two lovers to one another. To get close to God, so close that you can 'feel God's breath', is a powerful image of the intimacy that is at the heart of a message about God's involvement in the world. God need not be a distant creator or a stern moral authority, but may be as close as the air we breathe, and with the gentleness of a breath able to pour His Spirit into us, filling us with love that drives out fear and helps us become the people we're designed to be.

Spirit of God, as gentle as a breath of air, as powerful as a stormy wind, fill us and shape us today with Your love. Where we are afraid encourage, where weary refresh, where deflated fill us with the hope that love is at the heart of all things, and all things will come together in Your love. Amen.

BROADCAST SATURDAY 22 MAY 2010

May 23

Anna Magnusson

I've had a poem in my head for the past few days. We're clearing out our old family home, and I keep remembering how important the *sounds* of a house are. The poem is by Robert Louis Stevenson, and this snatch has been floating through my memory:

My house, I say. But hark to the sunny doves
That make my roof the arena of their loves, ...
And fill the chimneys with their murmurous song:
Our house, they say ...

When we first arrived as children in this old stone house in the countryside, my sister and I shared an attic room. I remember how different everything sounded from the town street we'd come from. The baby starlings skittered and twittered under the eaves. When someone ran a bath, the water pipes thumped and throbbed. At night, in winter, the wind battered and howled around the old roof, and I remember snuggling under the bedclothes, feeling safe from the storm.

There was the particular squeaky *click* when we opened the little cupboard door of our bedside tables. My sister and I kept our treasures there: comics, books, letters, chocolate. And each day, the clacking of my father's manual typewriter rang through the glass door of his study.

The weekend my sister and I worked our way through the rooms of the house, clearing and sorting, that soundscape played in our heads. We'll carry it with us, long after the house is filled with new voices and stories.

God, we thank You this morning that we can carry with us the sounds and sights of our past, and for the comfort they can bring. Amen.

BROADCAST FRIDAY 23 MAY 2014

May 24

Lindsay Allen

I sometimes wonder who's up and about and listening to the radio at this time. Shift workers coming to the end of a long night, perhaps, or people with a busy day ahead, determined to make an early start.

Or are you, like me, just one of those habitually early risers who, even on holiday, is usually up before six? I find that there's something special about the early morning, a quiet intimacy with the emerging day.

It's interesting to note how often the phrase 'early in the morning' crops up in the Gospels. Jesus tells the story of a rich landowner who went out 'early in the morning' to hire men to work in his vineyard.

Matthew records that 'early in the morning' a hungry Jesus was walking back to Jerusalem when he spotted a fig tree growing by the side of the road.

It was 'early in the morning while it was still dark' that the women made their way to the tomb on that first Easter Sunday. And after the Resurrection, the disciples, having spent a fruitless night fishing, noticed 'early in the morning' a figure watching them from the shore, not realizing that it was Jesus.

Perhaps most significant is Mark's observation that 'very early in the morning, while it was still dark, Jesus got up, left the house and went off to a solitary place, where he prayed.'

Early morning is a time to be savoured, a time to reflect, a time to organize our priorities and seek God's blessing and direction for the day ahead.

Heavenly Father, we thank You for keeping us safe throughout the hours of darkness and for blessing us with the gift of another day. We pray that we use it well and wisely. Help us to be kind today and generous to those in need, and keep us from sin. Amen.

BROADCAST TUESDAY 24 MAY 2011

May 25

Anna Magnusson

Here's a memory from my childhood. It was an evening in May, the light that soft grey of early summer. The countryside was still, except for the shush of wind in the trees. I remember we were on our bicycles, circling around the driveway in front of the living room window, which glowed yellow-orange in the gloaming. Suddenly a cheer rang out from the living room. Minutes later, someone — probably our mother — came out on the step and shouted, 'Celtic have won!'

It was 25 May 1967 and Celtic had just beaten Inter Milan to become the first British team to win the European Cup. I was seven. Even now, the memory of the grey light, the aimless bicycle circles, the warm air and the cheer from the living room are vivid. Except: we only moved to the countryside when I was eight. In 1967 we lived in a house on a street in Glasgow. So what am I remembering?

Memory is powerful, and memory is unreliable. Like the moment Neil Armstrong landed on the moon. I remember sitting on the living room couch, the flickering, fuzzy black-and-white TV screen, and there he is, jumping down. I'm aware of a voice saying, 'Okay, it's very late. Bedtime.' But my older sister says I wasn't allowed to stay up. I was never there. Was I?

It's a mystery, memory. Strong and vivid; elusive and fragile. To carry with us the imprint of our living, the sense and sound and feel of our lives — it's the only thing that breaks the lock of time and sets us free.

Eternal God, who is beginning and end, beyond time and in this moment: thank You for the gift of remembering. Amen.

BROADCAST MONDAY 25 MAY 2015

May 26

Mark Wakelin

The Civil Rights leader and Baptist preacher Martin Luther King would often argue that we should take seriously Jesus's command to 'love our enemies'. Given King's own experience of being beaten, stabbed, imprisoned and vilified by racists across America, his argument is worth hearing. He was quite clear: you can't expect to have what he called 'an affectionate emotion' toward someone who is hurting you, but that isn't what he meant by love.

He said instead that we should have 'a creative redemptive good will'. Both 'creative' and 'redemptive' are profoundly theological words. The creative mind that can think outside the box and the compassionate heart that can seek a way forward for everyone to gain are both the mind of God working to change the world. Change is enacted by seeking solutions rather than vengeance.

I find it hard to imagine how difficult it must have been for Martin Luther King to say and live this love. Being filled with hurt, anger, frustration and the feelings of injustice and insult would make it very hard to be creative or redemptive. A clue, perhaps, was something else he said. 'The older I get,' he claimed, 'the more I owe.' He had a profound sense of how much he owed to God. Developing his sense of gratitude for what he had received seemed to release a huge capacity to love, even for those who beat him.

Generous God, You pour out Your love upon us in the most gracious way. The whole of creation cries out that it is made, and Your love surrounds us like the air we breathe. Help us today to live aware of Your loving, that in our living we may love others well. Amen.

BROADCAST WEDNESDAY 26 MAY 2010

May 27

Lindsay Allen

With more and more families feeling the squeeze, travel agents are reporting a boom in stay-at-home holidays this year.

Friends of ours own a cottage on a tiny island off the coast of Connemara in the west of Ireland and we go down to it from time to time. When some of my church congregation ask me what heaven is like, I show them the pictures!

Sitting outside the half-door of the cottage on a bright May morning, the only sounds are birdsong and the quiet lapping of a sparkling sea. The fields are awash with wild flowers, the hedges covered in blossom like a late fall of snow and the Twelve Bens of Connemara are glowing purple in the distance. You wouldn't want to be anywhere else on earth.

When the busyness of life begins to take its toll, there is something in all of us that longs for a quiet place. A need to be refreshed.

Jesus's disciples record that at one point in his ministry so many people were coming and going that they did not even have a chance to eat. So he said to them, 'Come with me by yourselves to a quiet place and get some rest.'

True rest is more than a break from work. The Sabbath 'day of rest' — now, unfortunately, a thing of the past for most families — is a God-ordained space in the week for both physical rest and spiritual refreshment. David wrote in the most famous of his Psalms, 'He maketh me to lie down in green pastures: he leadeth me beside the still waters. He restoreth my soul ...'

And so I encourage you to find that quiet place in your own life where you find peace and refreshment.

Heavenly Father, we pray that in the busyness of our lives we do not neglect our spiritual wellbeing; that we set aside that quiet place where, through prayer and quiet meditation, our souls are restored, our lives refreshed and our relationship with You renewed. Amen.

BROADCAST FRIDAY 27 MAY 2011

May 28

Stephen Oliver

I've just come back from Geneva and a visit to the Large Hadron Collider where scientists recreate conditions that existed within a billionth of a second of the Big Bang. Einstein once said that he believed imagination was more important than knowledge. And I can see that. I'm not sure I understand half of what I was told in Geneva, but I suspect my failure was not so much the lack of knowledge as the limits of my imagination. But I have to say that I get excited by science and new ways of understanding the universe.

We often think that science moves forward by the onward march of inexorable logic. But history suggests that progress is by way of that 'Eureka!' moment, the leap of imagination.

Imagination is the foundation of human compassion: the capacity to imagine what someone else is going through. Imagination is what inspires art, which in turn fires my imagination. When David Hockney painted purple trees, it seemed surreal but it made me look at trees more closely and, yes, I began to see the colours he had seen. Imagination is what fuels vision and, for good or ill, human ambition.

For when I came away from Geneva, I realized that what had impressed me most was not so much the basic science as the fact that someone had the vision to build this instrument at all; and more than that, had harnessed the imaginative collaboration of 10,000 scientists and engineers from over 100 countries to build it and make it work. Now that *is* a miracle.

God of mystery and majesty, free us from all that constrains imagination and limits our dreams. By Your Spirit, illuminate our minds and expand our vision for a better world and safe future for all people. Amen.

BROADCAST WEDNESDAY 28 MAY 2014

May 29

Eugene O'Neill

On this day in 1982, in the great cathedral of Canterbury in Kent, Archbishop Robert Runcie greeted Pope John Paul II. It was the first visit to England by a pope; and its historical significance was dramatized when, standing before the chair of St Augustine, having knelt together in prayer, the two leaders embraced to thunderous and heartfelt applause.

Later in the ceremony came a quieter moment when Archbishop and Pope, together with other Christian leaders, processed to the Martyrs' Chapel in the cathedral. Uttering the name of a chosen contemporary martyr, each of them lit a candle and placed it in a seven-branched candlestick.

'Martyr' simply means 'witness', in the Christian tradition signifying witness to faith. Among these martyrs, some had stood against the totalitarianisms of the 20th century by proclaiming the freedom of the individual to believe; some — like Martin Luther King — against social injustices.

The last candle on that day was the most poignant: lit for the 'unknown martyrs' of the 20th century, the countless of any faith or none who had suffered anonymously. One writer has called them 'candles in the dark'.

'Martyr' can be seen as a problematic word in the context of faith; yet all these were non-violent witnesses to a belief that compassion and love are ultimately stronger forces than bitterness and hatred.

God of mystery and miracle, speak to us through our eyes and ears that we may grow spiritually into the people You want us to become. Amen.

BROADCAST SATURDAY 29 MAY 2010

May 30

Peter Baker

It was during this week in 1953 that news began to circulate of a remarkable achievement. A New Zealander and his Nepalese companion had climbed to the roof of the world. Mount Everest, one of nature's remaining and most formidable frontiers, had at last been conquered.

After decades of failure and 12 previous attempts, nine of which were British expeditions, Edmund Hilary and Tenzing Norgay finally made the gruelling climb up the south face. Yet, after all that, they could only stay at the summit for 15 minutes because of low oxygen levels. But it didn't matter: they had actually done it. Following months of preparation and weeks of climbing, and though exhausted, they reached the top triumphant.

And once someone had shown that the impossible was possible, many thousands of others, including the disabled, the very old and young, have since completed the climb of 29,035 feet.

But it all began in the foothills of the Himalayas with a single step. This is the way every significant journey we make in life begins, every obstacle we have to face, each challenge that towers above us. Taking the first step is always crucial — whether that's a decision to move on, or a commitment to face our fears, realize our ambitions or create our own piece of history on a much smaller scale.

It was reported that, before they descended, Edmund Hilary placed on the summit a wooden cross he'd been given. For the Christian, Jesus is the pioneer of faith and the cross upon which he died is history's greatest turning point.

Lord, whatever the challenges we might face today in work or at home, may we be willing to take that important first step. Grant us perseverance to keep going until we complete what we started. And may we trust Christ, the one who by his death and resurrection has pioneered the way for us. Amen.

BROADCAST MONDAY 30 MAY 2011

May 31

Alison Murdoch

A few weeks ago my husband and I were looking forward to a special weekend in the country. We were encouraged by a good weather forecast — it's going to be sunny and gorgeous, they said. So my heart sank on the Saturday morning as I woke up to that particularly British sensation of grey light around the edges of the curtains, soon to be followed by the pit-pat of rain. The fact that we'd been led to expect sunshine made it even worse.

'Less desire means less pain,' says one of my Tibetan Buddhist teachers When I first heard this, I found it startling. Desire is part of pleasure, right? Yet now I wonder if much of the time we're simply setting ourselves up for a fall. However convinced I am that a frothy cappuccino, a new piece of clothing or the latest gizmo will make me happy — when I observe more closely, how long does my happiness and satisfaction actually last?

Desire also creates a kind of blindness to what's actually happening around us right now. For example, we might miss out on the simple pleasure of a morning cuddle in bed on a rainy morning, in place of that bracing walk that we'd originally had in mind. Desire can also make us so caught up in ourselves that we fail to notice what we can do for the people around us — which is often a much more direct source of happiness and satisfaction than anything else.

The weather is like the government, said Jerome K Jerome: 'it's always in the wrong'. Maybe the 24 hour weather channel isn't the main story.

Let's pray that we can all find happiness and be open to the needs of others, regardless of whether the sun is shining this weekend.

BROADCAST FRIDAY 31 MAY 2013

June 1

Peter Baker

The transition from a white minority government in Rhodesia to a black-led government occurred on this day in 1979. Quite soon after, Robert Mugabe's ZANU-PF came to power and so began the path to a new post-colonial destiny for Zimbabwe. It has been a troubled journey; the country characterized like many African states by tribalism, the rising incidence of HIV/AIDS, human rights abuses and allegations of corruption.

It is the issue of land rights and reforms that proved so problematic for Zimbabwe at the very beginning and whose harmful consequences still continue into the present. The overwhelming majority of land at the time of independence was in the hands of the white settlers and their families. But of course they were not the original owners; the Shona, the Kalanga and the Ndebele tribes all laid claim to a share in the wealth of the land.

A lack of agreement over whose primary rights should be recognized and inadequate compensation to whites, who had been instrumental in developing the country, was followed by forcible government acquisition of farms and land holdings, accompanied by violence, murder and further economic meltdown.

There are no easy answers. And it is a global problem, not just an African one. But in this vital matter of whose land it is, maybe a worldview shaped by the Bible can help create a better understanding. According to that perspective, the land, everywhere, ultimately belongs to God the creator. He is the original owner. We are simply stewards whose job is to ensure that God's gift of the land is managed with justice, fairness and for the benefit of all, not just some.

Lord, the earth and everything in it belongs to You. Teach us in the West the value of a simpler lifestyle so that we will not exploit the resources of the world You have given us. We pray that governments may grant just access to land for all those denied it. Through Christ, Amen.

BROADCAST WEDNESDAY 1 JUNE 2011

June 2

George Craig

Looking back to the 1950s, it seems like a different world. One in which small suburban living rooms were crammed to overflowing with people transfixed by a tiny flickering screen in the corner of the room. Their main reason for being there on this day in 1953 was to see the coronation of Queen Elizabeth II. There seemed to be an atmosphere of patriotic enthusiasm about, which even a small boy like me couldn't miss. But for many, at least as big an attraction was the chance to see a television set actually working.

The technology then was pretty primitive – the screens not much bigger than a modern smartphone and the pictures black and white and, frankly, blurred. But it just seemed so ... *clever* that such a thing was possible. It gave people lucky enough to have access to a TV a chance to feel part of an event at which ordinarily they would just be distant spectators. Radio had done that to some extent but ... now the sound had pictures. I strongly suspect that one of the reasons that the Queen is so much valued by so many people is that the generation that grew up with her has – largely through television – been able to feel an involvement with her that just wasn't possible before.

But that was then. Things have moved on. For many of us television has become so much a part of our lives that we have long since stopped seeing it as a technological wonder. But maybe we've also lost our sense of wonder about being able to see and be part of events and experiences in ways that otherwise we couldn't have dreamed about. And to my mind, that's a pity.

Maybe we'll never get back the awe at the technology that people had in 1953, but it is good to pause and ask ourselves sometimes if we *should* try to recover the sense of privilege that our access to a world beyond ourselves can give.

Father, we are truly grateful for the opportunities with which technology enriches our lives. Make us sensitive to the responsibilities that come with them. Amen.

BROADCAST MONDAY 2 JUNE 2014

June 3

Eugene O'Neill

Almost every day we are faced with dilemmas: choices between doing the expedient thing and what we know to be the right thing.

Sometimes it isn't easy to know what the right thing is and a great deal of thinking is needed. But often moral choices are a lot more domestic than that: to remind the person behind the till that they've forgotten to ring in that item; to keep the expenses claims straight; to notice dishonesty and call it.

When it comes to conscience, few of us are called to make life or death choices even once in our lives; and it is often not obvious how our smaller choices matter.

On 3 June 1886, a Ugandan teenage boy, Charles Lwanga, was compelled to make such a decision. He and some of his companions — attendants at the royal court — were propelled into a dilemma by the demands of their king, Mwanga. Their choice ended in their execution.

Charles is now a saint, but what good did this sacrifice do? One of the prayers set for his feast day in the Catholic tradition says: 'in their lives on earth you give us an example.' The heroic virtue of this young African and his companions is a civic virtue. Their example — their choice — proclaimed the limits of the power of the state at the doors of personal conscience. It also asserted that, for a strong society to exist, people of powerful conscience are needed, because only they will ensure that honesty and right dealing — not expediency — are the foundations for action.

Creator and sustainer of all there is, You speak to us in the depths of our consciences; may they guide our individual choices and may these create a just and strong society. Amen.

BROADCAST THURSDAY 3 JUNE 2010

June 4

George Craig

Everybody in our village just south of Aberdeen liked our Billy. He and my father were cousins but had grown up together like brothers. He was an integral part of my childhood. He was someone who knew all there was to know about the places to set creels — lobster and crab pots — where to put nets, and how to do that in mountainous seas standing in a tiny boat just visible from the cliffs. I also knew him as one of the funniest human beings I've ever met. Yet even as a very small child I knew something else about Billy — he'd been rescued at Dunkirk.

He had a hard war. I'm pretty sure that he was wounded more than once and he certainly saw dramatic and unpleasant action — serving for the whole war, and in many ways never entirely recovering from it. But the Dunkirk experience was clearly — for him and for everyone else — something special. Even today most people know something about the extraordinary story of how, between 26 May and the 4 June 1940, nearly 340,000 troops were miraculously saved from capture by being lifted from the French coast by a motley flotilla of naval and private vessels.

What could have been remembered as a massive defeat — which it was — is actually remembered so differently. It's remembered for the heroism of the crews of the hundreds of small boats, people who put their lives on the line — indeed many of them gave their lives — to bring the army home.

It's surely the sheer improbability of the thing that makes it so special. The heroes were just ordinary people responding heroically to extraordinary circumstances. Billy never forgot that and nor should we.

Lord, we marvel at the example of those who were willing to risk their lives to save others at Dunkirk. In an often selfish age we are grateful for the reminder that it's in our service to others that we can make a real and lasting contribution to the world. Amen.

BROADCAST WEDNESDAY 4 JUNE 2014

June 5

Jane Livesey

Today is the day designated by the United Nations as World Environment Day. The theme of the day this year is 'Seven billion dreams. One planet. Consume with care.' The UN reminds us that the wellbeing of humanity is intimately bound up with the wellbeing of our planet and the responsible management of the planet's natural resources. In his homily at his inaugural mass in March 2013, Pope Francis said that it was part of our human vocation to be protectors protectors of people but also protectors of all creation, respecting each of God's creatures and respecting the environment in which we live. Pope Francis is shortly to produce his second encyclical, which also has the care of the environment as its theme. This is not coincidence. Whatever one's stance on climate change and global warming, it cannot be contentious to say that we should take care of our planet which, by and large, takes such good care of us. This is not always the case, as recent earthquakes and volcanoes have reminded us, but overall we have very good cause to be grateful to our planet.

Most of us take seriously our responsibility to be grateful to those who are good to us. We remember to say thank you and to treat them with respect and affection. Today reminds us that our planet deserves no less. Perhaps it is a good day to be attentive to some aspect of creation that we normally take for granted: to really look at a beautiful tree or plant or flower, or really listen to a bird singing its heart out and to say a heartfelt thank you to its (and our) creator.

Creator God, we thank You for your creation, which You have entrusted to our care. May we keep faith with that trust. Amen.

BROADCAST FRIDAY 5 JUNE 2015

June 6

Jenny Wigley

'Crossing the Rubicon', 'draw a line in the sand'— there's a whole collection of phrases that have made the transition from physical battles to metaphorical ones. The Allied landings on the beaches of Normandy in World War II have given us what may be the most familiar of them all: 'D-Day'.

It's come to be used as a term marking a turning point, and D-Day in 1944 was certainly that. But it was part of the much bigger picture of the war in Europe and the terrible human cost that it involved for both armed forces and civilians. Whether it's right or not to think of one single day when the war was won, D-Day was when Britain and her allies came to believe that the war could and would be won.

The image of the battle between good and evil features large in many New Testament writings. St Paul speaks of death as the last enemy, to be swallowed up in victory. It's a hope for the future but it's signposted — more than that, for Christians it's a guarantee — through the death and rising-to-life-again of Jesus Christ. That's the turning point, and Paul insists that this isn't just a dramatic reversal of fortunes for one person, but for all of us: Jesus's death and resurrection mark a change in the course of human history.

All sorts of spiritual battles remain, and the experience of death will be endured by us all, but St Paul makes his great statement of faith in his letter to the Romans: 'In all these things we are more than conquerors … not anything in all creation will be able to separate us from the love of God in Christ Jesus our Lord.'

Jesus our redeemer, in Your living and Your dying You opened for us the gate to eternal life; may the flame of Your love burn so brightly in our hearts that we fear nothing in this life, but hope for all things in the life to come. Amen.

BROADCAST SATURDAY 6 JUNE 2015

June 7

Tina Beattie

Today is the feast day of St Robert of Newminster, a 12th-century English Cistercian monk and one of the founders of Fountains Abbey in Yorkshire. Robert's biographers describe him as a kind and gentle man, merciful to others but strict in his personal regime of poverty.

Cistercian spirituality is based on the Rule of St Benedict. It's a weaving together of prayer, manual labour and a life of austerity. The Cistercians made a significant contribution to agriculture and technology in medieval Europe, and they were known for the architectural beauty of their abbeys, such as Tintern, Rievaulx and Fountains.

Today, these ruined buildings lend a haunting beauty to our countryside. They're tranquil places to visit, their contours softened by time, with few reminders of the violence which destroyed them in the religious and political upheavals of the 16th century.

Our quest for God expresses itself in sublimely creative ways, but it also sometimes drives us to terrible acts of destruction. The lives of saints such as Robert reflect the virtues of holiness and simplicity that all great religions seek to cultivate among their followers. But today also reminds us of the darker side of religion, because it marks the anniversary of the beginning of the siege of Jerusalem during the First Crusade in 1099.

Never before has it been so urgent for us to go beyond the violence and conflict of religious differences, to discover a shared vision of peace. With its rich diversity of peoples and faiths, our society today offers us unique opportunities for dialogue and understanding.

We ask Robert of Newminster and all the saints to pray with us, as we seek a more simple, peaceful and creative way of being together in the world. Amen.

BROADCAST TUESDAY 7 JUNE 2011

June 8

Stephen Shipley

'To describe his music is like trying to keep sunlight in a string bag.' That's the vivid way the creative gifts of Benjamin Britten were expressed at his funeral address in December 1976. This year we're celebrating the centenary of Britten's birth, and today sees the opening of the festival he began with his partner, the singer Peter Pears, and the writer Eric Crozier in 1948 in Aldeburgh on the Suffolk coast. It's an evocative place with a bleak, stony beach dotted with upturned fishing boats – and it's on that very beach that, during this year's festival, Britten's most famous opera, *Peter Grimes*, will be performed, inspired as it is by the vast East Anglian skies and moody sea.

So what is it that draws so many people to Britten's music? I believe it's the power he has to evoke the mysteries of life. 'I'm coming to feel more and more that all my music must be written to the glory of God,' he said on one occasion. However, like a lot of great artists, he wrestled with doubt and depression, and he would look back nostalgically to the clear untroubled faith he had as a boy. While he believed in a reality which works in us and through us, he wasn't sure he could give the name of God to that reality. But that's the experience of so many. Often we have to go through the darkness to find the way ahead.

'Ben will like the sound of the trumpets,' said the bishop at the end of his funeral address for Britten, 'though he will find it difficult to believe they're sounding for him.' They'll sound for us too – be sure of that – though maybe not quite so loudly! So let's be ready for them.

Pray then that each of us may discern God's will – His plan for us in the fullness of time. Amen.

BROADCAST SATURDAY 8 JUNE 2013

June 9

Jenny Wigley

As Carers Week begins, one responsibility that will be in many of our thoughts is that of caring for older people. My father-in-law was involved with a group of care homes for the elderly. And he would always insist that their work should be about 'the person not the problem'.

He tells the wonderful story of a very elderly lady who regretted that she'd never been up in an aeroplane. For her 100th birthday, a limo arrived at the care home to take her to the airport, where a plane was duly waiting to give her the thrill of her life. Now she had a tale to tell that was not just of a dimly remembered past, but of an experience she really could share with her friends.

There's a lovely account of care across the generations in the biblical story of Ruth. An elderly widow, Naomi, loses her two sons and tries to persuade her daughters-in-law to return to their own communities to find new husbands for themselves. Ruth refuses to abandon her mother-in-law, and instead takes a beautiful vow: 'Where you go, I will go … your people will be my people, and your God my God.'

In the story, the two women return to Israel, where Naomi finds a home and Ruth a husband. And having shared a past, they now find a future, as Ruth gives birth to a son who is to become the ancestor of a dynasty of kings.

To care for another means asking what is possible, not only what is necessary. However challenging such may be, we need to see not just a problem to be managed, but a person to be loved and a life to be lived.

Eternal God, we thank You for the gift of years and the fullness of life. As we care for one another across the generations, help us to find memories to cherish and a future to build that we may rest in Your power and trust in Your love. Amen.

BROADCAST MONDAY 9 JUNE 2008

June 10

Peter Townley

In the Thyssen Museum in Madrid there was one picture that drew me back again and again. It was the portrait of Henry VIII, wearing that familiar fur-edged velvet cap, painted in 1537 by Hans Holbein the Younger.

Looking at this well-known painting, which I had seen reproduced in books and magazines since childhood, I was transported back to my history lessons at school. I remembered those stories of his six wives and the need to secure the Tudor dynasty. I thought about the consequences of the break with Rome and the English Reformation – the bravery of such ministers as St Thomas More as they battled with their consciences. This complex King, who could be so ruthless and yet apparently so sensitive when he played the lute.

What intrigued me was that nobody else was stopping to look but, rather, moving quickly on. Then it struck me. Henry VIII might well have been part of my story and indeed my heritage, but he wasn't part of theirs.

It was a salutary reminder to me of the number of paintings of people or events that I must have walked past in galleries that have been seminal in a nation's history, somebody else's story, but not mine.

Of course, it's not just about nations and paintings. It's also about the stories of families, neighbourhoods, religious groups …

Today, whether it's about our global village, our nation or the people down the street, help us, God, to listen to each other's stories and to understand what has made us whoever we are. Amen.

BROADCAST TUESDAY 10 JUNE 2014

June 11

Marjory MacLean

Fifty years ago today, President John F Kennedy gave a radio broadcast to the American people and announced the introduction of a new law that was to become the Civil Rights Act of 1964. With a promised end to all sorts of injustices, including racial segregation in education and other areas of community life, Mr Kennedy must have seemed to many in the United States to be switching on a light of liberation, a light they would pursue until a time of real, longed-for freedoms. It must have seemed like his promises and policies were lamps illuminating a path into the future.

Fifty years into that future, we look back into history and we know that between that promise in June 1963 and the passing of the Act the following year lay the violent death of the President, suddenly ending the story of his political life and the changes it was bringing to his country. But the shining promise of civil rights was not quenched by his death, and at last prevailed over the course of the many years that followed. That was a light that shone beyond the life that created it, and that is always the legacy of the best-remembered people.

All around the world, men and women of faith are guided and comforted by the same promise that the goodness and kindness of today will shine through into tomorrow, even if we are not there tomorrow to notice it.

O light of the past, the present and all time to come, help us to see our path lit in front of us, guiding us on the way of making peace and showing love. Make us unafraid to serve those who come after us and care about the world beyond our own lives. Amen.

BROADCAST TUESDAY 11 JUNE 2013

June 12

Gillean Maclean

I made a new friend recently. I meet him each evening just as it's getting dark. Same place, almost the same time. He's an otter, and each night on my last walk with the dog, he crosses our path coming from the sea into the burn at the bottom of my garden. If I want to see him (and I can hardly describe the joy that meeting offers me at the end of each day), I have to watch the clock and the sky carefully. I have to allow for the slightly later sunset each day and judge the time of my walk with precision. He (or perhaps she) is the most regular of visitors to my garden. He's utterly reliable and yet he has no watch, no clock, no diary and no visible timetable. We humans are creatures governed by these things. We are at once fascinated and trapped by the relentless hound that is time.

A new exhibit in the National Museum of Scotland is a wonderful timepiece called the Midsummer Chronophage, a clock with no numbers or hands. The clock is designed to slow down or even stop occasionally just to remind us that everyone experiences time differently. On the top of the clock there's a huge insect that appears to be eating up the minutes. In my worst nightmares, the time-consuming insect swallows me down in one great gulp.

My friend the otter lives in harmony with the times and seasons. The sun and moon and the length of days are his clock. As creatures of the same God we travel very different paths and experience time in very different ways, but in our crossing I have glimpsed something of God's greatness that can encompass us all and that transcends time.

Timeless and ageless God of eternity, grant us the wisdom to use the time You have given us carefully and thankfully, and to set aside just a little of that gift today simply to wonder. Amen.

BROADCAST TUESDAY 12 JUNE 2012

June 13

Peter Townley

Reflecting on growing up in Manchester 50 or so years ago, I'm amazed to remember how sectarian the city was. If you made a new friend, one of the first questions to ask was whether the other child was a Protestant or a Catholic. Later on in life, the answer to that question could decide whether you got a job or not. If your surname didn't give you away, the name of your school did.

Even the two football teams were tarred with this particular tribal brush. And then, at Whit Week, the Protestants walked on Whit Monday and the Catholics on Whit Friday.

At the time of the Second Vatican Council, I remember as a choir boy our church having special meetings with the local Catholic parish. Little did I realize how significant these meetings were.

At one of these gatherings one of our Catholic neighbours, Mr Murtagh, stood up in the Church Hall and asked his Priest: 'Father, do you mean to say that we can now say the Lord's Prayer together?'

It was at this time that Pope John XXIII's *Journal of a Soul* was first published. He wrote: 'After three years of preparation, certainly laborious but also joyful and serene, we are now on the slopes of the sacred mountain. May the Lord give us strength to bring everything to a joyful conclusion.'

Years later, a fruit of this coming together in Barnsley, where I now work, is that we have the only purpose built Roman Catholic–Anglican school for 3–16 year olds in the country.

Let us thank God for all those who work to build up relationships across all kinds of boundaries and divides. Amen.

BROADCAST FRIDAY 13 JUNE 2014

June 14

Pritpal Kaur Riat

This week is Carers Week, a partnership of nine national charities. It aims to highlight the huge impact and contribution that carers make in society and to their communities. For many people in my community, caring for their parents is their most immediate concern.

A poem that has remained with me since my school days is Seamus Heaney's 'Follower'. The final verse contrasts how once the child was a nuisance, tripping and falling, but now, in old age, it is the father who stumbles.

In the circle of life, our parents first and foremost care for us, but then we in turn, as time goes by, may need to start caring for them, whether directly or through the provision we lovingly make for them. However, in a spiritual sense, caring for others should never be a nuisance – in fact it's really a blessing.

A line in Sikh scripture starts, '*Gurdev Mata, Gurdev Pita*' – which can be interpreted to mean that someone's first guru, or guide, is their mother, and their second guru is their father, even before their spiritual guru is discovered. Sikhs are therefore taught that caring for our parents is one of the most worthwhile and valuable types of service that we can offer.

There's been some pretty negative news about the caring professions recently, but reading about Carers Week has filled me with humility and admiration for people that perform such a role. They embody dedication, love, selflessness and sacrifice.

Let us pray for all carers, and that we – even if big sacrifices are uncalled for – can also help care for others in some small, yet meaningful way.

BROADCAST TUESDAY 14 JUNE 2011

June 15

Gillean Maclean

On 15 June 1996, the media reported that a huge explosion had rocked the centre of Manchester. Ten years later, the release of a video taken by a police helicopter showed the true devastation of the blast. The damage to surrounding buildings was such that a total regeneration of a major part of the city centre had to be carried out. The Prime Minister at the time, John Major, decided not to stop the ongoing peace talks. Today, 16 years later, we have peace and a parliament in Northern Ireland. But there are still people who are hurting from those many years of what became known as 'The Troubles'. The devastation caused by the horror that is sectarianism can perhaps best be seen from a distance and in hindsight. What is needed if we are to offer a more tolerant future to our children is a total regeneration of the building blocks of our religious traditions.

In Scotland most of us are ashamed of our sectarian past and the links between our religious affiliations and certain football clubs – though the problem in that context is different in its severity. And many supporters cheer their teams passionately for all the right reasons. So we know sectarianism is neither about faith nor about football, but about prejudice, and we would love to dissociate ourselves from that – but still we can't, not yet, not while the spectre still rears its ugly head from time to time.

All of us must learn to travel middle roads if we are not to see a repeat of the disaster that was 15 June 1996.

Almighty and eternal God of the one people, forgive us our divisions and help us today to celebrate diversity, to recognize the failings of the past and to regenerate our communities to reflect the oneness of Your holy nature. Amen.

BROADCAST FRIDAY 15 JUNE 2012

June 16

Gopinder Kaur

I'm particularly fond of the name of my newborn niece. It's Asisse, meaning 'blessing'. To Punjabi ears, the Italian town of Assisi, made famous by St Francis, must be a very blessed place.

Today I think of his prayer about seeking the serenity to accept what one cannot change, the courage to change what one can, and the wisdom to know the difference. Those I most admire somehow instinctively embrace this paradox that one can be dynamic and proactive in the world while still being able to accept, to let go and bow to a higher order. 'You must reach for the stars,' one saintly Sikh told me, 'but be as humble as the dust ...'

Today Sikhs mark the martyrdom of our fifth Guru, Guru Arjan Dev, whom we remember for his vision, creativity, love and service. We are indebted to him for the construction of the Harmandir Sahib, known otherwise as the Golden Temple, in Amritsar. He also meticulously compiled our scripture and generated numerous practical initiatives to support ordinary villagers, the sick and the downtrodden. All this preserved and propelled into the future a commitment to oneness, interfaith engagement and care for the world.

Yet, in 1606, the Guru spent his last days facing brutal torture under a new and less tolerant Mughal regime. His response was calm equanimity to the very end, as he left us the blessing of today's prayer:

May Your divine will be ever sweet to me, O God;
I beg only for the treasure of Your Name.

BROADCAST WEDNESDAY 16 JUNE 2010

June 17

Noel Battye

They tell me that John Wesley, who was born on this day in 1703, preached some 40,000 sermons in his lifetime. I don't know how many sermons I have listened to, but I can remember very few, so I'm inclined to identify with the writer who once said that listening to sermons is a bit like washing: it has its effect at the time, even if you forget the details afterwards.

Indeed, I would have to say, that of all the preachers I have ever listened to, only two remain in my memory, and those more because of who they were rather than what they said. One was the diminutive Mother Teresa of Calcutta speaking in the church of St Mary the Great in Cambridge about taking babies out of dustbins; and the other, in the same venue some time later, was the Russian Orthodox leader and writer of devotional classics Metropolitan Anthony Bloom, born 100 years ago this week. You couldn't possibly listen to two more different people — the tiny nun dressed in white, with her earnest walnut face telling us that giving wasn't giving unless it hurt, and the tall, stately, black-robed bearded figure speaking quietly and with authority about the inner life of the spirit.

Yet each one spoke with clear integrity and with an authority expressed in their eyes. One spoke with energy and zeal, the other with quiet calm. Neither had what was called the enthusiasm of Wesley, yet all three, I suspect, had one thing in common despite their different backgrounds, denominations and points of emphasis: something of that Holy Spirit which refuses to be defined by its methods of expression, sounding one day like a rushing, mighty wind and the next like a still, small voice, a breath of life, which is why we pray today:

'Breathe on me, Breath of God; fill me with life anew.'

BROADCAST TUESDAY 17 JUNE 2014

June 18

Ibrahim Mogra

Fasting in Ramadan is regarded as one of the Pillars of Islam. It is a unique act of sincere obedience to God. It is as if one is living like God who does not eat and drink at all. The degree of sincerity in this act of worship cannot be matched in any other kind of worship. When any person prays in company, others around them can see that they are praying. Their sincerity may be questionable. When any person performs a pilgrimage, others around them can see them. Their sincerity may be questionable. However, no one can tell whether a person is fasting or not. There are no visible signs. Only the fasting person and God know about it. God takes pride in the fasting person and says, 'The fasting is for me and I will personally reward the one who fasts.'

Fasting is like a personal revolution against everyday habits and conventions that enslave people. Before fasting, a person could eat and drink as they please. When Ramadan comes, it puts a stop to that. Now for a whole month they have to go without food and drink from dawn until sunset. It is as if they are being trained for unforeseen changes in life. Perhaps to be prepared for tougher times. Life is never the same. Circumstances always change. We all have ups and downs: healthy today, ill tomorrow; rich today, poor tomorrow; well fed today, starving tomorrow; self-sufficient today, reliant tomorrow; resident today, traveller tomorrow. Our circumstances change all the time. Ramadan trains us up to face some of these changes and uncertainties of life.

Dear God, help us to prepare for this life and the life here after. Amin.

BROADCAST THURSDAY 18 JUNE 2015

June 19

Ranjit-Singh Dhanda

Even at the age of 56, I find the closing supplication of every Sikh prayer a huge challenge. All Sikh prayers end with the reminder that God's Name is forever in ascendance and it is God's Will that everyone is forgiven and blessed. We're called upon to forgive and seek God's blessings for all, without discrimination. To live out this closing prayer requires enormous spiritual strength.

In the Sikh tradition there exists the concept of the *sant sipaahi*, or 'saint-soldier' – one who has the courage and fortitude to do good in the face of seemingly and quite possibly insurmountable problems. So where is this battlefield and what is the conflict? The battlefield and conflict is in fact one: the mind. Becoming saintly and doing good deeds to gain spiritual strength is the easy bit. That spiritual strength is required to keep doing good in adversity, to control one's own mind and to save it from the vices of anger, lust, greed, materialistic attachment and arrogance.

It is only once this mind is composed and at peace, having the spiritual strength to win these internal battles, that we can sincerely ask for the Lord's forgiveness and blessings for all from the heart.

Please Lord, bless our political leaders and each and every one of us with the spiritual strength, humility and wisdom to act with nobility. Let us all contribute selflessly and tirelessly toward achieving peace for all

BROADCAST TUESDAY 19 JUNE 2012

June 20

Noel Battye

The accession of the youthful Queen Victoria on this day in 1837 has always made a deep impression upon me since I first read various accounts of it, including that recorded in her own diary.

In much the same way, so did that recently re-released speech made by her great-great granddaughter, our present monarch, on her 21st birthday, when she vowed to serve this country for all her life, whether it be long or short. I suppose the reason it appeals to me so much is because I am of a generation for whom life vocations were a youthful thing.

Well over 90 per cent of my fellow ordinands were, like me, in their very early twenties. While in retrospect I can see why people would have questions to ask, to us it was entirely natural – our vocation in life.

The worldly-wise of later decades became rather suspicious about sheltered backgrounds; they spoke of the need for life experience, and of preference for those leaving other careers and so on, but I have never been entirely convinced.

I have always held before me the youthful models, if not of the 12-year-old Jesus in the Temple, at least of young Samuel in the shrine, the country boy David – youngest of an otherwise impressive family – and Jeremiah, the most reluctant of prophets who tried to evade his vocation with the words, 'I am but a youth.'

Almost 50 years on, I would have to say that whatever my many and undoubted shortcomings along the way, that youthful vocation is for me as bright and clear as ever, and I like to think that I still strive to fulfil it in the living of each new day.

Lord, we thank You for the young of every rising generation. Bless each one in his or her vocation and keep ever before them the vision of Your guiding light. Amen.

BROADCAST SATURDAY 20 JUNE 2015

June 21

Alastair McIntosh

Today is summer solstice. I grew up on the Isle of Lewis near the Callanish standing stones. It beats most locals why visitors want to gather for rituals there, often with rain and midges! But in keeping with the spirit, here's a story for celebrants at this morning's festivities.

Around 1695, the geographer Martin Martin spoke to a Lewis minister whose parish extended to the now-uninhabited Isle of North Rona.

Visiting the island, the minister had been greeted with: 'God save you, pilgrim, you are heartily welcome here; for we have had repeated apparitions of your person among us, and congratulate your arrival in this our remote country.'

Then one of the men processed around him, sunwise, uttering blessings of happiness. They gave him costly gifts of corn, too, 'as an expression of our sincere love'. He reported that the islanders took their surnames from the 'colour of the sky, rainbow and clouds'.

While their intentions touched the minister, he was troubled by their Hebridean sun blessing, and bid them give it up.

But, I wonder, might there not be a more integrated view? To early Christians, the sun often symbolized God. Might our religion, whatever it may be, serve, in those rainbow words from North Rona, 'as an expression of our sincere love'? So let these words of the 2nd-century Christian theologian Clement of Alexandria be my summer solstice prayer:

'Hail, oh light, for he who rides over all creation . . . has changed sunset into sunrise, and crucified death into life.' Amen.

BROADCAST MONDAY 21 JUNE 2011

June 22

Kevin Franz

One hot June day in London, searching for peace and shade, I was on my way
to the famous gardens at Kew. On the Tube I met an elderly Japanese man
on a similar quest and we travelled together. He told me how as a boy he had
witnessed the devastation of Hiroshima in the aftermath of the atomic blast.
Later, in 1967, he had been working as an engineer in the Suez Canal area when
the Six-Day War broke out, and he and his team found themselves in the midst
of the conflict. When we arrived at Kew, he invited me to go with him to the
Japanese landscape dominated by the great Gateway of the Imperial Messenger.
He led me through the Gardens of Peace, a calm and tranquil place with its
stone paths flanked by lanterns and a water basin. And he showed me a granite
block inscribed with a haiku which caught the mood of our encounter: 'Even
sparrows / Freed from all fear of man / England in spring.'

My Japanese companion was someone whose early life had been lived in a
militarist state, who had lived through the terrifying effects of weapons of mass
destruction, who had seen conflict close at hand. I'd simply been looking for
a peaceful place of shade and green spaces. Yet it was his gracious, peaceful
presence that enriched that day for me. He offered what Quakers call a
testimony to peace.

Today, as we recall the anniversary of Hitler's invasion of the Soviet Union
in 1941 and the murderous, terrible events it unleashed, some prayerful words
from Óscar Romero come to mind:

> Peace is not the product of terror or fear.
> Peace is not the silence of cemeteries.
> Peace is not the silent result of violent repression.
> Peace is the generous, tranquil contribution of all to the good of all.
> Peace is dynamism. Peace is generosity. Amen.

BROADCAST MONDAY 22 JUNE 2009

June 23

Eugene O'Neill

Saturday mornings in my early childhood were reserved for the pleasure of sleep. While other families seemed to rise with the light, my parents changed pace from the busy week and, with us, simply lay in bed — silent, long and late.

Except at this time of year. Like so many, I spent every June from the age of 11 until the end of university being examined. Even now, I still can't smell freshly cut grass without an uneasy feeling that I should be revising; or remembering the urging from teachers — and from the voices within — to achieve; or the sense of impending doom that it might all go wrong.

Now, as a school chaplain, the young people I meet seem so much happier than I was; but I'm sure much remains the same. Schooldays can feel like being a mouse on a wheel.

When I asked them recently, my friends agreed that none would want to go back to that world again. Though all are grateful for the encouragement of good teachers and the benefits of education, they rate these as their greatest achievements — before exams and career: love; commitment; true friends; the great satisfaction there is in not having to be the best. The simple pleasures that our parents loved — even the restoring inactivity of sleep!

Creator and sustainer, assist students and those preparing for exams. May they know Your calm. As You help us work and achieve, show us also the value of our humanity: that we are worth more than the work we do and the goals for which we strive. And when the fever of our duties is over, may we know a slackening of pace; and a space for soothing, savouring and restoration. Amen.

BROADCAST SATURDAY 23 JUNE 2012

June 24

Frank Sellar

A few weeks ago, my mother died. Someone asked me recently how I was getting on.

'Fine,' I replied, 'except for one thing that happened out of the blue which took me by surprise.' I was sorting through her clothes in order to take them to a charity shop, when I found some money in a coat pocket. It was only loose change, but for some odd reason it made me choke up and tears came into my eyes. Don't ask me why!

Losing someone who has been close to you is never easy, and yet it's an experience all of us must face as some stage. The familiar has gone. The opportunity to chat on the phone is no longer there, and the comfort of someone who has known and loved you is past.

St John's Gospel tells how Jesus visited the grave of Lazarus, his friend. After talking to the grieving sisters and seeing Lazarus's friends upset, 'Jesus wept.' It's the shortest verse in the Bible, and yet it speaks of his distress at death, and that gives me comfort.

And I find comfort too in something else he said that same day: 'I am the resurrection and the life,' he asserted. 'The person who believes in me will live, even though they die, and whoever lives and believes in me will never die'.

To place our hope and trust in the one who died but was raised again reminds me that, while parting may be painful, it need not be forever.

Heavenly Father, thank You that Jesus understands our loss and sadness. As we place our hope and trust in Him, let us find peace and serenity in You today and comfort and healing from You for tomorrow, and all we ask is for Jesus's sake. Amen.

BROADCAST MONDAY 24 JUNE 2013

June 25

Michael Ford

I've always thought that one of the greatest privileges in life is to sit with a dying person. It may be someone we love very much or a friend we know less intimately. It isn't easy, but I expect only those who've been granted the opportunity will know precisely what I mean.

Yet when I read newspaper reports of how a Hollywood director died 'surrounded by all his family', I also realize how fortunate he was. Such farewell gatherings aren't granted to everyone. I know of people who deeply regret the fact that they weren't there at the end because the patient died much sooner than anyone was expecting.

Ten years ago today, there was a great deal of interest in the fact that, for the first time on national television, viewers were shown the death process of a patient. Some hailed it as a landmark moment in broadcasting, while others questioned the ethics of transmitting such a personal event. From a scientific viewpoint, I can understand the audience fascination, but from a spiritual perspective I'm not so sure. For me, being alongside someone in their final days or hours is a sacred experience.

Last month my oldest friend entered the final stages of illness quite suddenly, and I was able to share some of that time with him. Much of our friendship had been forged by conversation and laughter. In those last hours, it was marked by silence and concern. But although the environment was clinical and functional, the side room seemed to take on a dignified, spiritual character of its own. Outwardly, there was efficient medical care; but, inwardly, a holy journey was beginning.

And so this morning we pray for all those who are dying. May the peace of God uphold and comfort them. Amen.

BROADCAST WEDNESDAY 25 JUNE 2008

June 26

Frank Sellar

If many of us think about torture at all, we may consider it to be something that happened in the Middle Ages, something that can on occasions even be the topic of humour, as in some British cinema farces. But there is really nothing funny or medieval about torture. On this United Nations International Day in Support of Victims of Torture, we need to know that torture is currently used in more than 100 countries throughout the world.

Torture can include many forms of suffering, both physical and psychological. Most techniques seek to prolong the victim's pain and fear as long as possible without leaving visible evidence, and can include beatings, electric shocks, stretching, submersion, suffocation, burning and sexual assault. Anyone can become a victim of torture, regardless of age, gender, religion, social class, ethnicity or level of education. And if we believe that all human beings are made in God's image and worthy of honour, then torture is also an insult to Him who creates us and loves us.

By designating the 26 June as a day to stand against torture, the United Nations is making a statement that all forms of degrading treatment or punishment are absolutely abhorrent.

So then let us pray for all who suffer today at the hands of governments or groups that use the infliction of pain on others for their own twisted purposes.

Heavenly Father, we acknowledge that Christ himself was humiliated and ill-treated at the hands of evil men. We pray for strength for those who are damaged and disturbed as victims. Come to the aid of those who suffer and grant opportunity for repentance to those who inflict wounds, and all we ask is for Jesus's sake. Amen.

BROADCAST WEDNESDAY 26 JUNE 2013

June 27

Eugene O'Neill

It is said that, among Catholics in late 19th-century Ireland, even the humblest rural cottage had three pictures on the wall above the hearth: Jesus carrying a burning heart; the Virgin Mary; and William Ewart Gladstone – the bearer of the promise of political freedom.

By the 1960s, a fourth image was that of John F Kennedy who, on this day in 1963, became the first serving American President to visit Ireland; and with his wife Jackie enchanted a nation with their charm and beauty

At the time, they seemed to offer a glimpse of another world – far-off, shimmering, perfect … yet, somehow, intimately present. Rather like Byzantine icons or the Madonnas of Renaissance art.

How is it that such images draw us? I'm intrigued by the number of major exhibitions of religious art that have packed London galleries in the last few years. The most striking, for me, was a collection of Spanish devotional art, 'The Sacred Made Real', perhaps because visual expressions of faith formed the backdrop to my childhood. And they still do. Later today, I'm going to see the Leonardo da Vinci drawings from the Royal Collection in Belfast to mark the Queen's Jubilee.

Some criticize religion as an escape from reality into a world of illusion – as unreal as the Camelot of the Kennedys proved to be. But much of Christian art holds even when it draws the eye to brutal realities such as the suffering of Jesus. In the beauty of images, I have found a source of inner strength, especially in hard times; and at other times wells of solidarity and consolation – even when politics has disappointed.

Author of beauty, who inspires the loveliness of nature and the creations of art, let them be sacraments of Your presence, bring to our senses what is invisible and open doors to the sacred. Amen.

BROADCAST WEDNESDAY 27 JUNE 2012

June 28

Michael Mumisa

Millions of Muslims in Britain and across the world will be observing the month of fasting known as Ramadan. According to the Qur'an, fasting is an act of worship that was prescribed by God in different forms to Abraham, Moses, Jesus and other biblical prophets before Muhammad. So Muslims believe that fasting is one of the ways through which they affirm their connection with traditions going back to Abraham.

Ramadan is also the month of charity and giving and, for many Muslims, a way of experiencing how the less fortunate among us feel when they go without food. Yet this way of thinking about fasting and poverty has the potential to turn what for many people are genuine hardships in their daily lives into a pious religious ideal. Poverty is much more than just lack of food. It is also about lack of access to decent education, healthcare, housing and fundamental human rights. The poor of any society, no matter how developed, are often the most vulnerable to fall victim to human rights abuses.

These are particularly very hard times for many. Christians, Jews, Hindus, Sikhs, Muslims and many others have been operating food banks up and down the country. We hope and pray that we will remain steadfast in our struggles against poverty and social injustices alongside people from other faiths and those of no particular faith. We pray for the wisdom to work together towards removing the structures and systems of our society that create and perpetuate poverty.

In the words of Muhammad:

'O Lord! Bring us the new moon with security and peace, and in harmony with what You love. May those who are fasting break their fast under Your mercy.' Amin.

BROADCAST SATURDAY 28 JUNE 2014

June 29

Eugene O'Neill

After his visit to Britain, Pope Benedict was reported to have been astonished at the beauty of the Anglican liturgy he witnessed at Westminster Abbey.

It was the spiritual depth and richness of the English choral tradition that moved him; and from this came his invitation to Westminster Abbey choir to sing later today in Rome at one of the most important events in the Catholic Church's year: the Mass on the Feast Day of St Peter and St Paul.

At this liturgy, newly created archbishops are given 'palliums' — woollen scarves emblazoned with crosses — worn as a symbol of unity with the Pope. Indeed, until the Reformation, the Archbishop of Canterbury himself wore a pallium — a tradition echoed in his coat of arms in which a pallium still appears as a heraldic device.

That England's foremost abbey — itself dedicated to St Peter — should send its celebrated choir to St Peter's Basilica seems wonderfully apt. Around 1,400 years ago, the then pope — St Gregory the Great — was prompted to send St Augustine to re-evangelize England after seeing British boys captured from the Angle tribe in the Roman slave market. Tradition holds that he remarked: 'They are not Angles — but angels.'

This is a remarkable statement of friendship by the Anglican Church; and from the Pope, a sign of a desire to receive from the Anglican tradition.

A sense of beauty is often linked to a craving for immortality; and Pope Benedict has often argued that a recovery of beauty will go hand in hand with recovery of belief in God.

Creator of Heavenly harmony, through music You communicate something essential, and feed the soul; may music's angelic beauty humble us and draw us out of ourselves toward You. Amen.

BROADCAST FRIDAY 29 JUNE 2012

June 30

Alison Murdoch

On this day in 1936, an unknown author called Margaret Mitchell published her first and only book: it was called *Gone with the Wind*. Three years later, the movie won an unprecedented eight Academy Awards, and went global. It's believed to be the most-watched film of all time, with an estimated 35 million cinema tickets being sold in the UK alone. Not to mention the TV repeats!

Whether it's indigenous folk tales or soap operas, Sherlock Holmes or the 'Twilight' series, storytelling has a vivid and powerful hold over the human psyche. Despite all the efforts of my schoolteachers, I remember *Gone with the Wind* much more clearly than any history or science lesson.

However, the power of the story also has its shadow side. For example, many of us are much better at remembering negative stories about ourselves than positive ones. How often does your inner critic take all your confidence away by reminding you: 'I've messed that up before … I'm no good at this … I can't, it's impossible!' We also use stories to develop fixed opinions of friends, family and strangers, forgetting that every human being is in a constant process of change.

The Buddhist practice of meditation enables us to identify the unhelpful thoughts and stories that arise in our minds before they turn into speech and action. Out of the thousands of thoughts we have each day, it can help us pinpoint those that will be most the helpful and constructive.

Let's pray that we can all find ways to nurture the positive mental habits that will bring happiness to ourselves and the people around us.

BROADCAST SATURDAY 30 JUNE 2012

July 1

Michael Mumisa

Among the British values that Muslims are being asked to embrace are 'personal and social responsibility'. What many people may not realize is that, in almost all Islamic theological traditions, social responsibilities are prioritized over duties and obligations to God or religious rituals such as fasting. The Qur'an states: 'Do not forget your responsibilities in the present world; and be good to others as God has been good to you.' (Qur'an 28:77)

According to Muslim tradition, Muhammad, the Prophet of Islam, declared: 'The best people, and the most beloved of God, are those who do things for the benefit of others.' For Muslims, social responsibilities are not limited to fellow human beings but extend to issues relating to the environment and animal welfare. For example, Muslims consider it *haram* (prohibited) to cut down trees unnecessarily even in a time of war, to waste water or to take part in any form of hunting as a sport. Muhammad warned his followers, saying: 'Whoever kills a sparrow or anything bigger than that without a just cause, God will hold him accountable on the Day of Judgment.'

He also prohibited them from using more water than necessary. His disciples asked him, 'O messenger of God! Can there be wastefulness while performing the ablution for a religious act?' To which he responded, 'Yes, even if you perform your ablution on the banks of a rushing river.'

For many Muslims, faith is a driver of personal and social responsibility. So our prayer today is:

Lord, grant us the wisdom to value the differences in our cultures, races and ideas. We ask You to forgive us our shortcomings. Amin.

BROADCAST TUESDAY 1 JULY 2014

July 2

Catherine Cowley

Many crises and difficulties can bring people together. Even when we're not directly affected, we can enter imaginatively into the suffering of those caught up in, for example, war, earthquakes, a tragedy in a family or community we identify with. We can feel solidarity with them. Economic crises, however, are different; rather than bringing us together, slumps can keep us separate, put us into competition with each other. Perhaps it's anxiety: if she keeps her job, does that mean I lose mine? Or the realization that there's no obvious way that we can both prosper. Rather than solidarity, fear can lead us to feel isolated.

In these circumstances it can be hard to hold on to the Christian vision that every human being is essentially social, and that we only flourish by acknowledging our interdependence. Our anxieties are real, but when concern turns to fear, it can drive us apart and fragment society even more.

The words 'Do not be afraid' are found throughout the Judaeo-Christian scriptures. They are often addressed to people in the midst of situations where fear would seem the natural and automatic response to what's going on. This is not suggesting a facile optimism which ignores the reality of the situation. Rather, it's saying that our anxiety shouldn't become the sort of fear which drives out the mutuality, love, trust and compassion that enable us to come through great difficulties with our humanity intact.

Lord, when our anxieties turn us in on ourselves, help us to be open to You, because we meet others at the depth at which we allow ourselves to be met by You. Amen.

BROADCAST THURSDAY 2 JULY 2009

July 3

Alison Murdoch

On this day in 1987, the former Gestapo chief Klaus Barbie was sentenced to life imprisonment in France, after a dramatic eight-week trial that gripped the world. Historians estimate that Barbie, also known as the 'Butcher of Lyon', was directly involved in the deaths of around 14,000 people before fleeing to Bolivia, where he was further implicated in the death of Che Guevara.

When I was a small child, we often divided our teams into 'goodies' and 'baddies'. If we'd known about Klaus Barbie, he would definitely have been a 'baddie'. As we got older, we enjoyed noisily spotting the goodies and baddies in the latest James Bond film. Children and young people have an inbuilt need to explore the difference between right and wrong, and establish a moral compass for their lives. Supporting this process, in a skilful way, may be the most significant thing that any adult ever does.

In December 2011, the Dalai Lama published a new book called *Beyond Religion* in which he argues that these key ethical issues should no longer be considered as religious business, but as human-being business. History demonstrates the appalling suffering that just one person can bring about, and as the world becomes ever more interconnected, the next generation will find they have even more power to help or to harm. After reading, writing and arithmetic, an education in ethics is arguably the most important thing in the world.

Let's pray that every child and young person can get the support they need to understand the difference between the actions that harm and the actions that help and heal.

BROADCAST TUESDAY 3 JULY 2012

July 4

Leslie Griffiths

Today is America's national day, a day for stars and stripes, a time of rejoicing for all our transatlantic cousins and friends. Three or four years ago, while on American soil, I was given the seat of honour for the formal public reading of the Declaration of Independence, one of the nation's founding documents. Its opening words trumpet an optimistic note: 'We hold these truths to be self-evident, that all men are created equal, that they are endowed by their Creator with certain unalienable rights; that among these are Life, Liberty, and the pursuit of Happiness.' What a world they point to, a world in which it would be bliss indeed to be alive. Unfortunately, as we know only too well, the reality is somewhat different. Too many men and women, in America as well as elsewhere, do not seem to enjoy many unalienable rights and their days are spent in the pursuit of survival rather than happiness.

A long time before the existence of the United States of America, St Paul issued his own declaration of independence. He came straight out with it: 'All men and women are sinners and fall short of the glory of God.' From that starting point he traced a path that would lead flawed human beings along the road of love and forgiveness, enabling them to break out of the prisons of despair to enjoy a life-giving relationship with their maker. They'd move out of slavery to sin into the glorious freedom of the children of God.

Dear Lord, show us Your mercy and help us to work hard to turn dreams into reality so that people everywhere may enjoy the Life, Liberty and pursuit of Happiness for which we all yearn. Through Christ our Lord, Amen.

BROADCAST SATURDAY 4 JULY 2015

July 5

Alison Murdoch

On this day in 1948, the National Health Service Act for England and Wales came into effect. Based on the principle that good health care should be available to all, regardless of wealth, it was an extraordinary, and some would say reckless, expression of compassion, generosity and universal responsibility. The NHS is now the world's largest publicly funded health service, treating over 3 million people each week.

If the NHS was a fairground stall, it would be one where everyone pays something and everyone takes something away, even if some prizes are worth more than others. In those terms, my husband and I would have struck jackpot last summer, if you can call it that, when he suddenly fell ill with a rare virus and spent over five weeks in intensive care. At a time of family crisis, money genuinely was the least of our worries. In contrast, friends in the USA live in constant fear of their medical bills.

The small Buddhist kingdom of Bhutan on the northern border of India has hit the headlines in recent years for its emphasis on Gross National Happiness. The Buddhist stance is that of course money is important and useful, but it can't buy happiness. So the Bhutanese bottom line isn't about GNP, exports and shareholder value, but about the mental and physical wellbeing of its population. These are same noble priorities that underpinned the NHS Act.

Let's give thanks for all the people over the centuries who have cared for others in times of illness and distress, whether rich or poor. Let's pray that, amid all the changes the NHS is going through, its founding principles of service and sharing can be strengthened and upheld.

BROADCAST THURSDAY 5 JULY 2012

July 6

Leslie Griffiths

Thirty years ago today, a young New Zealander was ordained as a Roman Catholic priest. It was his hope, on arriving in England, that he could become a Trappist monk — enclosed and away from the public gaze. But he was not allowed to take that path — 'you can't be a solitary until you've lived a life', he was told. So he went off into parish life and eventually arrived in the parish where I live. We got on famously and became firm friends. He was a fine pastor and dedicated to a modern view of the world, very much in the spirit of Pope John XXIII and Pope Francis. Then came his bombshell announcement that he wanted to leave the parish and become a hermit. Some people thought this move amounted to a rejection of them. In fact, he simply felt that he was now ready to live a life of prayer and contemplation, and that's what he's been doing for the last eight years. People might say — indeed, an energetic and activist Methodist like me might say — what's the point of that? What a waste. But I'd disagree. Like most of us, I'm generally so busy that my prayer life comes under great pressure. So what a comfort to know that my dear friend, 30 years a priest, holds me and others, those around him and the whole wide world, in his prayers. It's together — he in his solitary life and I with my busy diary — that we engage with the world and commend its needs to almighty God.

Dear Lord, bless all who open themselves to You today, whether alone or in the company of others. Help us to know that it's together that we sing Your praises and serve Your people. Through Christ our Lord, Amen.

BROADCAST MONDAY 6 JULY 2015

July 7

George Craig

I once had the privilege of meeting Trevor Hicks. His two teenage daughters were among the 96 people who died in the disaster at the Hillsborough football stadium in 1989. He is a remarkable man, and among the things I remember him saying, one in particular has stuck with me. He spoke about the way in which people react when they learn what happened to him and his family. He said that many people had problems knowing what to say, but only one reaction really upset him. That was when people who hadn't been through what he'd been through told him that they knew how he felt. His message was simple: if you haven't been there, you can never know how it feels.

Trevor Hicks's words seem particularly powerful today – the fifth anniversary of the 7/7 London bombings. Those injured and the families of those who died surely have a right to expect something from the rest of us. And surely all of us must want to do something to acknowledge what happened to them – and indeed to the victims of other, similar horrible events. But if we can't really understand what they've been through – and are still going through – what response can we make?

Well, I think there *is* something we can do. We must never allow 7/7 to slip out of sight, out of mind and into history. It's as real and painful for those it's affected today as it was in 2005. And that means that we, like they, need actively to remember it; we as individuals need to make it a part of our personal history. Memorials and ceremonies are important only if they express that – they are no substitute for it.

Father God, we lift up to You those who suffered and are still suffering as a result of the London bombings. We cannot begin to grasp what they have been through and we cannot ease their pain; but with Your help we can give them the respect they deserve by remembering and honouring them for their experience. Amen.

BROADCAST WEDNESDAY 7 JULY 2010

July 8

Ibrahim Mogra

This day in 2005, we were trying to come to terms with the terrorist attacks on London that had happened the previous day. The night before had been filled with joyful celebrations when the Olympics were awarded to London. The next morning, though, we were greeted by this terrible news. Four suicide bombers had attacked the London transport system. Fifty-two people had died and hundreds were injured. They were killed and maimed by their fellow countrymen whose anger and wickedness had blinded them. They had failed to see the human in each other. At an event held at the House of Lords some time ago, the former IRA volunteer Patrick Magee told us he only saw the enemy — not fathers, mothers, sons or daughters — when he planted his bomb in 1984 in Brighton's Grand Hotel. He did not see the humanity of his targets. Terrorists fail to understand that two wrongs do not make a right.

Justice is a crucial value. It is truth in action. It is the first principle of social life that governs all relationships. The most visible expression of justice is our treatment of fellow human beings, especially those with whom we are not friends.

The Qur'an says, 'Do not let the hatred of any people stop you from dealing justly. Deal justly, for that is closer to piety. Be firm in justice as witnesses for God, even in cases against yourselves, your parents or your relatives.'

Dear God, enable us to see the humanity of others and to respect life. Give governments the courage to serve justly. Remove all injustice and oppression. Indeed, You are The Fair and The Just. Amin.

BROADCAST MONDAY 8 JULY 2013

July 9

Leslie Griffiths

I'm a member of the House of Lords, and one of the loveliest things I do is welcome people in and show them round the magnificent premises of our national parliament. In recent months, I've taken the members of our church's Sisterhood – all ladies of an uncertain age, many of whom have survived World War II. They made their way with zimmer frames and Cockney banter, enchanting officials and members alike. The tea they ate was mountainous: sandwiches, cakes, scones with lashings of cream – all disappeared with great rapidity. They walked around the hallowed corridors as if they owned the place – which, of course, they did.

Most recently, I entertained four Year 11 pupils from a boys' school where I have some responsibility. Two of them were Muslims. It was Ramadan but they insisted that the rest of us should have lunch; they played a full part in our conversation even though their stomachs must have been aching for food. The family of one of these boys hailed from Kashmir, the disputed territory between India and Pakistan. Another was from Algeria and spoke fluent French and Arabic as well as English. A third was Jewish and spoke of his family's origins in Lebanon, the Gambia, Tsarist Russia and California. The fourth, a Chinese boy, is a brilliant pianist who wants to be a philosopher. How can anybody better that? I felt that my Christian faith was enriched by their company. And that my country was blessed by their citizenship within it.

Dear Lord, show us how to build a nation where we live with each other, learn from each other and laugh with each other. And then give us the wit and courage to work to build it. Through Jesus Christ our Lord. Amen.

BROADCAST THURSDAY 9 JULY 2015

July 10

Alison Murdoch

Many of us are about to face one of the most stress-inducing events of the year: going on holiday. It's ironic that a well-deserved break often starts with running for a train, queuing your way through a cattle pen the size of a squash court at the airport, or sitting in the biggest traffic jam of the year.

In 2008, the American scientific journal *Emotion* reported on a study of heart-rate recovery among people who'd just had a stressful experience. The researchers looked at three options. In the people who vented, sharing every detail with someone else, heart-rate recovery was worryingly slow. Those who replayed the incident to themselves were in the middle of the scale. Whereas the people who simply accepted the difficulty without any fuss had heart rates that either remained low or quickly recovered their natural balance.

The Buddha was also emphatic about the benefits of accepting the inevitable difficulties that life brings. If we can change an unwanted situation, great, but if we can't, then we might as well accept it. He used the image of a world where the surface is covered with stones and bits of glass. If it's not practical to cover the whole world with leather, then the least we can do is to cover our feet: that is, to develop a relaxed mind.

If this sounds obvious, then why do we still get hot and bothered when a plane gets delayed or a car sounds its horn? All it does is raise the temperature both for ourselves and the people around us.

Let's pray that, this year, holidaymakers can take a deep breath, keep a relaxed mind and accept that some things are simply beyond our control.

BROADCAST SATURDAY 10 JULY 2010

July 11

Cathy Le Feuvre

I'm fascinated by television programmes like *Britain's Got Talent* and *Fame Academy*. It's great when an unknown suddenly emerges – and someone who last week was working in a shop or as a cab driver suddenly becomes a chart-topper or a headliner in the West End.

I'm also amazed at the number of people who attend auditions really *believing* they have enough talent to be a superstar – even if the judges think otherwise.

We all have gifts, but we can't all be in the spotlight. The majority of us will just go about our lives quietly, hopefully using the talents and gifts that we have.

But not all of us have a great belief in our abilities, and some of us have yet to discover our gifts. We may think our contribution to life is pretty unimportant, especially compared to the great things we think others are doing.

But God has plans and purposes for each one of us, and we all have something to contribute – that's important to Him – even if we don't know it yet.

In the New Testament, in the first letter to the Corinthians, St Paul writes that 'God's various gifts are handed out everywhere; but they all originate in God's Spirit.' No gift is more important than another. Our inner selves are like our bodies. All the parts have different purposes and all are important in their own right.

God calls us all to be part of His work on earth. Each of us will have a path to follow and God will equip us accordingly.

Lord, You know us. With Your help may we discover and embrace the gifts You have given us, and then help us to explore ways in which we can use them to help improve our world and the lives of others. Amen.

BROADCAST FRIDAY 11 JULY 2008

July 12

Ibrahim Mogra

From the streets of our cities to workplaces and children's playgrounds, we can see a colourful mix of God's family. God says in the Qur'an, 'O mankind! I have created you from a single male and female and made you into nations and tribes so that you may recognize one another. Indeed the most honoured of you, in the sight of God, is the one who is most righteous. Indeed God is All-knowing, All-aware.' Black or white, man or woman – all are equal before God. He has honoured the children of Adam and so should we.

Muhammad (peace be upon Him) said, 'O people, indeed your Lord and Sustainer is One and your ancestor is one. All of you descend from Adam and Adam was made of earth. There is no superiority for an Arab over a non-Arab nor for a non-Arab over an Arab; neither for a white person over a black person nor a black person over a white person except the superiority gained through righteousness. Indeed the noblest of you in God's eyes is the one who is most conscious of God.' Muhammad also said, 'Indeed God does not look at your faces or your bodies or your family connections, but He looks at your hearts.'

In this week in 2001, the England race riots erupted. Whites and Asians turned on each other. Rioters destroyed cars and property, our northern cities burned while hospitals filled up with casualties. Racism had once again raised its ugly head, and it continues to this day in some places.

Loving God, help us recognize the humanity of others, to respect all human beings as equals, and to end racism. Amin.

BROADCAST FRIDAY 12 JULY 2013

July 13

Alison Murdoch

In my Christmas stocking last year I found a fridge magnet. It's headed 'Libra' – which is my star sign – with the comments: 'manipulative, flighty, indecisive, impatient, gullible and sulky. Escapist, extravagant, flirtatious ...', and so on. Instead of a set of scales, there's a woman trying to juggle shopping bags and cupcakes. It brings a smile, and hits the mark much more effectively than the usual astrological flattery.

Santa Claus – or rather, my husband – has clearly mastered the art of indirect communication. It wouldn't have been so easy to say this to my face. On the other hand, I can see that the things that rub us up the wrong way are also the things that polish us. Before I got married, for example, I considered myself a model of patience and reason. Now, every morning, there's an upturned loo seat to remind me that I'm not. I can either lose my cool, or else use the loo seat as a gentle reminder that I've still got work to do on myself.

My Buddhist teacher memorably says that 'the thought of liking problems should arise as naturally as the thought of liking ice cream'. Treating problems as an opportunity to learn can take away much of their sting. It's also a reminder that they don't just exist 'out there'. When something happens that we don't like, our minds easily slip into panic and exaggeration out of all proportion to the original difficulty, which delays the process of sorting the problem out.

Imagine a world where every problem is welcomed, even if not as ice-cream, then as an opportunity for developing understanding of ourselves and others.

Let's pray that we can each approach one difficulty we encounter today, not as a cause of irritation and anger, but as a source of insight and strength.

BROADCAST TUESDAY 13 JULY 2010

July 14

Claire Campbell Smith

The case of Meriam Ibrahim, sentenced to death for refusing to renounce her Christian faith, recently attracted huge international attention. She was convicted of apostasy — the abandoning of her religion — because, although she was brought up as a Christian, her father was a Muslim; and in Sudan, Muslims are not allowed to change their faith. Meriam showed immense courage, and the overturning of her sentence has been seen as a victory for religious freedom.

Just under 200 years ago today, a sermon preached in Oxford's university church was given the title 'National Apostasy'. The preacher was John Keble and his hearers were representatives of what he saw as a government misguided in its moves toward Catholic emancipation and the resulting impact on Church and state. Keble's sermon gave the first impulse to the Oxford Movement, which sought to reinstate ancient Christian traditions of faith and practice in the Anglican Church. The movement had wide influence but it also caused great controversy and its ideas were by no means universally accepted — indeed, many bishops refused to give jobs to priests who belonged to it. Yet the Church's ability to contain differing views meant that unity amidst diversity was maintained.

The same has been seen in the debate surrounding the enabling of women to become bishops in the Church of England, the final legislation for which goes before the Synod today. It's rooted in the belief that every part of the body of Christ is vital to its mission and is to be valued and cared for — a revolutionary model of interdependence in our diverse society.

Lord, may we live today with respect and concern for those around us, even those we do not understand or with whom we do not agree. Amen.

BROADCAST MONDAY 14 JULY 2014

July 15

Alison Murdoch

Around 2,500 years ago, a man sat under a tree in northern India, and achieved what is now called 'enlightenment'. Literally, the word means that he let go of all the psychological baggage he was carrying: all the accumulated anger, grasping and confusion which take away our peace of mind. Seven weeks later, the Buddha gave his first teaching on what he'd learned. This is the anniversary that Buddhists all over the world are celebrating today.

In that teaching, the Buddha made four key points. that our lives are pervaded by suffering; and this is why; that suffering can end; and how to achieve this. An advertising exec I once knew described this as the perfect marketing pitch — except for the word 'suffering'. The original term *dukkha* means something more like dissatisfaction of things never being quite as we'd like, of never really being at peace. Does that sound more familiar?!

The only reason the Buddha talked about dissatisfaction is because he wanted us to be free of it. His teachings are sometimes described as medicine — which nobody takes unless they see the need for it. When I first heard the Buddha's message, I was outraged. 'My life is full of happiness and good things! I'm coping just fine!' It was only when I thought more carefully that I realized how precarious that happiness really was, and that most of the time I was chasing after short-term distractions rather than addressing my long-term emotional and spiritual needs.

Buddhism isn't really about suffering but exactly the opposite: how to find happiness, satisfaction and peace of mind, and then use these qualities to be of service to others. Let's pray that people the world over can each find their unique way to do this.

BROADCAST THURSDAY 15 JULY 2010

July 16

Liz Adenjunle

I was once asked to visit an elderly woman at Homerton Hospital because she was close to death and she hadn't had any visitors. I sat and read to her, and it was clear from her expression that the human contact meant a great deal — because whatever our lifestyle, we need each other, and most of the time it costs nothing.

Loneliness is a common human experience. All of us, whether single or with a partner, whether for a short or long period of time, have experienced loneliness. Whatever one's background, life experiences or lifestyle, the truth is, we struggle without others. Even the Psalmist says to God in Psalm 25: 'Turn to me and be gracious to me, for I am lonely and afflicted.'

Loneliness is a recognized problem among the elderly — but within the last decade, a study by the Mental Health Foundation found loneliness to be greater among younger people aged 18–34 than the elderly over-55s — and one in four men who call the Samaritans' helpline mentions loneliness or isolation.

It needn't be grand gestures: a smile or a brief exchange of words to the person you see on the bus on the way to work can make all the difference to someone's life, in the same way that it does to us when we receive the same from others.

Another quote — this time from Psalm 147 — says: 'He [God] heals the brokenhearted and binds up their wounds.'

So today we recognize that, regardless of our lifestyles, we all feel lonely from time to time. We remember all those who are alone, or who feel burdened with loneliness, and we ask for Your comfort. And in Your love, let them know that they are not forgotten. Amen.

BROADCAST THURSDAY 16 JULY 2015

July 17

Nick Baines

I've been looking back at some of the momentous things that have happened on this day during the last few hundreds of years, and there are loads. I even remember some of them — like the many, mainly African, nations boycotting the Queen's opening of the Montreal Olympics in 1976 in protest at New Zealand's sporting links with apartheid South Africa.

I can even remember what I was doing that very day, because it's etched in my memory and has absolutely nothing to do with sport. It was the 18th birthday of a girl I fancied, and I managed to get an invite to her birthday party. I'd fallen in love with her, and it only took her another year to reciprocate! Today is her 50th birthday and I've been her husband for almost 28 years.

So, how are we going to celebrate? Well, we can't. We're at the Lambeth Conference in Canterbury, and so we'll have a family party later in August when we're all back.

The important thing, though, is to make sure we do celebrate. Individuals and communities need opportunities to party and express joy and thanks at the milestones passed. Surely it's not insignificant that Jesus — who managed quite easily to upset all the wrong people — was sometimes accused of being a bit too fond of partying. But it seems that wherever he went there was some sort of a great celebration. After all, his first miracle was at a wedding where he turned water into wine — and not the other way round.

Lord God, help us today to find something to celebrate. Open our eyes to the glories of Your world and the people we love. And particularly bless those who today celebrate their birthday. Amen.

BROADCAST THURSDAY 17 JULY 2008

July 18

Chris Bennett

As part of my work as a chaplain in the Titanic Quarter in Belfast, I am responsible for the pastoral care of a new community of people moving into a brand-new complex of apartments and offices – disparate people from all over the world finding themselves together in this strange, exciting new place. My post is a newly created one and presents something of a blank page, and to begin with I wasn't quite sure where to start. What can a chaplain offer to all the successful, trendy people in a vibrant new part of town?

I was thinking about this one afternoon as I sipped a creamy mocha on a comfy couch in a well-known coffee shop chain. Across from me, two friends, who obviously hadn't seen each other for a while, were catching up, swapping photos and stories and lots of laughter. Behind them, a group of young professional women were gathered in a knitting group (did you know that knitting is cool now?). Their conversation bounced around the group as their needles flashed back and forth. The door opened and a crowd of businessmen bustled in, ordered their coffees and grabbed a table. After a moment's pause, one man sat back and said to the group: 'So, how was everyone's day?'

It was my lightbulb moment. John Donne taught us that 'no man is an island', and in busy cities that truth is both more profoundly vital and more difficult to live out. We are built for community, to belong, to be part of families not just of blood relation but of city, of workplace, of interest and pastime, of shared passion. Perhaps a chaplain's job is to find as many places and ways as possible to say, 'So, how was everyone's day?'

Lord God, help all of us to seize every chance to build friendships, to grow communities, to 'only connect'. May we refuse to live an island life.

BROADCAST MONDAY 18 JULY 2011

July 19

Claire Campbell Smith

I'll soon be celebrating my half-century, and with that comes a certain amount of reflection on the ageing process. Today's cultural emphasis is on all things new, but I never cease to be fascinated by the old. I remember the awe I felt when I first visited London's Natural History Museum and was met by an enormous dinosaur. On this day in 1983, the museum unveiled a new dinosaur, *Baryonyx walkeri*, thought to have lived 125 million years ago and the most complete skeleton ever found in Britain. Equally awe-inspiring were the tombs of Egypt's Valley of the Kings; and this month, I'm travelling to Namibia, where I'll see rock art created by ancient African civilizations. The teenagers going with me have been seriously unimpressed by pictures of these rock paintings, but I'm hoping that will change *in situ*!

With an increasingly ageing population, we now have abundant opportunities to draw on the experience of those who have lived through different times, and have an alternative perspective to today's bias toward the immediate and the ephemeral. One of the many names given to God in the Bible is 'Ancient of Days'. This has inspired images of God as a very old *and* a very young man, who existed before time began and will do so for ever. Despite our increasing longevity, our lives on this earth will eventually end. But to us and to our world, whose frailty is highlighted by constant reports of climate change, the God of the past, present and future offers a perspective of eternity and invites us to trust in Him.

Heavenly Father, who orders all things for our eternal good, give us a firm trust in Your love and care, that, rising above our anxieties, we may rest on You, the rock of everlasting strength. Amen.

BROADCAST FRIDAY 19 JULY 2013

July 20

Sarah Joseph

My mother ran a model agency and worked full-time when I was growing up, so I spent a large amount of my time with my grandmother, whom we all called Nana.

Nana was born in 1909. Her father was an officer in the Royal Navy and her mother was a dressmaker — making garments for the ladies of court. She lived until she was 100 years old, and saw in her lifetime extraordinary technological change — from the advent of cars and roads to electricity into her home; from aeroplanes and rocket ships to televisions and computers. She also saw enormous social change. She recalled at age 11 the whole street coming out to see a man in a turban — a member of the British Indian Army — walking past. Yet as she grew older she embraced all people regardless of race, colour or creed.

She was also a profoundly spiritual woman, who drew from a deep religious well. From her I learned to pray, and I learned a rich religious vocabulary. Words such as grace, humility, self-sacrifice, redemption, character, virtue, faith, forgiveness and transformation featured in our everyday conversations. They were bound up in everyday life, not a thing apart; they were a way for her to explain how to live, not a school religious studies lesson.

The American writer David Brooks has, among others, written of the absence of a moral and religious language within the reach of young people. If it's vocabulary that allows us to think, then some young people may well have their moral, religious and spiritual experience limited by an absence of words.

Our Lord, give us the words to be able to think of You and Your Will for us. Grant us the language to know You, and to live in a manner pleasing to You. Amin.

BROADCAST MONDAY 20 JULY 2015

July 21

Chris Bennett

Everybody knows the end of the story of the *Titanic* — its resting place two miles beneath the surface of the icy Atlantic. Rewind to the start of the story and we find not tragedy but optimism, vision and breathtaking hope. *Titanic* and her sister ships were half as large again as their nearest rival. Their keels stretched nearly 900 feet along the slipways in the Belfast shipyards. Fifteen thousand men laboured for two years, building them panel upon panel, rivet by rivet. In their day these ships were the largest manmade moving objects in the world. When *Titanic* stood on the slipway it towered above its builders like a skyscraper.

Their working day was long, tough and dangerous, but I wonder if each of those men returned home to their beds every night with their hearts uplifted, knowing that their labours were creating a wonder of the world. Despite the *Titanic*'s tragic fate, we honour the vision of the men who built this extraordinary ship.

We all long to be part of something bigger than ourselves, and we sometimes need reminding that big dreams and great visions can become reality. At the dawn of the 1960s, John F Kennedy made the bold promise that man would walk on the moon before the end of the decade; today is the anniversary of the day in 1969 when his dream became reality. Each of us can have that man-on-the-moon vision for something.

Lord God, raise our eyes and our hopes to expect greater things. Disturb us when we are too easily satisfied or discouraged. May we return home to our beds tonight with our hearts uplifted, with the sense that our lives are making a difference.

BROADCAST THURSDAY 21 JULY 2011

July 22

Derek Boden

Recently there's been a lot of talk about pensions. How are state pensions to be paid for? Can private pensions ever to be as generous as they were? And more than all that, at what age are we going to be able to retire? If I'm to believe all that I hear and read, who knows where it's going to end?

A short while ago I met a friend of mine who is retired. I've known him for years but our conversation that day troubled me. He had been meticulous in his work and had contributed a lot to the community where he lived, but he was hurt … maybe bitter would be the right world. He told me he felt forgotten and neglected, even by many of those he'd helped through his work.

It made me think again about how I relate to valued people once they retire. It's all too easy to overlook the worth of those who, when they were younger, were so much prized. It also made me think about how many of us face retirement. Perhaps, as we retire, we need to find new attitudes and new activities other than the old workaday ones.

That's why I'm encouraged by another friend who grew his first tomato when he was nearly 80 and by a lady I know who took her advanced driving test long after she retired.

So whatever decisions are made about our pensions and whatever age we retire, we'd do well to remember there is life after our life's work.

So grant us, Lord, satisfaction in our working day, encouragement in our retirement, appreciation of those who are retired and the awareness of Your presence through all our days. Amen.

BROADCAST THURSDAY 22 JULY 2010

July 23

Sarah Joseph

Some of my favourite stories from the Qur'an relate to the Prophet Joseph. When I was younger, I'm sure it was the biblical stories of his rainbow cloak that I loved, or maybe it was because he was my namesake, but as an adult it's Joseph as an outcast, a victim of human trafficking, a refugee, that has inspired me.

Joseph was persecuted by his own kin, and left in a well to die. Traders found him and sold him on as a slave, and thus he was taken from his own land and found himself in Egypt. Handsome and educated, he was purchased by a wealthy merchant, but when Joseph rejected the advances of the merchant's wife, he was cast into prison and forgotten. There he interpreted the dreams of prisoners, and it is one of these men who mentioned Joseph to the King. Joseph was brought before His Majesty, interpreted his dream and stored the grain in a time of abundance, which saved Egypt in a subsequent time of famine. Through this he was able to save his own family who later came to Egypt looking for food.

The story reminds me of so many refugees I've met in my life – people who have been forced from their own lands because of war or persecution, and ended up in Europe and America. Their stories of the persecution from which they fled and the prejudice they have often received have been both inspirational and painful to hear. I remember, 30 years ago, there was a Polish boy at school who fled the then Communist regime with his family. He worked so hard to learn English and to study. He is a scientist now.

Our Lord, allow us to welcome strangers, treat them kindly and understand that they can benefit us as well as those in the lands from which they come. Amin.

BROADCAST THURSDAY 23 JULY 2015

July 24

Richard Hill

The infant clung to his mother. His cookie-encrusted face charmed fellow travellers, eliciting smiles at first and then polite conversations about children and cookies.

There's nothing particularly remarkable about this everyday kind of scene, except that it happened a few weeks ago on a crowded train on the Bakerloo line in London. Let's face it, travellers on the Tube have turned avoiding conversation and eye contact into something bordering on an art form.

The cookie-munching infant shattered the social conventions of the Underground. Not exactly a headline but transforming all the same. All it took was a smiling child to act as kind of unspeaking mediator, transforming my short journey from Baker Street to Paddington.

Earlier that day I'd been in the National Gallery – looking at Da Vinci's *Madonna of the Rocks*. It depicts Mary, the angel Uriel and the infant Christ blessing his cousin John. This iconic portrayal of the Christ-child, followed later in my day by my experience of the mother and infant on the train, made me reflect on how God enters into our unspeaking, gaze-averting human journey to create relationships.

The Bible tells us that there is 'One God and one mediator between God and humankind, the man Christ Jesus.' Christ, man or infant, he begins a new dialogue.

Father, thank You that Christ has come, transforming our humanity and engaging us in the divine conversation. In Jesus's name, Amen.

BROADCAST FRIDAY 24 JULY 2009

July 25

Ibrahim Mogra

The deluge of rain over the past few weeks has attracted interesting comments about climate change and the environment, including one that said, 'This is Britain, just get on with it!' Arguments from all points of view continue to be made. But on whichever side of the argument we stand, we cannot escape the fact that we continue to harm and damage our beautiful, fragile planet. Massive industrialization has literally changed the face of this earth, with huge swathes of forests disappearing by the day.

According to the Qur'an, the human being is God's steward on earth. This responsibility is a trust and each one of us as a trustee is duty-bound to use the earth's resources carefully and to preserve them and to leave them in a better condition for future generations. The wasteful habits that so many of us in the developed world have are a major contributor to the demise of this unique planet. Were we to make some simple changes to our lifestyles, we could certainly prolong its life. Consider the food and drink that we bin at every meal; the clothes that we discard yet are still fit for wearing; the soap we allow to dissolve in a water-filled dish; the shampoo, toothpaste and cream that we squeeze out more than required. If we could stop all this wastage, we would be making a huge contribution toward the preservation of vital resources. The Qur'an declares that God does not love those who are wasteful.

Dear God, make us not of the wasteful; enable us to appreciate your bounties and to use them sensibly. Amin.

BROADCAST WEDNESDAY 25 JULY 2012

July 26

Patrick Thomas

Armenian Christians have always treasured beautifully illuminated manuscripts. Many of the finest are preserved in the Matenadaran Library in Yerevan, the Armenian capital, which I revisited recently. Most of them have colophons: footnotes that give details of the scribe, the miniaturist, the donor and the history of the manuscript as it was taken from monastery to monastery.

Perhaps the most remarkable of these treasures is also the largest: a huge collection of illustrated homilies. It was once the prized possession of a monastery at Mush in Turkish Armenia. In 1915 almost all the Christian inhabitants of the town were massacred and their monastery destroyed. Among the few survivors were two courageous Armenian women, who decided to save the precious manuscript.

It was too heavy for one person to carry, so they divided it in half, each wrapping a portion around her body. One of the women, starving and ill, managed to reach the safety of Etchmiadzin Cathedral, the centre of Armenian Christianity. There she handed her part of the manuscript to the priest. The other woman died on the journey, but not before she had carefully buried her section of the ancient book. It was recovered at the end of World War I, and the two halves were reunited.

The manuscript has become a powerful symbol of those things that the two women were determined should not be destroyed: their faith, their culture and their history.

Heavenly Father, we live in a society which often seems to value only the trivial and the ephemeral. Give us grace to discern those things that have true and lasting importance, and the courage to preserve them and pass them on to future generations. Amen.

BROADCAST SATURDAY 26 JULY 2008

July 27

Andrea Rea

When I left home in Minneapolis, Minnesota, to come and live in Ireland, I don't think I thought about how long I'd be away from home. Twenty-five years later, I suppose I still haven't given it much thought. Well, you don't, do you? You get on with life, with what you do, your family and friends, and pretty soon things have taken their own direction. When I go back to America to visit, my school chums have done the same thing and their lives have moved on in other directions.

One friend in particular, though, got on with her life rather more quickly than any of us anticipated. She married halfway through university and had her first baby nine months after the wedding. Within a few years she seemed to be living a grown-up life far more associated with our parents' lives than our own. A visit to her suburban house revealed a side porch, a car in the garage, two kids, a dog and a budgie. I had just left home with an army surplus footlocker, a guitar case and little else. We talked for a long time on that visit, and Denise seemed a little dazed by her journey toward maturity but told me her philosophy. 'Bloom where you are planted,' she said — but I wasn't convinced. Surely we choose where we plant ourselves? It seemed too random, too much left to fate or some kind of predetermined destiny.

Now, more than 20 years later, I see the wisdom of Denise's thinking. She understood back then that you can waste a lot of emotional energy in regrets and looking back, looking over the fence, as it were, to the garden next door, instead of making your own plot the best it can be.

God of all that grows in the earth as well as in our lives and hearts, help us to value the place where we've been planted and to look after ourselves and those around us. Lord of life, help us to bloom.

BROADCAST FRIDAY 27 JULY 2007

July 28

Clair Jaquiss

A friend of mine was training to be a priest in the Church of England. The course was about theology, Church history, pastoral skills and spirituality. Wherever he would be placed after that course, he was learning to be both holy and down-to-earth, spiritual and practical.

There was also a module that ran alongside the academic work, called the 'Personal Project'. It was one part of what they call 'formation' — the moulding of the person following the example of Christ. It had to be relevant to the life of the Christian minister and was assessed at the end like all the other modules. People took saxophone lessons and sang in choral societies. They learned sign language or made greetings cards.

My friend had a long discussion with his tutor about what he should do. He was in a pressured job. He still had his academic work. They concluded between them that, for three hours each fortnight, he should spend time in silence. Not praying or in spiritual reflection in any formal way — just time alone and silent: a void. Not easy when we feel we've got to fill all our gaps with words.

The mystic St John of the Cross wrote about the dark night of the soul. This is often assumed to refer to the darkness of grief and sadness. God meets us there, too. But St John of the Cross's dark night of the soul was essentially a way of purification where activity and speech are set aside — a darkness of nothingness where God is invited; where there is simply the silence of being.

So our prayer: for the strength of mind to spend some time today in silence — without words or ideas, empty of images — to meet God without obstacles in the silence of faith. Amen.

BROADCAST THURSDAY 28 JULY 2011

July 29

Alison Murdoch

Last weekend I visited a friend who has a wonderful selection of fridge magnets. One of them made me laugh but also stop and think. It said: 'Seen it all, done it all, can't remember most of it.' It's so true — when I look back at the past year, or even month, my memory is like a leaky boat. That's one reason I take so many photos, but unless they're selfies, I may not even remember who all the people are.

The Buddha would argue that all this rushing here and there, the 1,000 things to see, do, eat or drink before you die, is missing the point. The view may be magnificent, but it can only be seen through the lens of the mind, and if the mind is cloudy or biased in any way, that's all we get. It's like experiencing the world through the equivalent of a tinted or dirty pair of sunglasses.

The practice of mindfulness meditation offers one method for experiencing the world with more spaciousness and clarity. Through finding some quiet time at the beginning or end of each day, and learning to take pauses when we find ourselves overloaded, it's possible to regain control of the mind just as if we were grabbing the wheel of a driverless car. The results can be extraordinary. Thousands of people in the UK report lowered levels of stress, better sleep, improved concentration and happier relationships.

Although there are some first-rate Buddhist meditation teachers, this isn't a religious trip but a basic human skill. As the Roman Emperor Marcus Aurelius said: 'Very little is needed to make a happy life. It is all within yourself, in your own way of thinking.'

Let's pray that each of us can find a moment today to pause and question whether we really need to see and do that extra thing.

BROADCAST TUESDAY 29 JULY 2014

July 30

Michael Piret

In a challenging little book he wrote just after the attacks of 9/11, Archbishop Rowan Williams addressed the important matter of how we *answer back*. He was in Lower Manhattan on the day of the attack, just a couple of blocks from the World Trade Center. Later, he had a phone call from a journalist in Wales. The journalist started speaking in Welsh. Now, the Archbishop knew his own words about that terrible day would have to be very carefully chosen, and he could be more precise in English. So would he answer in English or Welsh? Whatever language he chose, that was how the conversation would go on.

You can see the connection between that (very small) choice, and issues of war and peace. Do we respond to attack with attack, violence with violence — that is, do we answer back in the same language? Or do we try to answer differently? — since, whatever language we choose, that is how the conversation will go on. This principle is at work even in the most mundane exchanges and encounters of our daily lives. It might just be that we're spoken to rudely or unpleasantly at work, or in the local bank or supermarket. Will we answer back in the same way? Or might we, instead, stop and think for a moment, change the tone of the encounter, and resist being drawn into a cycle of attack and reprisal?

Help us, God, to use for good the power we have to shape our daily conversations. If we feel provoked or stung by unkindness or discourtesy, keep us calm, give us patience and imagination — so we can answer back in a tone that dares to be different. Amen.

BROADCAST FRIDAY 30 JULY 2010

July 31

Clair Jaquiss

I was at Manchester Airport the other day. It was like some kind of abandoned film set. There was no tumbleweed but instead what seemed like acres of empty marble flooring and stainless steel and glass. I guess we'd hit a quiet time. I was travelling for work and we'd missed the holiday rush — or maybe people were just being much more cautious and prudent about spending money on holidays abroad. Not easy times for those businesses relying on tourists.

Well — you don't have to go abroad for rest and relaxation, for exploration and adventure. Of course, a change of location does help to divert the mind from the everyday concerns and worries that grind us down. But then so also does travel in the imagination — exploring another world through story or music or in silence.

St Ignatius Loyola, whose feast day it is today, lived in the 16th century. He'd worked as a young man in the court of a Spanish duke and his dream was to be a great knight, but when a cannonball shattered his knee, he had time on his hands — time to think and reflect. He was converted as he was laid up, and discovered some very creative ways of praying. His spiritual exercises encourage the person praying to imagine themselves into the Gospel story as an observer or as one of the characters: perhaps a shepherd in the fields of Bethlehem, or as a servant at the Last Supper. This imagined world is a place where there is space to listen to others in the story, to question them and to discover God's purpose for us. At the beginning of the day Ignatius would dedicate it: 'for the greater glory of God'.

So Lord, help us to discover You in the riches of our imagination. Fill our lives with Your love so that in partnership with You we may build Your kingdom together. Amen.

BROADCAST FRIDAY 31 JULY 2009

August 1

Andrew Graystone

We expect so much of sport. In our culture we have invested it with an almost religious significance. And nowhere is that more evident than at the Olympic Games, with its rituals and ideals. We require that children take part in sport because we believe it will somehow make them better people. We prescribe exercise as a route to good health, a remedy for depression and a cure for obesity. We ask sportsmen and women to be role models, even if their qualification is not much more than skill with a football.

Then when we host a big competition, we expect it to be much more than a sporting event. We want the Olympics to bring peace between nations, to produce economic benefits and to leave a legacy of regeneration. I can't help but wonder whether the weight of expectations we place on sport risk crushing what is essential about it.

For some of the joy of sport is its sheer pointlessness. At its best, people run and swim and jump for joy. And when grown men and women compete in team sports, there's something childlike about it. We invest sport with great seriousness, but only because deep down we know that it's not serious at all. Someone wins and someone loses, and there is joy and disappointment, but the great thing in sport is that it doesn't *really* matter.

In Christian theology, creation itself is sometimes seen as a playful act of God. And looked at in this way, all sport is a sign of grace — of the playfulness of spirit that we can only enjoy when we know that in the end, in the fullness of God's time, all shall be well.

God who gave us a spirit of playfulness, renew in us the joy of competition, the fun of creativity and the exhilaration that comes from discovering all that we are and can be. Amen.

BROADCAST WEDNESDAY 1 AUGUST 2012

August 2

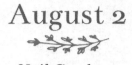

Neil Gardner

This weekend the Commonwealth Games – the 'Friendly Games', as they have been known and shown to be in Glasgow these last ten days or so – will come to an end. And within a day or two our national focus will shift from their closing ceremony to ceremonies and services across the country marking the centenary of the beginning of World War I. It was Sir Edward Gray, the then Foreign Secretary, who on 3 August 1914 famously commented: 'The lamps are going out all over Europe, we shall not see them lit again in our lifetime.'

'Lights out' is a military term used to mark the end of the day. In old Scottish regiments, it was often expressed in a plaintive tune played by the duty piper, and these days it's one of the features of the Royal Edinburgh Military Tattoo, when a lone piper appears high on the ramparts of the castle toward the end of the evening. But when the lights went out 100 years ago, we were not going to sleep: we were going to war.

As is so often the case, the Psalmist keeps things in reassuring perspective. 'Lord, you have been our dwelling-place in all generations, it is written. For a thousand years in your sight are like yesterday when it is past, or like a watch in the night.'

God of eternity, bring hope to those in despair, comfort to those who suffer and light to those who sit in darkness, through him whose light shines in the darkness, a light no darkness can ever overcome: Jesus Christ our Lord. Amen.

BROADCAST SATURDAY 2 AUGUST 2014

August 3

Marjory MacLean

Today is the anniversary of one of the most daring achievements in naval history, when in 1958 the submarine USS *Nautilus* was the first to sail under the North Pole from one side of the ice cap to the other.

Nautilus had been built just after World War II as the first ever nuclear-powered submarine, controversial in her potential but astonishing in her technology. She had already broken endurance records for submerging and for distance. To cross the Pole she had to be fitted with equipment to replace the ordinary compasses and gyros that would malfunction so far north. And in an earlier attempt she could not make it through the gap between a 50-foot-thick ice-shelf and the ocean floor, and had to turn back. In early August she made it through, right under the Pole itself. That must have been the ultimate nightmare for a claustrophobia sufferer, and the challenge must have felt of almost biblical proportions to the crew.

The Old Testament is most readable when its characters are filled with a sense of adventure and launch themselves into some great unknown – a desert, a battle, a campaign, a marriage, a change of career. Believers read the stories, trying to remember that these really pretty practical people did not know how things were going to work out and were undertaking great acts of faith.

In the worship of those times, in the psalms and hymns that have come down to us, utter trust is put in God for wise counsel and safe passage, for tasks achieved and for security.

> 'Lord, You show us the path of life. In Your presence there is fullness of joy; and in Your right hand are pleasures for ever more.' When daunting adventure faces us and we are willing to risk it or unable to avoid it, let us put our trust in You, Father, Son and Holy Spirit. Amen.

BROADCAST MONDAY 3 AUGUST 2009

August 4

Neil Gardner

The Scottish National War Memorial in the precincts of Edinburgh Castle is a poignant place at the best of times, but on a day like today, the centenary of the outbreak of World War I, it takes on an especially powerful significance. At its heart is the shrine of remembrance, where an ornate casket containing the names of those who fell in that conflict sits on top of a solid block of marble, which in turn stands firmly on Castle Rock itself. It is as if the names of the fallen are fixed not only to the castle but to the rock on which it stands, inextricably linked to the fabric and foundation of all that we hold dear.

I'm sure that's what Sir Robert Lorimer had in mind when he designed the shrine. I imagine he was less concerned about the occasional services that would be held there and are often rendered inaudible by the challenging acoustics of those marble halls. But that doesn't matter, for this war memorial, like all others, must be primarily a place for silence. 'For everything there is a season, and a time for every matter under heaven,' says the writer of Ecclesiastes. 'A time to keep silence and a time to speak; a time for war, and a time for peace.'

Loving God, we remember with thanksgiving all those whom You have gathered from the storm of war into the peace of Your presence and not least those who gave their lives in World War I. May we be taught to live by those who learned to die, and in the face of their sacrifice, when all is said and done, fall silent. Amen.

BROADCAST MONDAY 4 AUGUST 2014

August 5

Ernest Rea

A few months ago, I visited Jerusalem. I was travelling with a party of two Christians, two Jews and two Muslims to experience the spiritual significance of a city holy to us all.

On the first afternoon, we gathered at the Western Wall. We stood together and watched the extraordinary sight of Jews praying at the great wall which is all that remains of Solomon's Temple. I was uneasy for my Muslim colleagues. One, a woman from Blackburn, was wearing a headscarf. The other, an imam from Nottingham, was in traditional Islamic dress. They were subjected to suspicious and, let me be honest, at times hostile stares.

An Orthodox Jewish man who had been praying by the wall saw us; and he made his way over. I wasn't sure what was going to happen next. But he greeted us with a huge smile and, in halting English, he told us that he was delighted to see us and that we were all very welcome.

It was a moment of grace. We all felt we'd experienced a blessing. And it set the tone for the rest of our visit. The next four days were a time of learning about each other and understanding – to such an extent that, on our last morning, we all felt able to pray together.

Now I don't want to offer facile solutions to complex problems. It will be politics that decides the course of events in the Middle East. But I will never again dismiss the claims of those who say that peace and understanding can begin with a friendly word and a welcoming gesture.

Lord, we pray for peace in our hearts and in our homes, in our nation and in our world. Amen.

BROADCAST TUESDAY 5 AUGUST 2008

August 6

Shaunaka Rishi Das

My good wife, Keshava, likes to journey to the village of Nether Winchendon, a small village in Buckinghamshire. Her ideal spot is a wide field beside a flowing river, where the water is as clear as a window and decorated with trees, swans, dragonfly and fish.

Keshava loves this place for its peaceful atmosphere and its romantic setting. She brings her Krishna Book, her chanting beads and her lunch, and settles down for a day of thoughtful meditation. Being a devotee of Krishna, she finds the presence of the cows comforting and auspicious. They wander around munching, with wide eyes and a mellow walk, keeping themselves to themselves.

On one such glorious day, after a satisfying morning, Keshava packed her wicker basket and headed for the gate. On her way she noticed the cows in a herd and in her path, so she made to go around them. But they moved toward her and then she noticed that they were all looking at her.

Keshava stopped and the cows stared. Then they began to move forward as one; then to trot, all the time staring. Keshava dropped her basket, lifted her skirts and ran. The cows, as if in a Western, ran as well. Keshava shouted out Krishna's name, repeatedly. Where could she run to? And the only answer could be: the river. So, in she jumped, landing up to her waist, and turned to see the cows pulling up on the bank.

Then, immediate danger past, she surveyed these bovine thugs and shouted her indignation, especially given the fact that she was a vegetarian — I mean, come on!

Dear Lord, there are so many unexpected disturbances in our lives, such as when peaceful cows turn bad. Help us to accept distress, even when it comes from those we love, and learn to let it go. Hare Krishna.

BROADCAST MONDAY 6 AUGUST 2012

August 7

Michael Mumisa

This month, millions of Muslims all over the world will be observing the month of fasting known as Ramadan. Fasting during Ramadan is one of the five pillars of the Muslim faith. Muslims believe it to be an act of worship that was prescribed by God in different forms to all the biblical prophets before Muhammad.

This is also the month of charity and giving. When I was growing up and attending the koranic schools known as the *madrasas*, I was told that fasting is a way of experiencing how the less fortunate among us feel and the hardships that they go through in their daily lives.

I have since been wondering: can fasting from dawn after having had a meal, and breaking fast at sunset with another meal fit for two, be the only and most effective way of expressing our solidarity with the poor? Indeed, the month of fasting is the month when many of us gain weight due to excessive eating!

Is poverty only about food? Or should we be doing more?

Desmond Tutu, a man I admire greatly, once said that there is a tendency among some of us to view and present poverty as a religious ideal, the thinking that since God is on the side of the poor, poverty must be a good thing.

We hope and pray that we will remain steadfast in our jihad or struggles against poverty and social injustices alongside people from other faiths and those of no particular faith. We pray for the wisdom to work together toward removing the structures and systems of our society that cause and perpetuate poverty.

Our Lord! Bestow on us mercy from Yourself, and make it easy for us to deal with the difficult tasks that are before us! Amen.

BROADCAST SATURDAY 7 AUGUST 2010

August 8

David Bruce

Beside my desk at home I have a small wooden cross. It hangs on a thin cord, attached to a drawing pin on the wall. It is made of dark wood, and as an object of art or even a carpenter's skill, it is of little note. But I hope I never lose it. Its importance is that it was the parting gift to me from a priest of the Armenian Apostolic Church during one of several visits I made to his country after the ending of Soviet rule.

Its distinctive feature is the design of little buds that appear to grow from the ends of the branches of the cross — as if the branches themselves are alive and about to bear fruit. My friend and I had been talking about our personal and national stories — me of the Irish famine in the 1840s, its effect on our history ever since and how we have really never recovered. And he of the Armenian genocide perpetrated in the closing years of World War I and beyond — and of the national wound it created which refuses to heal, even today. As we parted and he pressed the cross into my hand as a keepsake, he said 'Never forget the cross, but also its fruit. Perhaps, in God's good grace, there might better days for us Armenians, as for you Irish.'

Father, we lift up to You the unsung heroes whose extraordinary refusal to be overcome by despair is an inspiration and a challenge to us all. Amen.

BROADCAST SATURDAY 8 AUGUST 2009

August 9

Shaunaka Rishi Das

Tomorrow is the celebration of Lord Krishna's birth, a great day in the Hindu year. Krishna, the most popular of Hindu deities, is a child — God as a child. And when I say the most popular of Hindu deities, I don't mean that there are many gods, but that there is one God manifested in many different ways.

Krishna is an Olympian, even as a child. He is a weightlifter, lifting Govardhan Hill with the little finger of his left hand, the body's weakest digit; he did the high jump from a mountain and without a net; he threw weights — a demon in the form of an ass, which he threw further than anyone ever threw an ass; and he won his greatest boxing bout with one punch, delivered to a demon bull — all this among other glories.

He comes as an avatar of God. He fulfils the role as a child who is a superhero. He protects his devotees and shares their love, and he thumps the rascals. Unlike other forms of God, he has no responsibilities (being a child), and is not even very concerned with religion. He just loves those who love him and arranges for that love to increase in their hearts, in order for their relationship to deepen and to become more intimate.

He shows his prowess, easily beating any hero or Olympian, to help us understand that our efforts are limited by our bodies and minds — and that there is a platform where we can exist without mundane limits.

Dear Lord Krishna, you are the strength of the strong and the ability in man. I limit myself by living in separation from you. Please bless my ability to appreciate your unlimited affection. Hare Krishna.

BROADCAST THURSDAY 9 AUGUST 2012

August 10

Marjory MacLean

When a crowd gathers, all sorts of things can happen. In Edinburgh during the Festival Fringe, cheerful crowds magically form in Parliament Square or outside the National Gallery, with people letting their hair down a little, enjoying the cleverness or humour of the showmen who are there to entertain or advertise their act. And on the very same evenings in Tottenham or Enfield or Birmingham, people spontaneously gather with darker intentions, letting their hair down too, joining together to do dreadful things they would not be seen doing alone.

The timeless stories of our great religious traditions have warned us about the power of crowds for thousands of years. On Palm Sunday, we Christians gladly imagine ourselves part of the crowd that threw palm fronds and cloaks on the road in front of Jesus's donkey, and shouted praise to their King. On Good Friday, we are reluctant to think of ourselves in the crowd that bayed for Christ's death and lapped up his torture.

It takes courage to insist on our dignity as individuals, to stand up when necessary against a crowd with all its temptations, energy and lack of inhibition. Whoever we may be, teenaged, middle-aged or old, living in the din of the city or in the silence of the countryside, we must finally be true to ourselves and to ourselves alone, gently but persistently holding on to what seems good and right.

Loving God, You have created us one by one and You hear each one of us speak with a unique voice, aloud to others or in our most secret thoughts. Do not let us choose to be only what we are in a crowd, but may we have strength enough to live lives that are counted and measured each for its own precious sake. Amen.

BROADCAST WEDNESDAY 10 AUGUST 2011

August 11

David Bruce

There is a well-known hymn written by John Henry Newman that comes to mind on this anniversary of his death on 11 August 1890.

Newman was an Oxford academic, an Anglican who began as a member of the evangelical wing of the Church of England. Later he converted to Catholicism, after which his Oxford career ended. So impressive was his contribution to the life of the Catholic Church in England that, in 1879, he was made a cardinal by Pope Leo XIII.

'Lead, Kindly Light' became a much-loved hymn, sung across most Christian traditions. It is said that when the *Carpathia* arrived to pick up survivors after the sinking of the *Titanic*, it was Newman's hymn that was being sung by those fortunate enough to have secured a place in the lifeboats. Many a believer facing despair has found a deep comfort from these words, which encourage us to take one step at a time, even when the darkness around makes taking a step of any kind a matter of faith. So we pray:

Lead, Kindly Light, amid th'encircling gloom,
Lead Thou me on;
The night is dark, and I am far from home,
Lead Thou me on.
Keep Thou my feet; I do not ask to see
The distant scene; one step enough for me.

BROADCAST TUESDAY 11 AUGUST 2015

August 12

George Craig

When I first met Georgina, she had just passed her 91st birthday. I'm pretty sure it was at that first meeting that she took me aside and said she had a secret to tell me. 'I'm 18 really,' she said, 'but they've given me this dreadful body.' And frankly the poor old body was showing signs of wear: her sight and hearing were failing and she wasn't nearly as mobile as she would have liked. It would have been enough to drag anyone down.

But it didn't stop Georgie. She carried on being 18 for another 12 years until eventually even her spirit couldn't make the exhausted body go on. Up to that point, though, you always had to remember that you weren't dealing with a frail old lady but a joyful and mischievous teenager.

Everybody who spent time with her came away feeling better about the world and themselves. She had a deep care for people that touched everybody who met her. She always looked out and forward, and however frustrated she might get with what she couldn't do any more, she simply made all the more effort to enjoy the things she could still do.

Which is what brings her to my mind so often. I'm fortunate to be pretty fit and well. I'm a lot younger than 91, but I spend so much time worrying that every twinge, ache or pain might signal the end that I have less and less time to simply enjoy all the good things I have. It isn't about depression – that's much harder and more complex to deal with. But it's about how our attitudes can impact us.

Many of us can be very impatient when we're told to focus on all the positive stuff that's going on in our lives. It seems just too simple. But Georgina, and many like her, are proof that it can work.

Lord, I thank You so much for the example of those who demonstrate the healing and strengthening power of living whatever life they have to the full and living it for others. Help us learn from them. Amen.

BROADCAST WEDNESDAY 12 AUGUST 2009

August 13

Stephen Shipley

Discussing spiritual matters and particularly faith is often strange to people. We tend to keep our spiritual motivation and our faith to ourselves, often for fear of offending others or out of fear of contradiction – or because we're unsure of the right language in which to express elusive concepts. And yet the state of the human spirit is fundamental to healing and wholeness. So every health professional, every doctor, every nurse needs to be easy and familiar with the language of the spirit in order to express the almost inexpressible.

Today is the anniversary of the death of Florence Nightingale. She was born into a wealthy family who opposed her wish to train as a nurse, but she finally achieved what she wanted and she headed her own private nursing institute in London. Her efforts at improving conditions for the wounded, especially during the Crimean War, won her great acclaim, and she devoted the rest of her life to reforming nursing care. But what distinguished her achievement particularly was her emphasis on everyone getting in touch with their *own* spirit. Yes, she insisted that her own training school for nurses be open and inclusive. Women were admitted regardless of religious affiliation, and were there to provide nursing services rather than try for death-bed conversions. Of course, that was right. Yet she believed nurses needed the resources of God to do their work well.

So on this day, when we honour Florence Nightingale's memory and ask God's blessing on all who work in the health service, let's pray that we may not be reluctant to use the language of the spirit and that we may know the vital importance of that spirit in healing. Amen.

BROADCAST WEDNESDAY 13 AUGUST 2014

August 14

Richard Hill

On this day in 1969, British troops were deployed on the streets of Northern Ireland to keep the peace.

I was just a little boy. I recall Mum sending me out with a flask of tea for some young soldiers who were guarding a bridge near our house. The young corporal asked me to open the flask – afraid it was a booby trap. He then asked me to taste the tea too – just in case something other than sugar had been added.

They were frightened young men, not certain whom to trust. I was a small boy entranced by their radios, rifles and uniforms.

I saw that fearful look on other occasions. Most memorably, in the 1980s when I was a young man. I can't forget the intensity and fear I saw in the young second lieutenant's eyes. He pointed his Browning pistol at my head and asked what I wanted – well, if I'm honest, what he actually said is unbroadcastable. I'm still not sure who was more afraid, him or me. All I wanted to do was to enter the police station on Belfast's Springfield Road to report that my car had been stoned by a crowd of youths. Clearly they weren't used to routine callers. Once he realized I wanted to make an enquiry, he holstered his pistol and reverted to polite interaction.

I guess he was simply afraid – he had reason to be back then. I hadn't exactly had a good day either!

St John in his first letter says, 'There is no fear in love. Perfect love drives out fear.'

There aren't any troops on the streets today.

As for perfect love? It's still worth working at.

God our Father: Give us loving hearts. Release us from those fears that hold us back. Amen.

BROADCAST TUESDAY 14 AUGUST 2012

August 15

Stephen Shipley

One of the many sublime moments in the thanksgiving service celebrating the life and work of the composer Sir John Tavener was the playing of an orchestral arrangement of his anthem 'Mother of God, here I stand now praying before this icon of your radiant brightness'. The service took place in a packed and wonderfully silent Westminster Abbey on a hot June afternoon, and it was a fitting tribute to an extraordinary musician whose creativity sprang from his religious faith. Many of his compositions held an appeal for audiences that did not necessarily identify with contemporary music or the theological values from which he started. However, their response meant a great deal to him: he took their engagement as an affirmation that his music was operating on a spiritual level.

Today, many Christians throughout the world will be honouring Mary, the Mother of God, for 15 August is traditionally the feast day of the Assumption of Mary. Now it's easy to become sceptical about the point of this festival, because the Bible contains no mention of Mary being taken up into heaven by God. The first Church writer to speak of it was St Gregory of Tours at the end of the 6th century. Nevertheless, let's not dismiss it as irrelevant dogma. Rather, let's acknowledge – as did that huge congregation at John Tavener's memorial service – that it's a sign to us that some day, through God's grace, we too may join Mary the Blessed Mother in giving glory to God. The story of Mary has all the magic beauty of a fairy tale – with one big difference. She actually existed – and she lived out God's will.

Let's pray then that through the struggles, pressures, tensions and hopes of each day, we too like Mary may be granted a glimpse of heaven and earth at one. Amen.

BROADCAST FRIDAY 15 AUGUST 2014

August 16

Catherine Cowley

Many of us find it difficult at times to say 'I'm sorry'. It means admitting, not only to ourselves but to someone else, that we were in the wrong. It means acknowledging the hurt and damage we have caused, and regretting it.

However, it can be even more difficult to say 'forgive me.' When we apologize, the initiative is still ours; when we ask for forgiveness, we hand that initiative over to someone else. We are vulnerable. We know that forgiveness cannot be demanded as a right, it can only be received as a gift. Perhaps they won't forgive, perhaps they'll hold it against us. Often, we fear that we are not worthy of forgiveness. This can be particularly the case when we stand before God and ask for mercy.

It is told of Napoleon Bonaparte that one day a woman whose son had been condemned to death for a terrible crime went to him to ask for mercy. He replied that justice must be done, and that the man did not deserve mercy. She replied, 'If he deserved it, it would not be mercy.' Napoleon pardoned him.

If Napoleon could see this, how much more will God, who is so often referred to in scripture as being 'full of mercy and compassion'. It is not the case that we must 'deserve' mercy before we can receive it. It is the very nature of mercy that it stands aside from questions of merit or just dessert. What we must do is ask for it.

God, give us confidence in Your loving mercy so that we can come to You for forgiveness in trustful hope. Amen.

BROADCAST MONDAY 16 AUGUST 2010

August 17

Michael Ford

When I learned that today was the feast of St Hyacinth, my mind immediately conjured up an image of a certain Hyacinth Bucket – 'Bouquet' – from the BBC sitcom *Keeping Up Appearances*. I couldn't help thinking of Mrs Bouquet with a halo over her head, something she would certainly have aspired to, especially if the vicar was on his way to one of her candlelight suppers.

But St Hyacinth was a person quite the reverse of Mrs Bouquet. Born into Polish nobility in Silesia back in 1185, he became a priest and devoted himself to the lowest in society. After meeting St Dominic in Rome, he was one of the first to receive the habit of Dominic's newly established Order of Friars Preachers.

With a temperament said to be predisposed to virtue, a spirit of prayer and a zeal for the salvation of souls, he became known as 'The Apostle of the North' for his missionary work from Prussia to Norway. Multitudes were converted, churches and convents sprang up, and many miracles were attributed to him. But what really draws me to St Hyacinth is that he never allowed these outer accomplishments to compromise his inner life. No missionary triumph would detract him from his daily discipline of prayer and recollection, and his dutiful desire to be alongside the sick in hospitals. Unlike his television namesake, here was someone who wasn't worried about keeping up appearances but proud to be known literally as a friend of the poor.

So this morning let us pray that we may follow in the footsteps of St Hyacinth, turning from ourselves toward those in need and showing solidarity with the poor, the sick and the forgotten of our world. Amen.

BROADCAST SATURDAY 17 AUGUST 2013

August 18

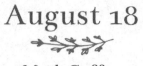

Mark Coffey

It was on this day in 1989 that businessman Michael Knighton appeared to have struck a deal to buy Manchester United for £20m. That's only a quarter of the price the club sold one player for 20 years later: Christian Ronaldo to Real Madrid. In the end, Knighton's deal fell apart, but the Isle of Man property tycoon had seen that global branding and television revenue were the future.

Manchester United is now estimated to be worth $2.23 billion with a global fanbase of 659 million people – nearly one in ten of the world's population. As a teacher who referees school matches every Saturday, I see that as a huge responsibility for the club's players who are role models for today's young people. Back in 1955, when the young Busby Babe, Duncan Edwards, cycled home from Old Trafford and was booked by a policeman for riding without lights, the manager, Matt Busby, fined him two weeks' wages for bringing the club's name into disrepute. Its reputation today owes as much to another Scottish manager, Alex Ferguson, whose discipline and values have kept the feet of many young superstars on the ground.

To its credit, the Football Association also sees the importance of developing both the player and the person. Psychological and social development is incorporated into all coaching drills as well as physical and technical competence. Sporting success is not just about the results of the England team, but the health, teamwork and life skills developed at the grassroots level of soccer.

Lord God, when everything seems to be up for sale, give us thankful hearts for the gifts of life and health. And in the beautiful game, may there be role models, coaches and mentors who value what money can't buy and teach young people lessons that remain after their playing days are past. Amen.

BROADCAST SATURDAY 18 AUGUST 2012

August 19

Michael Ford

The Spanish mystic St John of the Cross says the soul at dawn is like a sparrow on a rooftop, turning itself toward the Spirit of Love. It's a poetic image. Yet, as we discovered only last week, dozens of Muslim worshippers paid the ultimate price while worshipping God at dawn when they were shot dead during prayers at a mosque in Nigeria.

Each day, though, is an opportunity to renew our lives before God: to put the past behind us and reorient ourselves using the divine compass. I like the description of a Christian as someone who says, 'Today I am beginning again', a statement that finds its source in the resurrection of Christ. No sin, no mistake, no regret has the last word as we focus on the mercy of God rather than those things that plague us with feelings of guilt or shame. God is no tormentor of the human conscience.

Each day we're encouraged to set off again along a spiritual path which will never be devoid of trial or temptation. This is what conversion is all about: to begin again without fear. The Christian life can only be understood in terms of continually renewed conversion. And in this respect our lives become literally revolutionized. Revolution comes from the Latin, *revolutus*, to turn around. Christianity is about turning around again and again. In the words of Gregory of Nyssa, in the Christian life we go forward 'from beginning to beginning, across beginnings that never end'.

Creator God, as this new day dawns, may the morning star rise in our hearts to bring us the light of life and lead us toward the everlasting day. Amen.

BROADCAST MONDAY 19 AUGUST 2013

August 20

Mark Coffey

A friend of my auntie was recently looking after a neighbour's dog when they were off on holiday. Sadly and quite unexpectedly, it died. In a state of panic, she found a vet in a phone book who advised her to bring the dog in. So she packed the deceased dog in a suitcase, of all things, and set off by train. A man saw her struggling at the station and offered to help carry the bag. 'It's so heavy,' he said. 'What have you got in it?' Not wanting to mention the dog, she said, 'Oh, just the company laptops.' Whereupon the supposedly kind man ran away with the suitcase!

The story reminds me of philosopher Thomas Aquinas's distinction between real and apparent goods. He believed that humans were rational, but that they often mistook wrong for right and all kinds of misery resulted. So it is that some mistake theft of a suitcase containing a dead dog for gain, and still others mistake greed for satisfaction, lust for love or tyranny for power. Much of this has to do with our belief that pleasure and happiness are for the here and now. While for Aquinas virtue and happiness were interconnected, it was not necessarily in his lifetime. His monastic vows of poverty, chastity and obedience renounced the great temptations of money, sex, and power and still remind those of us living outside cloistered walls of an inheritance that can never perish, spoil or fade.

So here's a prayer of Aquinas', that we might desire real rather than apparent goods:

'Ever-living God, lead me, a sinner, to the banquet where You, with Your Son and Holy Spirit, are everlasting joy, gladness without end, and perfect happiness.' Amen.

BROADCAST MONDAY 20 AUGUST 2012

August 21

Michael Ford

As politicians seek ways of building up trust again with a disillusioned electorate, agents of the spiritual life continue to find fresh expressions to reconnect people with God. But it can't be done without the discipline of prayer. St Paul's first letter to the Thessalonians encourages all Christians to 'pray without ceasing'. It might sound a tall order. But if we try to see our entire life as a prayer, then we can move in and out of the more formal times with much greater ease. Living spiritually is not so much about saying prayers at certain times of the day but about cultivating a relationship with God *throughout* the day – and night. There are no quick and easy solutions – rather it's in the faithful struggle day after day that our deeper identity in God is hammered out.

I learned this from an American I corresponded with for several years. He'd been a Trappist monk before deciding to leave the cloisters and earn a living as a postman. In one of his letters he told me how, in the monastery, the focus had been on seeking God 'out there somewhere'. But once he'd quit, he suddenly found himself with the much more demanding vocation of *becoming* the presence of God to the families he met on his mail rounds. As they shared their stories with him, a new ministry unfolded. And his life of prayer became a prayer for life.

Creator God, open our eyes to see, our minds to know and our hearts to embrace, that our lives may be continually transformed into a prayer for a world in need. Amen.

BROADCAST WEDNESDAY 21 AUGUST 2013

August 22

Mark Coffey

There's a story from 19th-century Boston, when philosophical clubs were all the rage. A man is fascinated by the debate over free will and determinism, but he can't decide which club to join. In the end, he opts for the Determinists' Association. 'Why do you wish to join?' they ask. 'Of my own free will,' he replies, only to have the door shut in his face. Despairingly, he crosses the street to knock on the door of the Free Will Club. 'Why do you want to join?' asks the doorkeeper. 'Well, I was refused entry at the Determinists' Association and that left me with no choice.' With that, a second door shuts.

'My first act of free will shall be to believe in free will,' wrote the pragmatic thinker William James. For him, some things in life just couldn't be settled by reason and science alone. He saw the God debate as another such area of life, arguments and proof being of less interest to him than the difference belief made in people's lives.

Yet James may have made more progress in his search for God if he had first asked, 'If he does exist and is personal, am I willing to be known by God?' If God is personal, he's relational; more interested in transformation of the heart than reasonable belief in the head. Such a God can remain hidden from the learned and known to little children. Indeed, we may already have seen him face-to-face without even realizing it.

Father God, sometimes You seem elusive or hidden. Yet You have promised that if we seek You with all our heart, You will let us find you. Help us open our eyes today to the thousand places that You play. Amen.

BROADCAST WEDNESDAY 22 AUGUST 2012

August 23

Mike Starkey

If you had gone up to somebody in 1st-century Palestine and asked them what they knew about peace, they might have said: 'Well, it depends whose definition of peace you're talking about.' At the time, the word peace was used in two very different ways. There were two radically different visions of peace.

One was the *Pax Romana*. The Roman Empire had conquered most of the known world. And everywhere the Romans went, they installed military bases to prevent insurrections. They brought in a Roman legal system, and built a network of roads and seaports. The arts and architecture flourished, and it was a time of relative peace and stability. So they called it *Pax Romana*, incorporating the Latin word for peace.

But it was a very particular type of peace. It was peace as defined by a military superpower and implemented by the sword. It was peace brought about by the brutal suppression of dissent, by the crushing of rival powers, cultures and faiths.

But there was another vision of peace at the time which had nothing to do with power or coercion. The Hebrew word for it is *shalom*, or *salaam* in Arabic. It means more than the absence of war and conflict. It implies maturity, wholeness and community, harmony, security and friendship.

It's lovely that all these qualities can be contained in a simple everyday greeting. But it's agonizing to see how far this type of peace is from being an everyday experience in the Middle East and other parts of the world riven by conflict.

Lord God, at the start of this day I commit myself to praying for peace in our world.
And may it not be a **Pax Romana** *peace but a* **shalom** *and* **salaam** *peace. Amen.*

BROADCAST SATURDAY 23 AUGUST 2014

August 24

Ian Bradley

Sydney Carter, who was born 100 years ago this year, has been described as the greatest British hymn writer of the 20th century. Several of his compositions are still hugely popular today, notably 'Lord of the Dance', 'One More Step Along the World I Go' and 'When I Needed a Neighbour, Were You There?'

Carter served in the Friends' Ambulance Unit during World War II and he remained a Quaker throughout his life. He regarded religious faith as much closer to doubt than certainty. 'By faith,' he wrote, 'we travel from what is to what we hope for. The first truth to learn is that we cannot be certain about anything.'

'Lord of the Dance' is really a carol rather than a hymn. Based on the melody of an old American Shaker song, ''Tis the Gift to Be Simple, 'Tis the Gift to Be Free' (a message that chimed with his own Quaker faith), it returned to a popular theme in medieval theology in portraying Christ as the Lord of the Dance.

For Carter, this image conveyed a fundamental truth about faith. In his words, 'Scriptures and creeds may seem incredible, but faith will still go dancing on. I see Christ as that incarnation of the piper who is calling us. He dances that shape and pattern which is at the heart of our reality. By Christ I mean not only Jesus; in other times and places, other planets, there may be other Lords of the Dance. But Jesus is the one I know of first and best.'

Dance then, whoever you may be, I am the Lord of the Dance, said he, and I'll lead you all wherever you may be, and I'll lead you all in the dance said he. Amen.

BROADCAST MONDAY 24 AUGUST 2015

August 25

Mike Starkey

Back in 1985, a professor of Educational Psychology decided to look into what it was that helps people stay happy and emotionally well balanced. His name was Robert D Enright. He decided to carry out a survey of the academic literature on forgiveness ... and found there was none at all!

Professor Enright started to research forgiveness, and what he discovered was fascinating. He found that the ability to forgive can reduce anxiety and depression, and increase self-esteem. When researchers stick electrodes onto volunteers and ask them to think about somebody who's wronged them in the past, heart rates and stress levels rise. People who hang onto grudges and a desire for vengeance appear to have a greater vulnerability to heart attacks and a weakened immune system.

On the other hand, people who are able to put past grudges and vengeance behind them show a lower level of stress and greater calm.

One of the central themes of the Bible is forgiveness. Jesus tells the story of a man who is let off a huge debt but then shows no mercy to somebody who owes him a much smaller debt. We're encouraged to forgive others, in the same way that God forgives us. And forgiveness isn't about working up warm, fuzzy feelings about another person: it's sometimes a hard choice we make, an act of will which may take time.

Heavenly Father, I pray You'll keep me alert to this theme of forgiveness in the day ahead. Give me the humility to ask for forgiveness where I've done wrong and the generosity to forgive others who have wronged me. Amen.

BROADCAST MONDAY 25 AUGUST 2014

August 26

Andrew Martlew

St Peter's Basilica in Rome is an awe-inspiring building. It's probably the biggest cathedral in the world. It's full of magnificent altars and statues and gold and mosaics and people — great swirls of them which, at least for me, do nothing to detract from the magnificence of the building and its role as a reminder of the majesty of God.

Tucked away in a side-chapel, behind an armoured glass screen, is one of the great sculptural masterpieces of the Renaissance: Michelangelo's *Pietà*, commissioned on this date in 1498. Mary cradles the body of her dead son on her lap. She is young and beautiful. He is barely marked by crucifixion. Polished, glowing marble — a mere five-and-a-half feet high, even though in my mind's eye it's on the same magnificent scale as the Basilica itself. An object of perfect beauty both in form and content.

And every time I see it, ever so quietly I weep. Somehow this thing of beauty speaks to me not just of the pain and desolation of Mary, but of the grief of every mother who has ever held her dead son. And through her, it speaks to me of the suffering of the whole of humanity, and therefore also of the presence of God at the very centre of that suffering.

Heavenly Father,
You are with us at all times,
in sorrow, in sickness and in poverty;
hold us in Your loving arms
though the world seems full of sorrow and pain,
and cradle us as we struggle toward our home with You.
In Jesus's name we pray. Amen.

BROADCAST FRIDAY 26 AUGUST 2011

August 27

Mike Starkey

When I was a teenager, I wanted to be George Harrison. It didn't matter that it was the late 1970s and the punk bands of the day were writing off the Beatles as old has-beens. I wanted to be George, the spiritually inclined guitarist.

But these days, I have to say I also harbour a sneaking respect for Brian Epstein. There are famously dozens of contenders for the title of 'Fifth Beatle'. But if anybody deserves the title most, it's probably Brian Epstein, their visionary manager, who died on this day in 1967 at the age of just 32. And that's not just my opinion: Paul McCartney's on record as saying the same thing.

It was Epstein who spotted the potential of the band at a lunchtime performance in Liverpool's Cavern Club in 1961. He was the one who got them signed with George Martin's Parlophone label, after they'd been turned down by all the other record companies in London. It was Epstein's marketing skills that shaped the Beatles' early image. It was his management skills that helped propel them to international stardom. And it was his interpersonal skills that mediated between band members whenever tempers frayed.

These days I find I have an increasing respect for those who choose to avoid the limelight themselves but nurture and develop the gifts in other people; for mentors who help others become more fully the person they have the potential to become.

Lord God, help me take a moment today to say thanks for the unsung heroes who have helped me become who I am. And help me identify one other person for whom I can be a guide and a help on the journey of life. Amen.

BROADCAST WEDNESDAY 27 AUGUST 2014

August 28

Craig Gardiner

When, on this day in 1963, Martin Luther King delivered his iconic plea for racial justice, he was dreaming of a time when his children would be judged not by the colour of their skin but by the content of their character.

Amazing, then, to think that Barack Obama, America's first black president, was just two years old when the speech was made. There's no doubt that in electing him, the arc of American history bent further than ever toward a racially inclusive society.

But the dream of Martin Luther King always went further than who lived in the White House. He spoke often about *shalom*, the biblical idea of bringing heaven's peace and equity to earth. Picking up the words of the Hebrew prophet Amos, Dr King proclaimed that no one should be satisfied until justice for all 'rolls down like waters and righteousness like a mighty stream'. Echoing the prophet Isaiah and John the Baptist, he claimed that such a society would see the rough places being made smooth and the crooked places made straight, for only then, with freedom and peace and justice for all, would the glory of God be revealed.

It's worth remembering that Martin Luther King was as outspoken about poverty and violence as he was about ethnicity. In these days of austerity, it's the poor who often bear the greatest burden; and in a world bristling with weaponry it's typically the innocents who suffer first. And for each of us today there will be the choice to welcome or reject someone who is different from us, there will be the option of putting ourselves first or choosing costly sacrifice for others. There will be the chance to respond to someone with violence or with love. Every day we must choose which dream we'll live by and what world we leave for our children.

God of justice and mercy, bring freedom for all of us today — freedom from poverty, violence and prejudice, freedom to share, to heal and embrace. Amen.

BROADCAST TUESDAY 28 AUGUST 2012

August 29

George Craig

Last month I went for my annual visit to my family near Aberdeen. For years I used to call Scotland 'home', but every time I go back it's more and more obvious that it really isn't home to me any more. And that got me thinking about the whole question of belonging — which has always been a big issue for me.

As a child, I was moved away from an area my family had lived in for generations to London, a place where we had no connections at all. When I got to school, the children weren't hostile or unkind but they really couldn't understand a word I said. It was a horrible experience. That loss of belonging and the desperate need to get it back dominated my life for years.

Of course, belonging can have a negative side, for it can be just as much about excluding people as including them. But the need to be able to say, with absolute confidence, that this is my place or these are my people is a powerful one not just for me but, I believe, for a lot of other people too.

And it's our own experience of that which gives us such strong feelings for those whose uprooting has been immeasurably more radical and dramatic than our own. The Christian faith says a great deal about belonging.

One of the driving themes of the New Testament is that we, in the deepest possible way, belong to God. And that brings with it responsibilities about how we relate to each other; which means not just offering help or hospitality but also creating a community where strangers can really feel they belong. We can show pretty easily that we're here to help. To offer belonging is harder, but if we can remember our own times of feeling excluded, that can help us convince strangers that we really want them to feel that they are one of us.

'Our Father …' What a great opening, Lord, to a prayer that tells us and the world about where and to whom we belong. Make us a people in whom our own belonging isn't closed and exclusive but looks outward at our neighbours with love and acceptance. Amen.

BROADCAST WEDNESDAY 29 AUGUST 2007

August 30

Lindsay Allen

My fellow countryman Seamus Heaney died exactly one year ago today.

'Famous Seamus', as we called him, was a farmer's son from rural Ulster who became, as one of his obituaries put it, 'probably the best known poet in the world.' He took the ordinary things of rural life, like ploughing and cutting turf, and invested them with significance.

Seamus was an academic whose work extended far beyond the narrow confines of academia and enriched the lives of many. We are thankful for him and for people like him without whom the world would be a poorer place.

Yet there was something more about Seamus Heaney than even his amazing gift for language.

Despite all his literary success and academic achievement, with professorships in Harvard and Oxford and a Nobel Prize for Literature, Seamus remained the same unassuming, quiet man from County Derry, the rich earth of his boyhood still clinging to his boots.

In today's brash, celebrity-obsessed culture, where talent is overstated and a sense of self-importance seems to embody the shallowness of instant stardom, the quietly self-effacing Seamus Heaneys of this world are something of an enigma.

In his letter to the Romans (12:3), the Apostle Paul wrote, 'Do not think of yourself more highly than you ought, but rather think of yourself with sober judgment, in accordance with the faith God has distributed to each of you.'

Heavenly Father, thank You for the various gifts and abilities You have given to each of us. Help us to appreciate them, develop them and use them wisely for Your glory and for the good of others. Amen.

BROADCAST SATURDAY 30 AUGUST 2014

August 31

Anna Drew

It's strange, what we inherit from our parents – height, eye colour, a passion for classic cars or milky tea. Some say, hard as we try, in the end we all turn into our mothers. I find myself tuning into the same radio programmes, worrying about the weather, complaining about the price of petrol. I've even got her hands.

When I was a little girl I was fascinated by mum's hands – the creases on her knuckles and palms, the softness of the pale, freckly skin and – best of all – the grey blue mounds of the raised veins on the backs of her hands. And now perfect replicas are sitting on the ends of my arms. Whatever happens, I'll always carry that piece of her with me – and, though they're not supermodel hands, that's really special to me.

Christians often talk about God as 'our Father'. They believe that every single human being holds within them a little of the DNA of God. And that life is about trying to grow into this inheritance – to be a bit more like Jesus, day by day.

For me, it's all about the hands. Jesus said, 'My mother and brothers are those who hear the word of God and do it.' I think this is what brings to life the God-blood running through our veins. Getting stuck in to make this world a better place, seeing what needs doing and getting your hands dirty.

And maybe, if we take time to notice that trace of the Divine in others and the shared inheritance that connects us all, we won't be so quick to judge or dismiss. Perhaps we'll be surprised by our shared family resemblance.

Lord of hands and faces, hearts and desires, give us confidence in our divine inheritance – and the courage to get our hands dirty. Amen.

BROADCAST MONDAY 31 AUGUST 2015

September 1

Janet Wootton

This year, some of us have been commemorating the 350th anniversary of an event that changed life in this country, and eventually shaped not only the nation but the world.

By August 1662, 2,000 Christian clergy had been ejected from their churches for refusing to conform to the liturgical and theological demands of the Church of England that went against their conscience. They lost their homes and livelihood, and their churches lost much-loved leaders.

Today in 1662 would have been the first week following the ejection. Where would those faithful church people find their leaders and teachers? What would the ejected clergy and their families do now?

Well, over the following months and years, these nonconformists put their time and talents to good use. They were not allowed to teach or learn in the ancient universities, so they set up new academies. There they developed radical teaching methods that depended on enquiry rather than tradition, and taught the newly emerging sciences.

Their successors became founders of some of the great scientific and professional institutions in the late 18th and 19th centuries. They pioneered medical discovery and used their newly acquired wealth to ensure that advances such as the smallpox vaccination were available to the poorest in society.

They were at the heart of the industrial revolution and world exploration. Britain's story would have been quite different if the creative energy of these nonconformists had not been released. And so, for better or worse, would the world we live in now.

God of this rich and fascinating world, we thank You for men and women of lively intellect and compassionate spirit, who continue to push the boundaries of human knowledge, and open new insights for all to share.

BROADCAST SATURDAY 1 SEPTEMBER 2012

September 2

Anna Drew

This week marks the beginning of a new school year for many of our children and young people. Many adults, too, will be inspired by the opportunity for a fresh start — new enthusiasm, reinvigorated commitments.

Though my own school days are a distant memory, I still find it hard to restrain myself from buying new stationery at this time of year. Blank pages are calling to be filled, with the surety of productivity and success ... if only I had the right pen.

But this week also has me pondering what success really looks like. Is it to be found only in exams passed, in financial, social or academic achievements?

Jesus looks like the ultimate loser. He failed to go into the family business; instead he became an itinerant preacher, wandering the countryside with his friends. No home, no wife and family, no financial stability ... He got noticed, but not always for the right reasons. Deserted by his closest friends, he died a criminal's death.

And on that cross, Jesus became the biggest loser of all time — he lost everything. So maybe success looks a little different from how we expect? Maybe it looks like a disgraced preacher nailed to a tree for crimes he never committed.

Christianity is designed to be a religion of losers. We're asked to walk in the footsteps of a God who broke every convention of what a successful human being should look like. We're told that humility, vulnerability and love are what matter most, not bank balances or straight-A grades. And we pray for the courage to believe that this true.

God of losers and winners, challenge us with your definition of success. Mould our priorities that they might speak to the world around us of unconventional victories. Amen.

BROADCAST WEDNESDAY 2 SEPTEMBER 2015

September 3

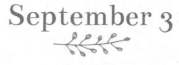

Bert Tosh

My late father served in the Royal Air Force for four years from 1941 to 1945. Many of the stories he told of his time in the Air Force were humorous, like the occasion when an American colonel gave him a cigar bigger than anything Churchill had ever tackled because my father happened to know the town from which the colonel's Irish ancestors had come. He would recall a particularly glorious summer in the Devon countryside when, in return for helping the local farmers, his unit received the best of agricultural produce, probably against all regulations.

He was rather proud of the fact he'd landed in Normandy three days after D-Day, but offered few further details, so I suggested to him he might like to see the film *Saving Private Ryan* with its recreation of the Allied invasion of Europe. He asked me why he would possibly want to do that and then refused point blank to countenance the idea. When I pressed him he said: 'They could never reproduce the smell – the stench of death and human decay.' He gazed into the distance for a moment and then changed the subject.

And I realized, as I realize this morning, 70 years to the day since Britain declared war on Germany, that for many people of my father's generation, there were memories that could not simply be put into words but relied on the senses to be evoked. And of course, that's not just true of those who served in World War II; it applies to many who serve in other places, such as Northern Ireland, Afghanistan or Iraq.

Lord, we think of all who carry painful memories they feel unable to share freely; may You be with them to calm them and to heal. Through Jesus Christ, Amen.

BROADCAST THURSDAY 3 SEPTEMBER 2009

September 4

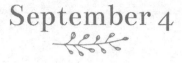

Lindsay Allen

As an Ulsterman, I'm all too familiar with the deep passions that can be aroused over questions of citizenship and national identity. Having been born in Northern Ireland, I can carry two passports, a UK one issued in Belfast and an Irish one issued in Dublin.

However as a Christian, I have, metaphorically, a third identity!

The Apostle Paul writes to Christians in Philippi and tells them, 'Our citizenship is in heaven.' He is reminding them that, although they have had the privilege of Roman citizenship conferred upon them, they are in fact also citizens of a much greater kingdom.

And the challenge for those who claim to be citizens of *that* kingdom is to ensure that their perspective on life is not determined principally by their nationality on earth but by their citizenship of heaven. So wherever I come from, whether it's from the UK or outside it, is of secondary importance. My outlook and my values, my response to events and my behaviour toward my fellow human beings must first and foremost be that of a Christian.

Heavenly Father, we thank You for the great gift of salvation and for the hope of eternal life through faith in Jesus Christ, Your Son. And though we live in the knowledge that our citizenship is in heaven, we pray that by Your grace You enable us live as good citizens in the cities, towns and villages in which You have placed us. Help us to be good neighbours, contributing to the wellbeing of our communities. Enable us to be loyal, honest, law-abiding and faithful until that day when You call us home. Amen.

BROADCAST THURSDAY 4 SEPTEMBER 2014

September 5

Janet Wootton

I have some very good friends in Aleppo, Syria. They belong to a small religious minority: Armenian Protestant Christians, part of an ancient community, indigenous to the region, but a small minority nonetheless.

Over the generations, they have contributed greatly to the community, establishing schools and healthcare facilities, and living peaceably and with joy alongside neighbours of different origins and faiths.

Like everyone else, we listen appalled to the news of deepening crisis and destruction. In a message at the beginning of the conflict, my friend (who is a leader in that community) wrote of his desire to see reform but not through violence, and of his concern at what would happen to the minorities under any new government.

This conflict has global repercussions. There are enormous questions about boundaries, regimes and ethnic and religious identities. But, for so many, it comes down to families and friends, tiny groups of people, caught in the disintegration of a world in which they had a place, a contribution to make and a life to live.

Before the conflict, my friend was hoping to do some research on the history of his community, to tell their story as part of the wider narrative. That wider story has now taken a dramatic and tragic turn.

God of all humankind, in this time of crisis, when mighty principles are at stake and futures are being forged, be with the ordinary people of Syria in their suffering and anxiety. Amen.

BROADCAST WEDNESDAY 5 SEPTEMBER 2012

September 6

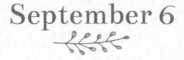

Nicholas James

A year ago today I was in Ethiopia, celebrating the new millennium a second time (their calendar works differently from ours).

The land is old and beautiful. Among its treasures is a set of tiny bones from thousands of millennia ago. They're hominid, not fully human — the remains of a great aunt of ours. Scientists named her 'Lucy'; the locals call her *Dinknesh*, or 'Shining One'.

But it was the northern hills that made me see again the special quality of Africa, a sense that this morning — like every morning — is the first morning of the world. Among the people of a distant village, I had no vehicle or phone or running water. Our life was lived by daylight, and every journey seemed to mean a lengthy climb. The landscape was a vision from the early chapters of the Bible.

Of all the things I might have missed, the one I did miss was the most surprising — I hadn't brought a mirror. I'd never realized before how much we use our own reflection to remind us who we are.

Yet even stranger was the way a sense of self was given back to me by other people, who seemed to make each chance encounter on the mountainside a thing of great significance.

Even in cities, the art of Africa is filled with scenes of village life — with yearning for a time of true community. A priest who'd worked in Zambia for many years once told me how he'd come to learn from this. Africans, he said, do not see God as being at the apex of a pyramid of power, which keeps descending through the world in forms of human status and subservience. Rather, they believe God holds us in his hands, keeping us together and enclosing us all in an unbreakable circle of love.

God of all peoples, open our hearts to Your encircling love. Fix in us the image of Your Son and help us to make communities that truly reflect Your purpose for creation. Amen.

BROADCAST SATURDAY 6 SEPTEMBER 2008

September 7

Claire Campbell Smith

As I packed to return home from working in Cairo this summer, a dull thud resonated across the city. It was a chilling sound in the warm night air – the second bomb that had exploded during my short time in Cairo, mercifully killing no one this time but leaving many injured. Such attacks have increased since the second of Egypt's revolutions in just four years and are part of the wider turbulence in the region. 'I don't fear the bombs', said an Egyptian friend, but they cast a dark shadow over a country whose economy is showing signs of recovery yet needs the stability that encourages investment and tourism.

On this day 75 years ago, bombs began to rain down on London at five in the afternoon, targeting the heavily populated East End docklands. Within an hour, vast areas had been blown apart and fires lit up the sky, but this was only the start. Night and day, the bombers returned, and by the end of the Blitz, eight months later, thousands had been killed and injured, and significant parts of London and other cities had been decimated.

Blitz is of course the German word for 'lightning', and in the awe-inspiring description of heaven in the Book of Revelation, we're told that lightning flashes forth from the throne at its centre. But seated on the throne is a lamb, apparently slain – a representation of the crucified Christ, who shares in the world's suffering, bore its pain on the cross and will one day usher in a kingdom of justice, righteousness and peace.

God, our refuge and strength, bring near the day when wars shall cease, and poverty and pain shall end, that earth may know the peace of heaven, through Jesus Christ our Lord. Amen.

BROADCAST MONDAY 7 SEPTEMBER 2015

September 8

Stephen Shipley

Tuscany was the scene of one of the most influential and sustained artistic revolutions in history, and nowhere is this more evident than in the beautiful city of Florence. I want to take you there in your imagination this morning – to the convent of San Marco, founded in the 12th century and enlarged 300 years later when Dominican monks moved in and one of their number, Fra Angelico, began a remarkable series of devotional frescoes. If you're able to visit the convent at the beginning of the day, wandering around the cloister and contemplating the images in each cell is a wonderful experience.

Today there's one that's particularly significant because this is the day Christians celebrate the Virgin Mary – on her birthday! So, if you look at the Annunciation scene that Fra Angelico has painted in the corridor between the cells, you'll see a loggia looking into a garden, bringing the mystery of the Incarnation from the distant past into the present. And there's Mary, her arms clasped in adoration, her eyes staring into the angel's in a deepening trance as if the gaze will never break.

Painters, poets and ordinary people have all been drawn to the scene of the Annunciation. Its sheer loveliness has brought out the loveliest in us. But it's also Mary's character that attracts and intrigues. Her acceptance of God's will, her readiness to embrace life and not draw away from it, is required of us *all* if we're to be bearers of faith, hope and love in a world desperately looking for the means of its salvation. A former Secretary-General of the United Nations, Dag Hammarskjöld, once described his own motivation simply in terms of saying 'Yes' to something beyond himself. Such was the choice Mary made.

May God help us to make this choice too: Amen.

BROADCAST TUESDAY 8 SEPTEMBER 2009

September 9

Nicholas Buxton

I always like to start the day with a few moments of quietness, and yet silence is often something that many of us find difficult, or even a little disturbing. We talk about an 'awkward silence' when people run out of things to say to each other. But why should silence be awkward? Why do we feel it necessary to avoid silence at all costs, even if it means talking rubbish or filling the air with noise in order to keep silence at bay? Why do we find it necessary to break a silence, becoming uncomfortable or even embarrassed as we desperately try to think of something to say?

The truth is, we need periods of quietness in order to put a little distance between ourselves and all that, quite literally, consumes our lives. To be silent is to let go of our unnecessary preoccupations with the past and the future, and to become aware of the still centre behind our internal commentary, allowing in turn for the possibility of an encounter with the reality that simply is 'what is'. In many religious traditions, the mind is likened to a pool of water, in which we are only able to see our reflection when its surface is completely still. This is not to say we must try and force the mind to be quiet, but rather that it is simply a state we reach when, like a fire deprived of fuel, distractions naturally fade away. In other words, we don't have to try to be quiet: we just have to be.

So let's pray that in those precious moments of quietness and peace, we may know the beauty of silence that is the deepest reality of what we are. Amen.

BROADCAST FRIDAY 9 SEPTEMBER 2011

September 10

Stephen Shipley

'A greater musical genius England never had,' wrote the 17th-century biographer Roger North of Henry Purcell. Purcell is one of four renowned composers we're celebrating particularly this year, so it's appropriate to reflect for a moment on his life. He lived all of it in London, through the Plague and the Great Fire, in a city that was busy, dirty, crowded, unpredictable but always buzzing. He learned his musical craft as a boy chorister at the Chapel Royal and then served in the court of Charles II, witnessing the lascivious behaviour and wanton excess that gave such excellent fodder to contemporary diarists. He watched as King James dug his own political grave and looked on as the Glorious Revolution brought William and Mary to the throne. And then, when opportunities for court musicians waned, he turned his attention to the world of the theatre, and here too his compositions were affected by events and the politics behind them.

I've always felt a special affinity to Purcell because his death — at the early age of 36 — occurred on 21 November, my birthday! He was buried close by the organ in Westminster Abbey, the place he'd served as organist for 16 years, and where flowers are laid regularly on his anniversary. His epitaph reads 'Here lyes Henry Purcell Esq., who left this life and is gone to that blessed place where only his harmony can be exceeded.' It's an apt tribute to someone who wasn't afraid to write daring music that often reflected both the splendour and the turbulence of the age in which he lived. But it's also an indication of the risks he was prepared to take — especially when composing for the Church.

So Lord, may we also not be afraid to gamble all on Your Almightiness and to dare everything in Your great service. Amen.

BROADCAST THURSDAY 10 SEPTEMBER 2009

September 11

Claire Campbell Smith

Sirius is the brightest star, its name deriving from the Greek for 'glowing' or 'scorcher'. In Ancient Egypt, the rising of Sirius signalled the first day of the year, when the Nile flooded and the planting season began. In the modern calendar, this falls today, although with a leap year coming up, it's tomorrow that the new year celebrations, still observed by the Egyptian Coptic Church, will take place. I say celebrations, but the liturgy, which captivated me in Cairo this summer with its mesmeric chanting, will commemorate the Church's martyrs, their blood symbolized by the wearing of red vestments. This year, it'll take on a deeper significance, remembering the beheading of 21 Coptic Christians by ISIL.

For the ancients, this day was the First of the Month of Thoth, the god depicted with the head of an ibis, whose curved beak resembles the crescent moon. Thoth was the scribe of the underworld. Egyptians believed that when you died, your heart was weighed on an enormous scale against a feather, representing truth and justice. Thoth recorded the verdict. A light heart showed a sinless life of good deeds, earning you a place in the afterlife. But a heart heavy with the weight of wrong-doings would be devoured by a beast — a second death, in which you were annihilated.

St Paul says that we'll all appear before the judgement seat of Christ. But his message, read during the Coptic New Year liturgy, conveys an understanding very different from that of Ancient Egypt: 'If anyone is in Christ, the new creation has come: the old has gone, the new is here! All this is from God, who reconciled us to Himself through Christ, not counting people's sins against them.'

Lord, thank You for Your saving act, a gift to all who trust You today. Amen.

BROADCAST FRIDAY 11 SEPTEMBER 2015

September 12

Alison Twaddle

At this time of year, rural East Lothian, where I live, is already well into harvest season, and in some places the land is already being re-ploughed, the rich breast of the earth overturned again by powerful machinery, ready for a new sowing.

While we rejoice in the combination of creation, invention, labour and skill, we are aware of other worlds where harvests are not so rich, where the dust cannot support a root and where centuries of skills are being lost. Women, who for generations have fed their children good things, are asking why the sun is getting nearer. And elsewhere farmers see their land flooded by rising sea levels or parched by the lack of rainfall as the seasons they have lived by for generations no longer change with the old rhythms. They too have questions to which there seem to be no answers.

But we do not live in different worlds: we share one creation. We have each developed the skills necessary to draw the best from God's providence in our place. Mothers have learned how best to feed their children; farmers have known their land and passed on that knowledge to each generation. The challenges that face our generation, as we face up to the consequences of our earlier rush to exploit creation's gifts, are challenges to be faced together, recognizing both the opportunities brought by new technologies and the gifts of the old skills of those who have lived close to the land in every age and place.

It was to one world that Jesus came; to a world in need of His saving grace. Help us, Lord, to be part of the building of His kingdom in our time. Guide us in the path of seeking justice and mercy, of sharing wealth and poverty, so that we may renew our commitment to be disciples of Jesus, who came so that all might have life, abundant life. Amen.

BROADCAST SATURDAY 12 SEPTEMBER 2009

September 13

Scott McKenna

About 30 years ago, I was working toward a Duke of Edinburgh's Award. I did community service with Tayside Police. Among other things, this involved attending a lecture given by a senior officer. During the lecture, someone entered the room, handed a piece of paper to the officer and then left. At the end, we were asked to describe the person who had entered the room earlier. Incredibly, there was no agreement among the young people present even as to the gender of the person, let alone a description of height, build or hair colour. For the police, in a real situation, an accurate description is vital.

And although we used the same words, we didn't always mean the same thing. Words can have multiple meanings. For example, God is sometimes described as a Shepherd, Husband or Lamb. Images and metaphors can be helpful, but they *can* be a hindrance: God is not a Shepherd, Husband or Lamb. If by *existence* we mean being born, growing, maturing and dying, then God does not exist, at least not in that usual sense. God is beyond existence. All thought about God is provisional. In sermons and prayers, silence between words may be the most God-filled moments. When asked about prayer, Mother Teresa said she said nothing; in silence, she listened. When asked what God said, she replied: God said nothing; in silence, He listened.

Be still. Be aware of God's presence around you and within you. Be aware of God's breath in your breathing. May the stillness and silence of your soul be filled by the eternal silence of God. Amen.

BROADCAST THURSDAY 13 SEPTEMBER 2012

September 14

Janet Wootton

In the last couple of weeks, there has been a lot of talk about the place of Parliament and Congress in major decisions about intervention in Syria. This has given rise to much discussion about the nature and value of public opinion, which is often swayed by the prevailing mood, and of the nature and value of dissent.

This has often been contrasted with religious faith, which is seen as dogmatic and hierarchical. And yet churches such as the Baptist, Independent and Congregational have been practising forms of democratic government for 400 years or more; and we have long-held wisdom to add to the debate.

In earlier generations, the monthly church meeting was a valuable arena in which people learned and honed debating skills, which they then took into national and local government, or into some of the great social campaigns, such as women's suffrage or labour rights.

In a church meeting, the aim is not to solicit people's opinions, but to seek the mind of Christ through debate and discussion, trusting that each person will have a measure of that wisdom. We tend to work through consensus rather than by majority vote, though there are times when taking a vote allows the voices of dissenters to be heard and recorded while the majority decision is carried.

At its best, this is a powerful and radical way of being a church – indeed, of being human together.

Living God, we pray for all those who have to make life and death decisions in our time. Where there is a chance to seek peace and reconciliation, help us, as a human community, to take it. Amen.

BROADCAST SATURDAY 14 SEPTEMBER 2013

September 15

Alison Twaddle

I never knew my maternal grandfather. He was a chief engineer in the Royal Navy and, although he survived action in World War I, he was lost at sea when his tug went down with all hands in a freak storm in the Bay of Biscay in 1929.

When my mother died a few years ago, I found an old shoebox full of postcards that her father had sent to her from his postings, mostly in the Mediterranean and the Far East. They are sepia photographs, some tinted in pale pinks and greens that highlight the blossoms and palm trees of the Nile and Hong Kong. The messages, however, say little about his adventures or the exotic places he had visited. They consist, rather, of simple words of encouragement from father to daughter: 'Be a good girl for your mother.' 'Try hard at your lessons and practise your spelling.' 'You must always wear your lace-up boots.' And, intriguingly: 'Never poke the fire from the top.'

Here was a man charged with great responsibilities, the safety of his ship and the lives of those who served under him dependent on his engineering skills. But he was also a father, with other concerns, a man remembering the family he had left behind: the little girl who wasn't a great scholar; who hated the boots she had to wear to correct a malformed foot; who tried to help around the house, but who was missing her daddy.

For each of us, this day will bring a range of demands on our time. There may be decisions of huge significance to be made, but underneath that will be the constant of our nearest relationships.

Help us, Lord, whatever our responsibilities, not to lose touch with those closest to us, who may need to know that amidst all the pressing concerns of our life and work, we care especially for them. Amen.

BROADCAST TUESDAY 15 SEPTEMBER 2009

September 16

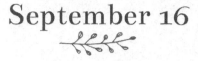

Janet Wootton

A few years ago, I was at meetings in South Africa, and took the opportunity to go on a tour through a gold mine in Johannesburg. This was partly personal, as a childhood friend of mine had gone to South Africa to make his career in gold mining, and died there in his early adult years. As a tourist, of course, I was not exposed to the dangers and the harsh conditions, but I wanted to pay my respects to my friend.

I hold no romantic ideas about mining. I grew up in West Yorkshire and later in the Midlands, surrounded in those days by pitheads and slag heaps, and stories of tragedy. Mining has always been a dangerous occupation. Accidents happen a long way from safety, and dangers such as fires or floods develop unexpectedly and travel fast.

Additionally, it is often those who have the least opportunity or choice in life that end up working in so difficult and hazardous an environment, with the consequence that safety measures are sometimes neglected.

On this day, as recently as 1986, fire and toxic fumes swept through the gold mine at Kinross in the Eastern Transvaal, killing more than 170 men, mostly black, unskilled labourers, working at depths of up to 12,000 feet, in one of the worst disasters in mining history.

God of the deep places of the earth, we hold before You the memory of all those who have died in work-related disasters. We pray for people who will go to work in hazardous occupations today, and for all who have the health and safety of others in their care. Amen.

BROADCAST MONDAY 16 SEPTEMBER 2013

September 17

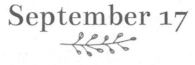

Joe Aldred

As a 15-year-old, I arrived in England from Jamaica to join my parents in September 1968. We lived in Smethwick in the West Midlands. My arrival was five months after the 'Rivers of Blood' speech by the then Conservative MP Enoch Powell; and Smethwick was one of the more racially sensitive areas at the time. When Mr Powell included in his speech the words, 'Like the Roman, I seem to see the river Tiber foaming with much blood,' I doubt he could have envisaged the furore that would ensue.

Growing up in rural Jamaica, I was oblivious to the challenges racial difference posed. I knew only that I was a human being made in the image and likeness of God; and so was everybody else. It hadn't dawned on me that the world was so strongly divided into racial and ethnic groups and that some believed themselves superior to others. I had a lot to learn.

And when on this day, 17 September, in 1993, the far-right British National Party won its first local election seat on the Isle of Dogs, it appeared that the challenges of the 1960s were a recurring racial and political nightmare. More recently, as a member of the Birmingham Faith Leaders Group, I had the privilege, with others, of encouraging tolerance and cooperation between people of different faiths and ethnicities, and to pray as well as act for all God's children to live together as one human race.

Creator God, as we struggle to live with the difference You have created, may we Your creatures, made in Your image and likeness, never give up the pursuit for tolerance, cooperation, peace and prosperity. And in our time, may we speak of and to one another in ways that lead to the good of all. Amen.

BROADCAST MONDAY 17 SEPTEMBER 2012

September 18

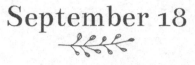

Alison Twaddle

On the 18 September 1961, the world was shocked by the death of the UN Secretary-General, Dag Hammarskjöld, who John F Kennedy called 'the greatest statesman of our century'. He died when his plane exploded on approach to Ndola airport in what was then Northern Rhodesia. He had been on a mission to broker peace in the worsening situation between the Congo and its breakaway province of Katanga.

Five years ago I was visiting HIV/AIDS projects in the Ndola diocese of Zambia, and one of my hosts suggested taking time out to visit the memorial built at the crash site. It's a modest building, evocative of a bird's wingspan in flight, and the approach to it, through the ever-encroaching trees, suggests a straight flight path to a runway, sadly never quite reached. The cause of the explosion has never been established.

Inside the museum itself are tributes to Hammarskjöld's unstinting work for peace during his term of office. He was a deeply spiritual man, yet one who did not find that his inward journey of discovery removed him from engagement with the everyday needs of his fellow human beings. This is summed up in a quote from his only book, *Markings*, that I noted at the time: 'In our age, the road to holiness necessarily passes through the world of action.'

This seemed singularly appropriate to the work I'd witnessed the church undertaking to help those living with HIV and AIDS, and hence our prayer for today:

That our desire to be closer to You, Lord, will reveal to us ways in which we can bring Your love to those we meet in our ordinary lives this day. Amen.

BROADCAST FRIDAY 18 SEPTEMBER 2009

September 19

Monawar Hussain

Our television screens have recently been filled with the distressing images of waves of human beings on the move, uprooted from their homes, cut off from their families and totally dispossessed of everything because of war and conflict. In Syria alone, the numbers are utterly shocking – over seven million displaced internally with some four million in refugee camps in neighbouring countries and now in the European Union. This has been described as the worst refugee crisis since World War II.

The Qur'an informs us that God 'has bestowed dignity on the children of Adam' (17:70). Human dignity is inherent, irrespective of one's religion, ethnicity, economic or social standing. A holy tradition informs us that on the Day of Judgement, God will ask:

> O son of Adam, I asked food from you but you did not feed Me. He would say: 'My Lord, how could I feed Thee, whereas Thou art the Lord of the worlds?' He said: 'Didn't you know that such and such servant of Mine asked food from you but you did not feed him, and were you not aware that if you had fed him you would have found him by My side?

When I see images of border guards beating refugees with batons, I see the smashing of a part of our collective human dignity and the shutting of gates on our common humanity.

May God bless those who feed and water the hungry, and offer shelter to the destitute. Amin.

BROADCAST SATURDAY 19 SEPTEMBER 2015

September 20

Janet Wootton

I am a complete convert to Facebook. I didn't find it on my own: my mother, who is in her 80s, asked a few years ago if we would help her get set up with a computer. So that Christmas, she bought a laptop and hub, and we helped her get online.

The next minute, she had signed up, and we have been racing to keep up ever since! With a widely scattered family and equally global friends, this has been a great way of keeping in touch. The quirky and the tragic, the moment of joy and the shared sadness, all find their place. Many of my friends share my faith, so we are also part of a praying community.

And I have discovered emoticons – you know, the little smiling and scowling faces: they just suddenly appeared among the options. There is an enormously long list of them, so I try to choose with care – I use those that stand for 'honoured' and 'delighted' a lot, as I work with some wonderful people.

On the other hand, I value solitude. There is a 'feeling lonely' icon which looks appropriately sad. But I want one that expresses 'Ah, at last I am on my own!' Surely lots of us would use that from time to time, when all that connectedness gets too much.

God, who created us as individuals in a community, we thank You for new ways of being in touch, overcoming loneliness and sharing news of family and friends. We thank You too for the gift of solitude, when we can gather our thoughts and simply be. Amen.

BROADCAST FRIDAY 20 SEPTEMBER 2013

September 21

Jane Livesey

Today I am going to a wedding. I have known the groom since he was 12. This year his mother died tragically at the age of 56. She was within metres of completing a walk on South Africa's Table Mountain when she collapsed from heat stroke and died three days later, just as her two children landed at Johannesburg Airport and before they could see her to say goodbye. Di was one of those people, and thank God we all have some of them in our lives, who was gentle, self-effacing and full of integrity. To know her was to have been enriched – and I am one of many to have been so enriched.

The great German Protestant theologian Dietrich Bonhoeffer, a man whose own integrity led him to the concentration camp in Flossenbürg and execution in April 1945, had it right when he said that nothing can fill the gap when we are away from those we love, and it would be wrong to try and find anything. We must simply hold out and win through. That sounds very hard at first, but at the same time it is a great consolation, since leaving the gap unfilled preserves the bonds between us.

At today's wedding there will be a Di-shaped gap both in the church and afterwards. But she will be there in the minds and hearts of all who loved and continue to love her – and thus the bonds are preserved.

Lord, we ask You to help us to 'hold out and win through' when those we love are taken from us suddenly and unexpectedly, trusting that nonetheless the bonds between us are not broken. Amen.

BROADCAST SATURDAY 21 SEPTEMBER 2013

September 22

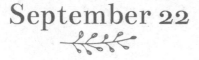

Edward Kessler

There is a special kind of English called 'Sir Humphrey talk'. If he thinks the Prime Minister is about to launch something crazy, he says, 'Courageous, Prime Minister.' If he thinks he is totally wrong, he says, 'Up to a point, Prime Minister.'

I was thinking about this when I was asked about the favourite occupation of Jews: arguing. You might call Judaism 'The Holy Argument.'

Nearly every rabbinic text consists of the following: Rabbi X says this; Rabbi Y says that. Take a standard Jewish text of the Torah, the Five Books of Moses, called in Hebrew *Mikraot Gedolot*, which has a little bit of biblical text and around it an ongoing rabbinic argument. There is Rashi's reading of the verse. There is his grandson Rashbam's reading. There is Ibn Ezra. There is Ramban. There is Sforno.

Each page is an extended argument. If you were to describe the religious literature of rabbinic Judaism, one description is that it is an 'anthology of arguments'. Another is that it's a millennial chat room.

What do we call those arguments? Arguments for the sake of heaven. But these are not only arguments for the sake of heaven. They are arguments with heaven itself. After all, Abraham argues with God. Moses argues with God. Jeremiah argues with God. So does Job.

Argument is central to the Jewish search for meaning, and our commentaries celebrate the diversity of the interpretations.

Jeremiah says, 'My word is like fire, an oracle of the Eternal, and like a hammer that shatters a rock.' Just as a hammer divides into several sparks, so too every scriptural verse yields several meanings.

Thank you, Lord, for providing diversity in the heart of the scriptures. May we celebrate Your unity through the diversity of human existence. Amen.

BROADCAST SATURDAY 22 SEPTEMBER 2012

September 23

Dónal McKeown

A few years ago, after a family event in my home parish, one of my nieces — then six years old — came up to me with a childlike twinkle that we adults can only dream of imitating. 'Uncle Dónal, I know why you wear that wee red hat on your head.' In a somewhat patronizing tone I replied, 'Why, love?' 'It covers your bald patch,' she said and turned on her heel. That shut me up!

Liturgists will give other profound explanations for the wearing of the zucchetto — the truth about its historical origins, development and what purpose it serves. But the little niece had somehow intuited that I was conscious of the growing hairless spot on the crown of my head. She had sensed a truth that I had scarcely acknowledged.

As adults we play many games — at home, at work and even with ourselves. Sometimes it is hard to know what's true. We've all felt betrayed at times by people we thought were honest. Most of us have lied to ourselves more often that we might care to admit. The truth isn't always easy to recognize, accept or live with. But Jesus said that the truth will set you free. And St Paul said that speaking the truth in love was one sure way of helping us to grow together. Today my prayer is simply that I can be a little better able to love my bald patch and rejoice in the truth.

Lord, You are the source of joy, and we pray to You: help us to understand that our heaven begins today when we seek and learn truth. May the faces of those who use Your name shine with the joy of Your Son. Amen.

BROADCAST TUESDAY 23 SEPTEMBER 2008

September 24

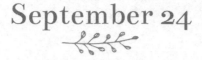

Monawar Hussain

Eid Mubarak — Happy Eid. Today is the beginning of the three days of celebration of the festival of Eid al-Adha. At this time, Muslims remember Abraham's willingness to sacrifice his beloved son. Our tradition is that this was not Isaac but Ishmael, his first-born, who was replaced with a ram that was sacrificed in his place. But what is the point of this story and does it have any meaning for us today?

For Sufi Muslims, Abraham and Ishmael's story is one of intense love of God. Both had lost themselves in the infinite ocean of Divine Oneness and had obliterated any desire for anything else but God. For Sufis, one must sacrifice all desire for anything other than the face of God.

There is also a meaning within Abraham and Ishmael's story for the world. Nearly half the world's population live on less than £1.60 a day. That's more than 3 billion people, with about half of those living in extreme poverty on half that daily amount. One billion of them are children and, according to UNICEF, 22,000 under-fives die each day through poverty.

Materialism and the insatiable appetite to consume more and more also endanger our planet. Abraham's challenge to all of us is to ask what we are prepared to sacrifice to feed our fellow human beings and what we are prepared to do to ensure that our world is sustainable for future generations to come. These are some of the greatest challenges facing humanity.

May God bless our world and our country — and may we always be among the nations that support the poor and the needy. Amin.

BROADCAST THURSDAY 24 SEPTEMBER 2015

September 25

Jonathan Wittenberg

Some people love DIY; others hate it. I've always loved it, which is just as well, because Jewish people are now busy building their succahs in preparation for the festival of Tabernacles which begins on Wednesday night.

A succah is a small hut. The walls can be constructed from anything, but the roof must be made of leaves and branches, spread thickly enough to make it shady inside. During the week of Tabernacles, we're supposed to eat our meals in the succah and even sleep there – if the great British weather permits.

The succah simplifies us. Our lives in the West today are often over-complicated, full of possessions and issues. We need too much and consume too much – trends encouraged by our market-driven society. The small succah, with its covering of leaves and decorations of fruits and vegetables, reminds us of what truly matters.

This summer I walked for several days with donkeys in the Pyrenees. The man who arranges the treks, which are quite challenging, has a remarkable vision. He himself travels with his family for months each year with no more possessions than a donkey can carry. 'I like to start with little,' he says, 'and finish with less. My riches are the people I meet on the way.'

The succah also focuses us on our real wealth: human companionship, food and shelter. It sharpens our concern for those who lack even these necessities. It teaches us not to get lost in our own world too much.

God, help us to remember what truly matters: the basic everyday needs of all people, human companionship and a respectful and grateful relationship with creation.

BROADCAST TUESDAY 25 SEPTEMBER 2007

September 26

Edward Kessler

Today is Yom Kippur, the Day of Atonement, when Jews offer prayers of contrition. Proclamations of remorse serve not only to apologize to the offended party but are also offered in the hope that the life of the penitent can return to normality as quickly as possible. But does saying 'sorry' guarantee a passport to normality? Is a statement of remorse equivalent to being repentant? In sum, what is repentance?

In religious terms, repentance is a prerequisite for divine forgiveness and mercy — God will not pardon us unconditionally but waits for us to repent. In repentance, we must experience genuine remorse for the wrong we have committed and then convert our penitential energy into positive acts.

So there are two stages in the repentance process. First, a negative stage: ceasing to do evil. And, second, a positive stage: doing good.

In Judaism, penitential energy is summarized in one word, *teshuvah*, which literally means 'returning'. The motion of turning implies that sin is not an immovable stain but a straying from the right path, and that by the effort of turning, the sinner can redirect his destiny. '"Return unto Me and I shall return unto you," says the Lord' (Malachi 3:7). God urges Israel to repent and not to be ashamed to do so, because children should not be ashamed to return to a parent who loves them (Deuteronomy Rabbah 2:24).

Teshuvah results in forgiveness because God desires our repentance. The rabbis describe God's appeal in these words: 'My sons, open for Me an aperture of repentance as narrow as the eye of a needle and I will open for you gates through which wagons and coaches can pass.'

We praise You, O Lord, who shows mercy and compassion to all. Amen.

BROADCAST WEDNESDAY 26 SEPTEMBER 2012

September 27

Jonathan Wittenberg

I greatly miss my teacher Rabbi Hugo Gryn, who was such a well-known voice on Radio 4. He used to say that people belong to one of two groups: they're either dividers or harmonizers, either quarrel-mongers or peacemakers. (Actually, I think we all have our worse, as well as our better, moments.)

But we must try to be peacemakers.

Today is the first day of the Jewish festival of Succot. The succah, a hut covered with a canopy of leaves, is a reminder of peace. 'Spread over us the canopy of your peace,' we pray.

It's easy to divide the world into 'them and us'. My heroes are those who don't do that, who strive to fulfil a more embracing vision.

It's easy to affirm our own identity by degrading and demonizing others, by excluding them from the canopy of peace. That's why gangs need other gangs to fight. Throughout history there have been states that behaved like such gangs. I learned this when growing up in a family of refugees from Nazi Germany. But no state, no society and few individuals are completely free from elements of xenophobia.

The rabbis taught: 'Seek peace and pursue it.' Pursuing peace means actively trying to understand others. It means listening to how they interpret the world; hearing what hurts them; seeing ourselves from their point of view. It can be challenging, but it's humbling and enriching too. It deepens our humanity and expands our horizons.

My heroes are those who have an inclusive vision, whether great prophets like Nelson Mandela or ordinary teachers working with Palestinian and Israeli children together.

God, don't let us leave it to You to bring peace. Give each of us the courage and vision to create harmony and understanding. Amen.

BROADCAST THURSDAY 27 SEPTEMBER 2007

September 28

Edward Kessler

It is not an accident that the most famous Jewish jokes are about the family.

Three elderly Jewish ladies are sitting on a bench talking about – what else – their children. 'My son,' says one, 'is such a wonderful son. Every month he sends me £500.' 'You think that's special,' says the second. 'That's nothing. Every month *my* son sends me £1,000.' 'Ach,' says the third. 'My son spends £500 a week on his psychiatrist. And what do you think he talks about? Me! Only me!'

Families are not always easy – there is occasional stress – yet it is through the family that the world acquires a human face. Through parents and grandparents we have history.

And through their children and grandchildren they have posterity.

And through the family we experience a complex choreography of love – what it means to give and share, to grow from obedience to responsibility, to learn, challenge, rebel, make mistakes, forgive and be forgiven, argue and make up. Without the family we would not know what life's most basic concepts mean.

My parents recently celebrated their 60th wedding anniversary, and they have taught me how to be a son as much as my children have taught me how to be a parent. And since I have had children of my own, I have also learned what it feels like to create something you cannot control.

Their marriage is the redemption of loneliness in which they can face the future without fear. Not because they are optimists (although they are), not because of blind trust (although they trust), but because they know they give one another support, understanding and strength.

We thank You, God, for helping us create and sustain our families. Amen.

BROADCAST FRIDAY 28 SEPTEMBER 2012

September 29

Karen Smith

Many of us may recall the dreadful day in January 1986 when, just after take-off, the space shuttle *Challenger* experienced what was described as a 'major malfunction'. Few who saw the explosion broadcast live on television will forget the sight of the huge curling plume of smoke in the sky, a sure sign of catastrophic failure.

The space shuttle programme was stopped, and given the devastating loss of seven astronauts, including a school teacher, it would perhaps have been understandable if the programme had been axed. Yet, two years later, on this day in 1988, a new space shuttle, *Discovery*, was launched.

I am in awe of those who are willing to explore new frontiers. Over the years there have been many courageous scientists, doctors and journalists who have ventured forward, often putting their own lives in jeopardy for the good of others.

While some of us are not great risk-takers, there is a sense in which at some point we are all required to step out into the unknown: a new job, a project at work, moving house. Life is never free from change and chance. Sometimes it may seem that the path we take is filled with twists and turns, and there are times when all we can do is stop and wait.

In those waiting moments, we may feel out of control and anxious. When I have felt like that, I often recall some of the words of Psalm 46: 'God is our refuge and strength, a very present help in trouble. ... Be still and know that I am God.'

Loving God, we pray for guidance for those who are seeking to make choices for the future. Help us all to put our trust in You, our refuge and strength. Amen.

BROADCAST MONDAY 29 SEPTEMBER 2014

September 30

Andrea Rea

The film star James Dean died prematurely in a car crash 60 years ago today. Dean's popularity grew quickly in his short life, through his performances in a handful of films that cast him as a moody, rebellious teen and young man. After his tragic death at the age of 24, Dean's mystique grew and he became a symbol of disaffected youth with his edgy, slightly dangerous aura and matinée-idol good looks. He's also looked to as an example of unrealized potential, and of someone who has stayed, truly, forever young.

There is a lot of pressure these days to stay young. Youth, as George Bernard Shaw said, is wasted on the young, and those of us who can no longer call themselves young know the truth of that for sure. But it might be better to stop pining for what used to be, and do what we can to deal with what actually is.

I'm reminded about a story I saw recently about a man who had an exciting career as a photographer of rock bands and solo artists at a world-famous music venue. Advancements in photography caused his professional prospects to narrow, and he ended up taking a job at the venue as a stagehand — moving equipment around for the rock artists that still come to play. He loves the job, and his favourite part of it is sweeping the floor of the stage, late at night, when everyone else is gone. He gets as much joy and takes as much pride in that work as when he rubbed shoulders with stars. He once photographed Bob Dylan, who wrote the song 'Forever Young' for his son, wishing him the blessing of busy hands, doing things for others, a sense of truth and a strong foundation.

Lord God, grant us wisdom to know that staying forever young is not a matter of fame or appearances, but of walking in your light and taking pride in what we can do for others. Amen.

BROADCAST WEDNESDAY 30 SEPTEMBER 2015

October 1

Karen Smith

Today has been declared by the United Nations the 'International Day of Older Persons'. While attention is often focused on youth in our society, it is estimated that there are 600 million people over 60 in the world. This will double by 2025 and reach two billion by 2050.

Concerned that dated stereotypes have often presented a false picture of ageing, the World Health Organization is keen to celebrate the contributions of older people. Many serve as volunteers in hospitals or in charitable work. Others care for family, friends and neighbours.

Of course, growing older is not without difficulties. Some people struggle with poor health, and at times, whatever our age, we may look back and feel weighed down by regret. We may wish we had been more patient, kind or long-suffering.

While we may lament some past word or deed, Christian faith reminds us that God stands ready to love and forgive. As the writer of Lamentations puts it: 'The steadfast love of the Lord never ceases; his mercies never come to an end; they are new every morning.'

It is sometimes difficult to live each day looking forward. Life may bring crushing disappointment or grief that seems to cloud the future. A 93-year-old friend of mine is one of the most positive people I know. In spite of the trouble she has experienced in life, she told me that she has learned to live every day in a spirit of thanksgiving to God. She believes God is faithful and she knows God's mercy will never come to an end. For me, such faith is both an inspiration and a challenge.

Loving God, be with those who have difficult decisions to make today. Give us all the peace of knowing that You are with us. Amen.

BROADCAST WEDNESDAY 1 OCTOBER 2014

October 2

Simon Doogan

A few weeks ago, the news was full of a research project demonstrating that teenagers who regularly smoke cannabis risk long-term damage to their IQs.

Then I discovered that way back on 2 October 1974 results of a strikingly similar study had been published: smoking cannabis may cause brain damage. Now, as then, a rush of protest came from those brandishing proof on the other side of the argument. What strikes a spiritual chord with me, however, is the reason why so many resort to drug use in the first place: the need to escape.

'When you're stoned, a problem can come up, and it takes a while to get your stuff together to be able to deal with it,' said a heavy user interviewed for the 1970s study. But then you read that he was in the US military and that smoking dope was his way of getting through the Vietnam War.

It's what we all feel from time to time, the desire to lift ourselves out from the heaviness of our situations. If we could only just turn down the pressure, even for a short while, fill our consciousness with something less preoccupying, less painful.

It's not that we don't want to square up to the reality of it all, it's that we feel we just can't do it in our own strength. Even though we know deep down that escape only ever really means postponement.

Loving Father, we pray for all those who seek escape in the taking of drugs, especially those exposing themselves to permanent harm. For the sake of Your Son who knew the anguish of life at its most intense and desperate, may they know today that, with You, they are never alone. Amen.

BROADCAST TUESDAY 2 OCTOBER 2012

October 3

Neil Gardner

One of my most famous predecessors as minister of Canongate Kirk on Edinburgh's Royal Mile was the Reverend Robert Walker. While not necessarily a famous name, he has certainly become a famous figure as the subject of Sir Henry Raeburn's iconic painting *The Skating Minister*. Cutting a dash in his top hat and frock coat as he skates sedately around a frozen Duddingston Loch, he looks every inch the sombre Presbyterian dressed in black from head to toe. Except that's not quite true. For if you look closely enough, you will see that his buckled shoes are fixed to his skates with pink straps!

The devil's in the detail, they say, but I'm more inclined to see this as a sign of the Skating Minister's lighter side, perhaps a subtle hint even of that period known as the Scottish Enlightenment in which he lived. Raeburn painted plenty of other leading figures of that distinctive era, distinguished professors of philosophy and theology among them. But he always depicted them in more conventional portraits, standing or sitting. The Skating Minister is the only one who has become so famous not for what he said or what he thought, but for what he did.

Let us pray: Father forgive us for the times when we fail to match the noble things we think and say with our actions, those times when, through all that we think and say and do, we fall short of the standard You have set for us in the life and teaching, in the death and rising of Your Son Jesus Christ. And may what we do today be truly for Your glory. Amen.

BROADCAST MONDAY 3 OCTOBER 2011

October 4

David Chillingworth

One of my children worked for a while as a hospital cleaner. One day he was given the job of cleaning the stairs: four floors of them – like painting the Forth Bridge. I was visiting some people in the hospital. I dropped in and out on him a few times during the afternoon – and he was still at it.

I think this morning of that army of people who are already at work now: cleaners and maintenance staff, workers who keep trains, buses and planes running, people in the water and power industries, healthcare workers. Maybe there is less sense of community around today – but in a complex modern society, we're dependent on the work of many people who we never see. We all depend on people not just doing it but doing it faithfully and well. That's part of the dignity of it.

There's a verse of a hymn by John Keble that says: 'The trivial round, the common task / Will furnish all we ought to ask; / Room to deny ourselves – a road / To bring us daily nearer God.' Every job has routine and tedium. Family life and child-rearing have more than most. The work of the priest is no different. I would plod on saying to myself: 'Don't ask what good will come of this. Just know that it is part of what creates a society of value and care.'

But John Keble's words go further – investing the commitment which we give to work with something of the spiritual. Where there is sacrifice, commitment and self-denial, God is in there as well.

At the start of the day, we remember those who work unseen and whose work makes possible the life and work of thousands of others. May they find fulfilment and satisfaction in knowing that in serving others they are serving You. Amen.

BROADCAST THURSDAY 4 OCTOBER 2007

October 5

Mary Stallard

For my seventh birthday, a family friend brought me a locket from Assisi, with a tiny picture inside of St Francis and the wolf which, according to legend, he tamed. I'm reminded of that story at animal blessings and pets' services which are often held around now to remember Francis.

But perhaps more important than his affinity with animals, Francis' life story speaks a message of hope for those involved in conflict. Much of our experience of life and relationships includes aspects that are broken, fragmented and contradictory. Perhaps we tend to think of saints as perfect people, and yet, like the stained-glass windows in which they're frequently depicted, often what makes them special is that somehow, through the broken parts of their lives, God's light and grace has shone with a particular brilliance.

Francis, born in late 12th-century Italy, had a turbulent home life. He was a rebellious and difficult youth, but as an adult Francis heard God speaking to him in prayer and began to live a simple life, dedicated to serving others. He attracted a group of friends and began a religious order that now exists worldwide and is characterized by its strong commitment to disciplined living, material poverty and faithful companionship.

In his youth, Francis fought as a soldier and suffered the indignity of imprisonment by enemies. Yet rather than Francis becoming consumed with a desire for revenge, his Christian faith inspired him to change his lifestyle, dedicating his energy and his gifts toward peacemaking. His life tells an amazing story of transformation.

God of change, when our lives are troubled, help us like Francis to look outward to address others' needs rather than inward to our own; and to discover Your joy and healing in simpler, more generous living. Amen.

BROADCAST MONDAY 5 OCTOBER 2009

October 6

Tina Beattie

In November 1977, President Anwar Sadat of Egypt was invited to address the Israeli Knesset. In his address, he said that 'amidst the ruins of what man has built and the remains of the victims of mankind, there emerges neither victor nor vanquished. The only vanquished remains man, God's most sublime creation.' Sadat called for people to 'stand together with … courage and boldness to erect a huge edifice of peace that … would be a beacon for generations to come.' Why, he asked, 'should we bequeath to the coming generations the plight of bloodshed, death, orphans, widowhood, family disintegration and the wailing of victims?'

That edifice of peace has not yet been built. Still the people of the Middle East are tormented by violence, yet they're also giving birth to fragile visions of freedom and hope. This requires great courage, for those who seek peace often become victims themselves. Sadat was assassinated by extremists in the Egyptian military on 6 October 1981. Today is the 31st anniversary of his death.

Sadat exhorted people who are victims of violence to become those who fill the earth with peace. Let me finish with his words:

'You, bewailing mother; you, widowed wife; you, the son who lost a brother or a father; you, all victims of war — fill the earth and space with recitals of peace. … Turn the song into a reality that blossoms and lives. Make hope a code of conduct and endeavour. The will of peoples is part of the will of God.' Amen.

BROADCAST SATURDAY 6 OCTOBER 2012

October 7

Neil Gardner

My parish of Canongate, the lower half of Edinburgh's famous Royal Mile, can trace its history back to 1128, when King David I, son of the saintly Queen Margaret, first founded it. He'd gone hunting in what we now know as Holyrood Park, but in those days it was thickly wooded and ideally suited to hunting. But legend has it that in the course of his favourite pursuit, the King was unseated from his horse and confronted by a fierce white stag bearing down on him with its sharp antlers.

Finding himself on his knees, he turned not unnaturally to prayer and asked that God might spare him a rather gory death, and as he prayed he suddenly caught a vision of the cross of Jesus between the antlers of the stag. And the stag stopped and withdrew quietly to the forest, and the King vowed that he would build an abbey as close to that spot as possible. And so the story of the Abbey of the Holyrood, or Holy Cross, began — nearly 900 years ago. To this day, the emblem of the parish is the cross between the antlers of the stag.

And so this day let us turn too to prayer: Lord God, in the midst of all the challenges and opportunities of this coming day, help us to discern Your will and purpose for us. Help us to trace the cross amidst all the dangers and distractions we encounter, and to focus on it and by its help to find the way forward. And all this we ask through him who died on the cross but rose again triumphant from the grave, Jesus Christ our Lord. Amen.

BROADCAST MONDAY 7 OCTOBER 2013

October 8

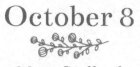

Mary Stallard

I've never been a particularly confident driver, and an accident two years ago badly increased my nervousness on the road. Coming around a blind bend, another driver lost control of their vehicle and drove into me. Although both cars were wrecked, neither of us suffered serious physical injury; but for weeks afterwards I found it really hard to drive, and I was often in tears at the wheel, anxious that I'd be involved in another crash. I was determined not to give up. Gradually, over many months, I regained a sense of calm on the road, but it's taken me a long time to reach the point where I can enjoy driving.

I've noticed recently that I'm much more relaxed in the car when I'm in the grip of another strong emotion – whether it's happiness over something beautiful, sadness caused by loss or failure, or even anger after a row!

It might sound odd but I'm thankful now for the experience of the accident, because it's helped me to grow so much. Not only has my driving improved, but I'm now much more aware of the impact emotions can have upon the whole of my life and behaviour.

I've been surprised at the subtle power that fear can gain if it's allowed free rein, and I'm glad that our Creator has equipped us with a whole range of tools among our other feelings, which, when acknowledged, can help us toward wholeness.

Jesus was supremely gifted at recognizing and naming people's fears and helping them to be released from situations where they were trapped or anxious. St John reflected upon this, describing how Jesus embodied 'the perfect love which casts out all fear' and which points toward the fullness of life.

Creator God, You ordered this world with time and space for everything and every emotion. Help us to be aware of our own and others' feelings and to be led more by love than by fear. Amen.

BROADCAST THURSDAY 8 OCTOBER 2009

October 9

Musharraf Hussain

One of the most misunderstood contemporary terms is 'jihad'. It is used regularly in media reporting and is almost always connected with violence and bloodshed. This is troubling, as the term within the Islamic tradition means 'to toil, to exert oneself, to strive and to struggle against difficulties'. Razi, one of the leading commentators on the Qur'an, argues 'that there is nothing in the word to indicate that this striving is to be effected by the sword'. On returning from a battle, the Prophet informed his companions that they were returning from the lesser jihad to the greater jihad. Perplexed, the companions asked, what was the greater jihad? The Prophet replied that it was human beings' struggle against selfish desires. The Prophetic traditions explain more fully the richness of the Islamic understanding of jihad.

'A man asked: "Should I join the jihad?" The Prophet replied, "Do you have parents?" The man said yes. The Prophet replied: "Then perform jihad by serving them!"

'"What kind of jihad is better?" The Prophet replied, "A word of truth spoken in front of an oppressive ruler."'

Sufi literature is rich with stories of how Sufis have overcome their lower selves to achieve human excellence. One of the key ethical teachings of Sufis is the idea of *husn-e-zan* — that is, having a good opinion of others. We can only live by such a teaching if we have first encountered our selves and understood our faults and shortcomings.

May we always seek out the good in others. Amin.

BROADCAST THURSDAY 9 OCTOBER 2014

October 10

Tina Beattie

Today is World Homeless Day, when we're invited to reflect on what it means to be homeless.

Homelessness can take many different forms. When we see refugees fleeing from war and tyranny, running barefoot from bombed houses and shattered lives, we see homelessness in its most dramatic form. We recognize homelessness on our streets when we see people sleeping rough or selling *The Big Issue*. If we're honest, those of us who have homes sometimes resent such intrusions into our insulated worlds. We don't want these reminders of social exclusion and economic brutality. We don't want to think about what it means to be overwhelmed by poverty, abandoned by one's family, or simply unable to cope with life's demands. Yet to be deprived of a home is to be deprived of so much else as well, for home is where our fundamental human needs are met — the need for love, warmth, companionship and security.

Sadly, for people of my generation, houses have too often been regarded more as commodities and investments than as homes where people love and grow together. In order for a house to become a home, it must absorb the lives of the people who live in it, grow with them and around them, and become part of who they are. These things take time. A new house might be exciting to live in, but a home is a mature and time-worn space of belonging.

My people will abide in a peaceful habitation, in secure dwellings, and in quiet resting places, says the prophet Isaiah. May that be our prayer for all who are homeless today. Amen.

BROADCAST WEDNESDAY 10 OCTOBER 2012

October 11

George Craig

This year has seen the opening of the dramatic and beautiful new museum in which the remains of Henry VIII's flagship, the *Mary Rose*, are displayed. But for many of us the very mention of the *Mary Rose* brings back memories of this day in 1982 when for the first time we saw her rising slowly through the water — miraculously brought back into the light after 437 years on the sea bed.

It is astonishing how much of the ship somehow survived. The new museum allows you to go close enough to really feel the scale of the structure.

But for me, from my first sight of the hull, it was the image of the teeming humanity trapped inside the ship as she sank that drove almost everything else from my mind. There were huge numbers of people crammed into every corner of the vessel — probably well over 400 of them. One of the most remarkable things about the recovery of the wreck is the extraordinary collection of intimate personal items — from clothing to tools — that were retrieved. And these objects somehow bring abstract history down to the life and death of the individuals who used to own them, some of them no more than children.

If we're not careful the past can just become lots of dates and events which, while fascinating, don't connect with us in any personal way. When we are confronted with racks of worn shoes, suddenly the people who wore them are real and their lives — and deaths — are real too.

The New Testament has many stories of Jesus surrounded by crowds yet still focusing on the needs of individuals. The traces of humanity on the Mary Rose are a valuable reminder that the great sweep of history past and present is actually made up of countless individual stories of ordinary people just like us.

Father, help us to remember that just as You love us as individuals, we should learn to recognize, respect and value each other the same way. Amen.

BROADCAST FRIDAY 11 OCTOBER 2013

October 12

Chris Edmondson

She stood there quietly sharing her story, occasionally with tears in her eyes, and you could have heard a pin drop. An apparently ordinary, middle-aged woman recounting an extraordinary and painful story – the murder of her son seven years before, as a result of a random knife attack. A young man about to be married – a case of being in the wrong place at the wrong time.

And the audience? A group of 30 male prisoners and me, along with others visiting the prison that day, were privileged to be flies on the wall for this extraordinary encounter. I think of it today, on the anniversary of the death of the prison reformer Elizabeth Fry in 1845.

What we witnessed is part of a programme called 'restorative justice'. It works on the premise that crimes need to be viewed less as violations against society and more as violations against individuals and in terms of the effects they have on them. When seen through the restorative lens, the all-important questions are not so much around 'Who is to blame?' as 'What can be done to make things better in the long term, for victims, the offender and the community?'

That particular prison visit will remain long in my memory, as I saw a woman, without bitterness, motivated by her Christian faith. She was able not only to forgive those who had taken her son's life, but also to help the men in her audience, some of whom had committed equally serious crimes, to realize at a deeper level the impact on their victims and to see the possibility of repairing the physical and emotional damage caused by crime.

Lord, give all today who may feel the need for revenge or retaliation the grace to follow the costly steps of Your Son in the way of restoration and healing. Amen.

BROADCAST MONDAY 12 OCTOBER 2009

October 13

Richard Frazer

Frank was a big, scary bloke. He'd been in and out of jail, his shaved head revealed some nasty scars, and he used to come to church during the day and just hang out the whole time, intimidating the tourists and making us all feel uncomfortable.

One day I got a call to say that Frank was very agitated. When I ran over to the church, I discovered that he had taken a massive overdose and was trying to end his life. We got him to hospital and he recovered. And a few weeks later, he was back – and more in his right mind. We sat together in the calmness of our beautiful medieval sanctuary and he asked me, 'Don't you know why I've been coming here?' I replied that I certainly knew he was upset about his father dying. I also thought quietly to myself that he was probably hoping someone might give him some money. He said, 'I just need to hear a word of forgiveness.'

The reason for his repeated visits suddenly dawned on me. He felt that his wayward life had been the cause of his father's untimely death. He wanted to be forgiven and to know that he didn't have to carry that feeling of shame for the rest of his life. Until that moment, we had been *managing* Frank, 'risk-assessing' him, perceiving him as a threat or a scrounger. Now I realized that he was teaching me about Christ, who comes to us often in the stranger's guise.

Lord Jesus Christ, you come to us in the most unlikely people. Make us more attentive and aware of your presence where we least expect to find you. We ask this in the hope of being surprised. Amen.

BROADCAST TUESDAY 13 OCTOBER 2015

October 14

Monawar Hussain

Today is the Day of 'Arafah. Over three million Muslims, from all four corners of the earth, representing a diversity of cultures and ethnicities, and speaking every conceivable language, will be gathering at the plain of 'Arafah in Saudi Arabia as part of the hajj pilgrimage, which every Muslim must perform at least once in a lifetime. The men will be dressed in the *ihram* – two simple, unstitched, white pieces of cloth; and the women in their traditional dress. Once the *haji* is in a state of *ihram*, he takes the oath to hold all life sacred; he is not to hurt or harm anything, not even a fly, or to be rude or offensive to another.

Today, there will be no way of knowing who is rich and who is poor, who is a professor and who is an ordinary labourer, who is a prime minister or a president, who an ordinary civil servant. All those outward identities are stripped away and one becomes totally absorbed in this mass of humanity. The whole day is spent in worship, meditation and prayer. There is a one-to-one conversation with God, seeking His forgiveness for oneself and one's loved ones, sharing one's sorrows, and seeking peace for those who have departed from this world. In tradition, the Prophet (peace be upon Him) has said that God says to the angels on the day of 'Arafah, 'Look, My angels, at My servants. They come dishevelled, dusty, arriving from every deep ravine. Bear witness that I have forgiven them. They will return [home] like the day their mothers bore them.'

O Merciful God, grant us to treat others with respect and rejoice in our common humanity. Amin.

BROADCAST MONDAY 14 OCTOBER 2013

October 15

Martin Graham

Today is the feast day of St Teresa of Ávila, one of the greatest saints in the Church calendar. One remarkable thing about St Teresa is that she died either on 4 October or on 15 October 1582, because her death came around midnight as Catholic countries in Europe made the switch from the old Julian calendar to the Gregorian calendar. By the time the correction of the 1600-year-old Julian calendar was made, it was 11 days out of sync with true time.

There are many varied ways of marking time across the world. Even if we don't feel controlled by a watch on our wrist, we still have our internal body clock telling us, sometimes pleading with us, that it is time to be going to sleep.

The seasons move on, time marches forward and just as nature moves through the seasons during the course of a year, so too do we move through the seasons in the course of our lives. In the springtime, life begins and with it is born the hopes and dreams for tomorrow. Then summer arrives. The hopes and dreams don't fade, things just become more realistic. But more importantly, life is being lived. Then autumn arrives and with it energy begins to fade, life slows down. And then winter comes upon us. It seems like life has stopped and nothing is friendly. The winter seems to destroy all that the other three seasons have created and built up.

Perhaps, as we start a new day, maybe begin a new job or enter a new phase in life, we could take St Teresa's prayer as our own:

Let nothing disturb you, let nothing frighten you, all things are passing away: God never changes. Patience obtains all things. Whoever has God lacks nothing; God alone suffices.

BROADCAST WEDNESDAY 15 OCTOBER 2014

October 16

Joe Aldred

I can recall vividly the occasion of my consecration as a bishop. There I was, kneeling humbly as other bishops from my denomination prayed over me. Rising to my feet, I felt the full weight of the responsibility that was now my lot. But was I up to the job? I was not at all sure. And that sense of being challenged has never left me. Yet I try not to do my job as though I were uncertain of myself – that would hardly inspire confidence. And I hear on the grapevine that most people's experience of me is of someone who is confident. Maybe that's because I have learned to suppress my shyness and uncertainty; also, because of my main coping mechanism, that of preparing well, leaving little to chance.

We all tend to remember those challenges when, for the first time, we took up some responsibility, such as a new job, getting married or becoming a parent. And alongside becoming a bishop, I can recall many occasions of first-time nerves that equate with assuming the spiritual authority and oversight of a bishop. These days I am a bishop without a portfolio, and this reminds me that in a sense all of us are overseers of one sort or another. At a minimum, we each have authority and oversight over our own lives. I know from my years of pastoral experience that, like me, many do what they do in spite of a sense of being challenged. It is by God's grace and the help of his Holy Spirit that we are able to shoulder our responsibilities.

Oh God, whatever our sphere of authority and oversight today, give us insight, confidence and strength to fulfil our role with grace and effectiveness. Amen.

BROADCAST SATURDAY 16 OCTOBER 2010

October 17

Shaunaka Rishi Das

In my 13th year, I sat in front of the fire one evening with my father. I liked to sit up with him when everyone else had gone to bed and all was quiet.

On this evening he asked me what I thought of drinking. In Ireland this only means the drinking of alcohol. I wasn't sure really. I *did* know that I didn't like the taste of drink.

My father said that I would have to make a choice at some stage to drink or not to drink. He, a teetotal all his life, said he chose not to drink for religious reasons and also because there was alcoholism in the family. He didn't know if it was a scientific fact that alcoholism ran in families, but some said it did and he didn't want to take the risk. He wanted to be responsible to my mother and to his children, and to be a good citizen. He couldn't do this if he developed cravings he might lose control of, and he thought that he had a personality that could become dependent, so he chose to refrain.

Having said that, he recognized many people could drink moderately, and that a sip of wine was good for the digestion. The choice was mine. He knew I would soon come under pressure from friends to have a drink, and wanted me to make an informed choice. I remain impressed by his broadminded approach and the trust he placed in me to make my own choice. I also chose to refrain.

I pray that we all get the chance to make good choices, to be shown the choices, to respect others' choices, and to offer others as broad a range of choice as our trust allows. Hare Krishna.

BROADCAST SATURDAY 17 OCTOBER 2015

October 18

Noel Battye

Today is St Luke's Day. In earlier times, whenever there was a late, warm spell around this time of the year, they used to call it 'St Luke's little summer' — whether because of the date or because it said something of the saint's character isn't quite clear. But what is clear is that the person who comes across in the writings of this young medic is one who is both warm and open.

Luke might have been responsible for more than a quarter of the New Testament, but there is little or no reference to himself in those two beautifully written books called 'Luke' and 'Acts'. Yet, somehow, the very incidents he chooses to relate speak volumes about the writer.

Luke paints, like an artist, some of the most vivid pictures, which many of us remember from childhood, including the Nativity. He alone tells of Zacharias in the Temple, Mary's visit to Elizabeth, the shepherds abiding in the fields. The parables Luke chooses to tell are often encouraging: the Good Samaritan, the woman who loses a coin and then finds it again, the wayward son who goes off the rails and in the end is restored to his family. When it comes to dealing with the final judgment, it is not all in terms of gleeful damnation, weeping and wailing and gnashing of teeth, but sad individual tragedies — the rich man who in the end finds he has to leave everything behind, and that other rich man who longs for his brothers to learn from his mistakes.

Nor was it all a matter of talk for Luke. Right at the end of his life, writing from prison and awaiting execution, St Paul tells how in his final isolation, 'Only Luke is with me'. Luke, the unobtrusive one, was there, standing by him to the end.

Lord, thank You for those who, while drawing little attention to themselves, make life better for others — whose warmth we sometimes take for granted but whose care and encouragement mean so very much. Amen.

BROADCAST TUESDAY 18 OCTOBER 2011

October 19

Stephen Wigley

This weekend marks the beginning of One World Week, and there is a whole range of events planned right across the country to remind us of how it is one world in which we live and one world whose resources we must learn to share. In 1987 this same lesson was brought home in a quite different way, with the stock market crash that began in the Far East, moved to the US and then wreaked havoc in London and across Europe. On Black Monday, as it came to be known, share prices in New York fell more sharply than during the Wall Street Crash of 1929. Thankfully, the impact was not as long-lasting as that earlier fall which led to the Great Depression. But the realization that the world's economic wellbeing can be so vulnerable to crises in financial markets has never really left us — even today, there is still some debate among economists as to the strength of the recovery some years on from the most recent crash in 2008.

It's hard to avoid matters of finance. Jesus was well aware of this, and it's also a topic he spoke a fair deal about in the Gospels: how to deal with debtors, budget for building work, pay a fair wage — and how servants should be trusted with money. But above all he warned against people putting their faith in money alone: you should focus instead, he said, on building up 'treasure in heaven', in relationships, acts of charity, things that will last. Maybe this weekend we can spend a bit more time investing in these things instead.

Heavenly Father, You teach us in Jesus where real treasure is to be found, in those values and relationships which endure; help us today not to be so preoccupied with material matters that we lose sight of those lasting values on which our lives depend. For Christ's sake, Amen.

BROADCAST SATURDAY 19 OCTOBER 2013

October 20

Michael Mumisa

Recently we witnessed the case of Rimsha Masih, a young Christian girl in Pakistan who was accused of blasphemy and arrested under Pakistani law. A Pakistani *mullah*, or Muslim religious teacher, was later arrested for falsely accusing her.

This incident reignited the debate among Muslims across the world about whether such blasphemy laws have any legitimate basis in Islam. Pakistani jurists who defend such laws have always argued that they are indeed Islamic. Many Muslims living in multi-faith and secular societies have been quick to point out that the Rimsha Masih case is another example of why Muslims should re-establish the pluralist traditions that Islam was once known for.

What is more important to me as a person of faith? Is it to live in a society in which a set of religious beliefs and all aspects of social morality are defined and enforced by law on citizens, or a society in which citizens are free to express and safeguard their beliefs and values?

Whenever I reflect on this question, I am reminded of the words from the Qur'an:
'Whosoever will, let him believe, and whosoever will, let him disbelieve ...' (18:29).
'Let there be no compulsion in religion!' (2: 256).
'Unto you your religion, and unto me my religion ...' (109:6).

In fact the Qu'ran recognizes the great diversity and variety in the human family: 'O mankind, truly we have created you male and female, and have made you nations and tribes that ye may recognize one another' (49:13).

'Our Lord! Forgive us our sins and let not our hearts entertain any unworthy thoughts or feelings against anyone. Our Lord! You are indeed full of kindness and Most Merciful.'
Amin.

BROADCAST SATURDAY 20 OCTOBER 2012

October 21

Joe Aldred

Some years ago I read Dale Carnegie's book *How to Win Friends and Influence People*. And one of the nuggets I have treasured since is that whatever the world may think of the vilest sinner, be they a mass-murderer, gangster or mugger, each individual actually sees him or herself in a more wholesome way — even when they acknowledge the seriousness of their crimes. I now tend to want to know more whenever I hear of a person or group tragically lashing out. I do not need to look too far back to my own racial history of slavery and colonialism to read of rebellions and the struggle for liberation that resulted in tragedy on both sides.

The Christian faith highlights Jesus's teaching simultaneously to free the oppressed and to turn the other cheek. Superficially these two ideals don't go well together, and yet we are called to hold them in creative tension, model them and show even to those who are marginalized by their own criminality that God the liberator is on their side. Wrongdoing should never be condoned, but discerning the boundaries of right and wrong is not always as obvious as we hope it might be, especially where abuse and a life of constant fear have diminished human experience. At times human actions are such that we find it difficult to ask why people did what they did; condemnation is inevitable. But justice and peace go together. And mercy can follow in time. There but for the grace of God go I.

O God, give us the gift of discernment to see with Your eyes; to protect the weak and vulnerable and to temper justice with mercy. Grant that like Jesus we become the friend of the marginalized, the victimized and the oppressed. Amen.

BROADCAST THURSDAY 21 OCTOBER 2010

October 22

Shaunaka Rishi Das

When listening to *Farming Today*, I once heard a report that explained that without using pesticides, up to 20 per cent of a crop can be lost, which seems unfortunate.

On the other hand, people are concerned about the bee population, saying that without bees pollinating crops, we could lose an even greater percentage. Others are concerned about animals, birds, trees, plants and herbs – whose very survival can be compromised by human activity.

An old Indian story tells of the bag of rice left in the marketplace. A bird came and landed near the bag. It took the few grains it needed and flew away. A mouse found the bag, scratched a small hole in its side and ate its fill. A man arrived and, not finding the owner, took the whole bag.

For the bird and the mouse, it was just a bag of grain, available to all. For the man, ownership was important. If he couldn't identify an owner, then he claimed ownership himself, and took the lot. His ownership benefited only himself, and deprived others. It was a thoughtless and extreme act, which we'd usually identify as greed. Maximizing profit can also be seen as extreme if it deprives others.

The Upanishads are a collection of philosophical works, ancient in origin, and sacred to Hindus. One of the books, the Isopanshad, the cream of the Upanishads, opens with the following verse:

'*Everything animate and inanimate within the universe is controlled and owned by the Lord. One should therefore accept only those things necessary for himself, which are set aside as his quota, and one should not accept other things, knowing well to whom they belong.*' *Hare Krishna*.

BROADCAST WEDNESDAY 22 OCTOBER 2014

October 23

Stephen Wigley

In recent months we've become all too aware of the growing refugee crisis triggered by the fighting in Syria, as thousands flee across the borders into Jordan, Lebanon and Turkey. The scale of the problem is mind-boggling: recent estimates are of two million people displaced, including over a million children. But sometimes it's the very numbers that make us forget that each one represents an individual human life.

Thinking about this, a personal story brought me up short. It was on this day in October 1956 that the Hungarian Uprising began, led by Imre Nagy, as students and workers rose up against Russian rule. After some initial success, the Red Army moved in to brutally suppress the revolt and, in the chaos that followed, some 200,000, mainly young people, fled abroad.

We came to know one of them when we moved as a family to live in Rome in the late 1960s. For us, Rome was an opportunity to spend some time enjoying a new and different lifestyle. For Lazlo and family, it was the place where he'd had to build a new life after fleeing his home. He'd succeeded — but he always carried the memories of what he had to leave behind.

I guess that's true for all refugees; it's certainly true to the experience of the Bible. Much of the Old Testament is shaped by the experience of exile and the longing to return home; and in Matthew's Gospel, even the infant Jesus and his parents know what it's like to flee to safety in Egypt. So as we hear reports of refugee crises and are challenged by emergency appeals, may we be reminded that behind all the numbers lie individual stories.

Loving Lord, You show in the stories of the Bible Your care for the exiled and the refugee; help us to show that same concern for those caught up in fighting and having to flee from their homes today. For Christ's sake, Amen.

BROADCAST WEDNESDAY 23 OCTOBER 2013

October 24

Shaunaka Rishi Das

Every year I attend a conference which takes place in a beautiful Krishna temple nestled in the Tuscan hills above Florence.

The temple building was once owned by Machiavelli, and now houses a Krishna-centred art collection, a splendid vegetarian restaurant and grounds that flow through different levels of romantic grandeur.

As part of the conference we spend a day in Florence sightseeing and, at the end of a hot day walking from cultural icon to artistic masterpiece, there is nothing better than an Italian ice cream. But this year our Florentine guide had deserted us. We, an international group, were left to negotiate that old Hindu chestnut of a question, whether the ice cream contained egg or not.

In my enthusiasm to serve my colleagues, I began to run from shop to shop asking if the ice cream contained egg. Not being able to speak Italian, I pieced together the few words I knew, and found that no one seemed to understand me. Eventually other members of the group caught up with me to find that I was pointing at the ice cream saying '*sans uovo*', without egg – though unfortunately *sans* means 'without' in French. As Italians saw it, I was running into their shop, pointing at the ice cream and insisting 'Saint Egg'.

This had my colleagues in fits of laughter, especially as we found out that all the ice cream in town was without egg – and to this day the story is still rolled out for fun: the day that Shaunaka beatified an egg.

Dear Lord, as enthused as I am in my convictions, too often I rush into action with a poor fund of knowledge. Sometimes the results are funny but sometimes my ignorance amounts to prejudice, rash judgment and disturbance. May I take the time to think before I act and to put relationship before conviction. Hare Krishna.

BROADCAST MONDAY 24 OCTOBER 2011

October 25

Nicholas Holtam

I haven't got used to going into church since the builders have been in. It's not just that St Martin-in-the-Fields, that much-loved but dirty London church, has had a lick of paint and now looks clean. What seems to have made the biggest difference is that the coloured glass that was put in at the end of the war has been replaced by clear glass, like the Georgian original. Even with the scaffolding still up on the outside of the building, it lets in so much more light and makes the building dance, especially in the early morning.

And what I am looking forward to once the external scaffolding has come down is the visual connectedness of what happens inside the church with what's going on outside. Being able to see through the glass, above street level, should help us to pray for the needs of the city around us.

The priest and poet George Herbert wrote what has become a favourite hymn: 'Teach Me My God and King, In All Things Thee to See'. The verse that strikes me this morning is:

> A man that looks on glass,
> On it may stay his eye;
> Or if it pleaseth, through it pass,
> And then the heavens espy.

Glass separates an inner from an outer world. It reveals that there is a reality beyond the limited horizons of the present, a larger beyond from which light breaks in and gives a glimpse of eternity.

Lord God, may we delight in the rooms and buildings that set our horizons. May we learn to live together creatively in the limits of time and space, illumined by the light that comes from beyond in which we glimpse eternity. Amen.

BROADCAST THURSDAY 25 OCTOBER 2007

October 26

Stephen Shipley

Corbar Cross is a tall, simple, wooden cross erected by a group of Christians in the 1980s as a prominent landmark on a hill overlooking the Derbyshire town of Buxton, on the edge of the Peak District. It's a hill I walk my dogs up most days, but last month, just as the Pope arrived to begin his five-day visit to the UK, the cross was sawn down in protest. There's been much anger and sorrow expressed by the local people — and not only by those who go to church. For a week the cross remained where it had fallen, upside-down, spiked by metal railings, ugly and defeated. Plans are afoot, though, to replace it before too long.

One of the Buxton clergy set up a Facebook group — 'Corbar Cross Outrage' he called it — and it's provoked a lot of discussion about the cross's purpose. Some, I'm glad to say, see it not only as a symbol of suffering but also of forgiveness — and there's no doubt that good is going to come out of this whole unfortunate incident. One positive thing already is that most people aren't making sentimental assertions about the cross's function. Christians believe it was the price Jesus was willing to pay so that men and women could inherit eternal life and he had no intention of being distracted by those who would water down what it meant to follow him. He too ended up on a hill, fallen, ugly and defeated — but it didn't finish there.

At the start of another new day, we may encounter incidents that disturb, even shock us. We pray God will restore hope and peace to our troubled world, and that he will lead us through the pain of the dying Christ to the joy of his resurrection. Amen.

BROADCAST TUESDAY 26 OCTOBER 2010

October 27

Karen Smith

Theodore Roosevelt, whose birth in 1858 we remember today, was known as a person of action who tried to achieve justice and fairness at home and abroad. His efforts for world peace were recognized when he was awarded the Nobel Peace Prize in 1906.

Teddy, or TR as he was known, said on one occasion: 'In any moment of decision, the best thing you can do is the right thing, the next best thing is the wrong thing, and the worst thing you can do is nothing.'

A gregarious figure, it seemed that little could daunt Teddy Roosevelt. Yet, like most of us, he had moments when he was helpless to change his circumstances. When his wife died shortly after giving birth to their daughter, he was overwhelmed by grief and wrote in his diary: 'The light has gone out of my life.'

It seems to me that this is an apt description of the pain of bereavement. Losing someone or something we love or care for deeply may leave us feeling isolated as if somehow we are left alone in the darkness. The Psalmist knew this to be true and yet believed that God was still near: 'The Lord is my light and my salvation, whom shall I fear? The Lord is the stronghold of my life of whom shall I be afraid? ... Wait for the Lord, be strong and let your heart take courage; wait for the Lord!'

At times, of course, waiting is all we can do ... yet, in those moments, Christian faith teaches that God waits with us. While we may feel alone, God will not abandon us.

Lord, make us ready maybe to recognize You in unforeseen circumstances — and to respond. Amen.

BROADCAST TUESDAY 27 OCTOBER 2015

October 28

Stephen Shipley

Listening a few months ago to an engaging edition of Radio 4's *The Reunion* brought back many happy memories of the celebrated television drama *Brideshead Revisited*. It was filmed in the magnificent surroundings of Castle Howard in Yorkshire, and the 1981 cast list read like a roll call of the theatre world – Jeremy Irons, Anthony Andrews, Diana Quick, Claire Bloom, Laurence Olivier, John Gielgud … It attracted huge audiences and quite rightly won numerous accolades.

Evelyn Waugh, the author of the original novel, was born on this day in 1903 and he described the book's theme as 'the operation of divine grace on a group of diverse but closely connected characters.' And it's that grace which gives the story its religious dimension – the suggestion that God allows us to make or mar our lives and yet never lets us go completely. 'Underneath are the everlasting arms', as the Bible puts it. Of course we're bound to encounter some people who seem to display no sign at all of the operation of divine grace, but most of us will at some time or other have experienced a sense of wonder at the mystery of the world and of our own existence, some revelation of the meaning and possibilities of life, some feeling of being drawn to particular people.

'To know and love one other human being is the root of all wisdom,' says Charles Ryder, the narrator in Waugh's *Brideshead Revisited*. But that all turned sour for him in the novel and, at least in the short run, it led to misery and ruin. And the reason? Because he treated his earthly love as a rival to divine love instead of a pointer to it. Our relationships can often be complex interactions, too.

Let's pray that all our encounters today may be open to that grace which God promises will never fail. Amen.

BROADCAST THURSDAY 28 OCTOBER 2010

October 29

George Pitcher

Today sees the last dawn of British Summer Time and our clocks go back an hour tonight. That means that the next time I join you for *Prayer for the Day*, on Monday morning, it will effectively be around a quarter to five 'in old money', though it will be a tad lighter outside because quarter to seven will have come back to join us, if you follow me. I vow at this time of year to rise only with the sun, though I tend to drop that resolution in June.

I shouldn't really make light of the encroaching dark, though, because the hour change raises serious issues. It's said that lives could be saved by keeping lighter evenings, that Scottish agriculture would prosper and carbon emissions would be cut. Let's remember that those suffering from Seasonal Affective Disorder have a particular reason to dread this time of year.

And the seasonal mood changes for all of us, the weather and the dark make summertime seem a very distant memory. This time of the morning is often called an 'ungodly hour'. They say the darkest time is the hour before dawn — the time when the most depressing thoughts trouble us.

But there's also hope in that saying — because it tells us that however dark it gets, a new dawn *will* come. So let's take that thought and roll with the season and take to heart the words of the Minnie Louise Haskins poem: 'Go out into the darkness and put your hand into the Hand of God. That shall be to you better than light and safer than a known way.'

Let's pray for God's strength in the shortening days ahead, confident in the knowledge that there is a light in our lives that no darkness can extinguish. Amen.

BROADCAST SATURDAY 29 OCTOBER 2011

October 30

Karen Smith

On this day in 1960, Sir Michael Woodruff performed the first successful kidney transplant in the UK. Discovering that one of his patients had an identical twin brother, and believing that this might reduce the risk of rejection, the operation was successfully undertaken.

Today, transplants are carried out on a regular basis in hospitals around the world. While organ donation is a personal choice and not everyone may feel able to be a donor, the gift certainly offers life and hope to another person.

Many years, ago, I met a woman, Mary, who had given one of her kidneys to an older man in her church. Apparently, he had a very rare blood type, which at the time made it difficult to find a donor. When Mary discovered that she had the same blood type, without hesitation she volunteered to help. Some time after the operation, I met her and listened as she spoke about her experience. At the time, I remember being struck, not just by the fact that the gift had been given freely or even sacrificially, but by its cost.

The idea of costly giving is something we may not consider very often. Yet Christian faith teaches that generosity is not without a price. Love often requires that we give up something in order to be able to give: the loss of a grudge in order to forgive, forgetting the slight in order to restore a relationship. Love can hurt.

Jesus knew this to be true and yet constantly challenged his disciples to love more. 'A new commandment I give to you,' he said, 'that you love one another; just as I have loved you, you also are to love one another.'

We thank you, O Lord, for those who by word or deed have reminded us of the nature of love. Amen.

BROADCAST FRIDAY 30 OCTOBER 2015

October 31

Roger Hutchings

I suppose if you're a child, and someone's bought you a pumpkin and a mask, you may be looking forward to tonight. If you're a particular kind of grown-up, well, I gather Hallowe'en costumes for parties are all the rage. But then if you're elderly and live on your own, perhaps you view the prospect of 'trick or treat' with little enthusiasm.

Long ago, Christians tried to take over a pagan festival marking the end of summer by nominating November 1 as All Saints' Day, or All Hallows', so tonight is the eve of All Hallows' — Hallowe'en. The process has backfired a little, though, with a whole industry providing spooky stuff of all kinds. Indeed, some Christians feel that it encourages young people to dabble with potentially dangerous forces, and a number of churches put on special 'safe' parties to try to prevent this. Others feel it's harmless fun.

Beyond our shores, All Saints' is a public holiday for many of our continental neighbours, when whole families, including children, will visit the graves of their ancestors, and place chrysanthemums and other flowers in their churchyards.

There are, then, many reasons to offer prayers today — for children, that they may be kept from harm, for the lonely or weak, that they may not be afraid. We can pray too for ourselves, so that we may continue to learn from the saints who have lived before us. In the Book of Revelation, there's a verse that describes the song of the saints and martyrs in the presence of God: it can be on our lips this morning.

'Blessing and glory and wisdom and thanksgiving and honour and power and might be to our God for ever and ever!' Amen.

BROADCAST SATURDAY 31 OCTOBER 2009

November 1

Neil Gardner

This summer I visited Seton Collegiate Church in East Lothian for the first but certainly not the last time. Though no longer in use as a regular place of worship, the church occupies a peaceful woodland setting, all beautifully maintained by Historic Scotland. Dating from the 15th century, it was more intact than I expected, and contains a number of fascinating monuments, one of which in particular caught my eye. It was erected by Lady Isabel Seton in memory of her husband James, the first Earl of Perth, who died at Seton in 1611 'in the twentieth year of his age' and contains the following inscription by William Drummond of Hawthornden:

> Insteed of epitaphes and airye praise,
> This monument a lady chaste did raise
> To her lord's living fame, and, after death,
> Her bodye doth unto this place bequeath,
> To rest with his till God's shrill trumpet sound;
> Thogh tyme her lyf, no tyme her love can bound.

It's a charming verse which seems particularly appropriate for this All Saints' Day, when we are encouraged to remember and give thanks for all those whose lives were bound by time, but whose love, influence and example are boundless. Though time her life, no time her love can bound.

Almighty God, we give special thanks today for all those who have gone before us — for those who led saintly lives and are obviously to be admired; and for those too who in quiet and unassuming ways have left us an example to follow. Give us grace to do that in this life, that we might come to share with them the joys of that life which are everlasting. Amen.

BROADCAST THURSDAY 1 NOVEMBER 2012

November 2

Shaunaka Rishi Das

I was born in the small Irish town of Wexford, a sea-faring and market town of about 15,000 people. We were a Catholic community. There was a scattering of Protestants among us who, though thin on the ground, were conspicuous because for us they were different. Not that there was anything wrong with them – just different.

Although this seemed a tolerant understanding, it formed a strong impression in my mind for, as a child, difference feeds every possibility, all abnormal – as we were normal, and they were not.

One Sunday, my father took two of my siblings and me off to mass, as was normal, but we didn't go to our usual church in Rowe Street. We went to the chapel at the end of the street, St Iberius's, the Protestant church. We had never been inside this building; it belonged to *them*. My father asked permission of the vicar for us to attend. We went to the gallery and sat there throughout the service. He told us to be silent and not to utter a sound – in effect to be as respectful as we would be in our own church.

After the service my father took us outside and said, 'Now, was that very different from a mass in Rowe Street Church?' We all agreed that it wasn't, and he said, 'So there, Protestants are not very different', and that was that.

We all traipsed home for Sunday dinner, slightly bewildered, but clear that we were not very different. This simple experience has helped me to always question my prejudice and explore difference, and I owe a lot to my father for his wisdom.

Thank You, Lord, for such a guide and for feeding so many new possibilities in my life by making difference normal. Hare Krishna.

BROADCAST TUESDAY 2 NOVEMBER 2010

November 3

George Pitcher

We do find it easy to judge our world leaders. We'll decide they're good or bad as easily as we judge pubs or television programmes. Take a couple of American presidents.

It's exactly 75 years to the day that Franklin D Roosevelt was elected by a landslide in 1936 to serve his second term as President of the United States. And today is also the seventh anniversary of George W Bush winning *his* second term as President.

The two leaders are separated by half a century and faced very different worlds, but I think I can guess how we would rank them. Roosevelt, the great World War II leader, supporting Britain through Lend Lease and then joining America to the heroic battle to drive the Nazis from Europe, is likely to appear near the top of the presidential league. Bush, committing America to controversial wars in Afghanistan and Iraq, is likely at the moment to appear somewhat lower in the popular presidents' league.

But these aren't contestants on *The X Factor*. Let's remember that both presidents took their country to war in the wake of direct attacks on the United States – Roosevelt after Pearl Harbour, Bush after the 9/11 terrorist assaults on New York and the Pentagon. We're entitled to consider whether they got those judgement calls right, but that's not an end to it.

Ultimately, we should be less hasty to judge the men than to learn from their actions.

Let's pray that today's leaders do learn from the great conflicts of the past, that decisions to wage war are always and only taken as a last resort and to protect the world from danger. And that we all honour those lives that have been laid down in previous conflicts by continually striving for God's peace, building His kingdom here on earth. Amen.

BROADCAST THURSDAY 3 NOVEMBER 2011

November 4

Leslie Griffiths

The moat of the Tower of London is filling with poppies — ceramic poppies — one for each of the 888,246 British and colonial service men and women who died in World War I. The visual effect is overwhelming; it resembles a rising tide, a surge of colour, a stark reminder of the heavy cost of war. In this centenary year, the promise to remember them seems to have added poignancy and urgency.

Today marks the anniversary of the death of a man commemorated by one of those poppies, the poet Wilfred Owen; he died just one week before the end of the war. He was decorated for his courage in the heat of battle. But his poetry speaks of the horrors experienced in the trenches — the wailing of shells, the monstrous anger of the guns and the stuttering rifles' rapid rattle. And also the separating of lovers, the holy glimmers of goodbyes and, each slow dusk, the drawing down of blinds.

The consolations of religion meant little to Wilfred Owen. Its prayers and rituals seemed to him so hollow. That echoes my own experience at the very beginning of my ministry. Whenever I'd visit the geriatric men's ward of our local hospital, I'd be greeted by a chorus of baleful comments from a small handful of veterans of World War I who, the minute they saw my clerical collar, erupted against me. War empties life of meaning; it robs men and women of their humanity. We must surely resolve to work for the day when swords will be beaten into ploughshares, spears into pruning hooks, and peace prevails.

Dear Lord, make me a channel of Your peace. Where there is hatred, let me bring Your love. For Christ's sake, Amen.

BROADCAST TUESDAY 4 NOVEMBER 2014

November 5

Roger Hutchings

As the fireworks fill the night sky tonight, and the noise reaches into our homes, not many, I think, will be remembering that there are religious overtones to the occasion. The people of Lewes remember, though: because Protestants were martyred there in 1555 and for years they have burned on 5 November not only Guy Fawkes (who was a Roman Catholic) but also images of the Pope. I'm not a Catholic, but if I were, I'd be deeply saddened by that. In fact, I *am* both saddened and offended by it.

Burning an effigy of the Pope is just one example of the negative ways in which people keep alive the divisions of the past and the prejudices of the present. It makes little difference whether those divisions are political, military or religious, or whether, as is often the case, they're a complicated mixture of all three. It makes no difference whether the prejudices are to do with class, race or beliefs. They can be reinforced for each generation, and perhaps even more importantly, they can be passed on to the next generation. Fireworks, marches, demonstrations, even folksongs can all have that kind of influence.

It hardly seems necessary to spell it out, but we each have a responsibility in this — to learn from the past, of course, but then to leave behind what can mar or destroy good relationships for the future. The Christian agenda is about understanding, forgiving, finding ways to restore what's damaged or broken. As St Paul puts it, 'put away from you all bitterness and wrath' and 'do not let the sun go down on your anger'. Perhaps we can remember those words as the sun goes down and the fireworks come out tonight.

Grant us, O God, the grace to overcome past ills and to forgive one another as in Christ we have been forgiven. Amen.

BROADCAST THURSDAY 5 NOVEMBER 2009

November 6

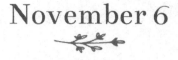

Leslie Griffiths

Memory's a strange and wonderful thing. Just consider this. A letter arrives in the post. I don't have to open it to know who it's from; the handwriting gives the game away. As soon as I see the envelope, I can picture the person who wrote it, someone who's known me since I was a child. At the very sight of it, warm and vivid memories flood into my mind. Before I start to read, I've been transported back in time. See what I mean?

And I could add so many examples to show the way apparently innocuous events are charged with the possibility of opening our minds, awakening us to old pleasures (or fears, of course) and reminding us that the past hasn't gone forever. It lurks barely below the rim of our consciousness, just waiting for its moment to greet us. It could be a place we pass through, a snatch of music we hear, someone's face, the bite of an apple — any one of so many things that releases an energy we didn't know existed.

It isn't that our minds stretch back to a disappearing past; it's more the past rising up to claim the present. I get this feeling every time I take bread and wine in a service of Holy Communion. 'This do in remembrance of me,' Jesus said, and those words do the trick every time. Time isn't just an ever-rolling stream that bears us all away. It's with us, in us, around us, bubbling away beneath the surface and always waiting to surprise us.

Dear Lord, live with us today, go with us into the day's work. Give us a sense of Your abiding presence with us in all we do. We thank You for all that is past and trust You for all that is to come. Amen.

BROADCAST THURSDAY 6 NOVEMBER 2014

November 7

Jasdeep Singh Rahal

From the middle of next week it will be Diwali: one of the major festivals
celebrated worldwide by Hindus, Sikhs and Jains. Each year, for five days,
clay lamps filled with oil are lit and adorn houses, shops and Hindu temples
to welcome Lakshmi, the goddess of wealth and happiness. For Hindus, the
festival also commemorates the return of Lord Rama after 14 years of exile,
during which he had fought and defeated the demon king, Ravana. On Rama's
return, people were joyous and lit their houses to celebrate his victory over evil.
a victory of light over darkness.

In this season of Remembrance, we recall how light has triumphed in other
dark times. Researching for the British Army Museum, I discovered that Hindu
soldiers formed the majority of the British Indian Army in World War I. Many
of these men were decorated for their acts of valour and bravery.

In the battle of Cambrai one November night in 1917, with his regiment cut
off and surrounded by the enemy — under fire, and across a six-mile stretch of
open ground — one Hindu soldier managed to deliver and return a vital message
to brigade headquarters. For this action, Gobind Singh Rathore was awarded
the Victoria Cross: Britain's highest award for gallantry.

The Diwali message of victory of good over evil is a metaphor for the conflict in our own
lives. Let us strive with courage to fight and win the internal battle between light and
darkness within our own minds.

BROADCAST SATURDAY 7 NOVEMBER 2015

November 8

Sam Wells

I had a cousin who was a few years older than me. When my cousin was four, a consultant told my aunt, 'This boy is severely autistic. You must bring him up like a dog.' So that's exactly what my aunt did, with clear instructions, routines and disciplines.

My cousin died ten years ago aged 46. At his funeral the reserved front rows were not well filled. The wider family had never got over the original diagnosis, and few had formed a real relationship with him. But the rest of the church was packed with friends and acquaintances.

Witness after witness came forward to tell of how my cousin sang so gladly in the choir that his expression was an icon; of how he played the piano with such gusto it gave others the courage to try; of how he delivered the daily papers to the old folks' home with faithfulness and cheerfulness. Was this really the person I had always been a bit scared of and was later taught to feel sorry for?

At the end of the service, my bewildered father glanced from the full-to-bursting body of the church to the empty reserved front pews with a tear in his eye. 'Look at all these people,' he said. 'They knew who he was. They saw who he was. We were told to see him as a dog. We never saw him until today – until he died. And then today we truly saw him, for the first time, in the community he created around him.'

God of mercy and grace, be close to all who live with a severe mental or developmental disability, and with all whose lives are lived alongside them. Make them a blessing to all Your people, and show us Your face in theirs. Amen.

BROADCAST THURSDAY 8 NOVEMBER 2012

November 9

David Anderson

Kabul is a city that sounds like it ought to be sneezed out when you speak its name. Given the air quality we're experiencing on our current operational tour of the city, this analogy seems fitting. *Dust on the Paw* is a novel written by Robin Jenkins, the Scottish author, about life in Kabul in the 1950s. It reflects on the ethnic, sectarian, political and cultural differences of the people and the place through the lens of the political and diplomatic life in the British Embassy. It might have been written for today. The phrase 'dust on the paw' comes from the 11th-century Persian poet Firdausi. He writes: 'the powerful ones of the earth were the lion's paw, and the humble the dust on it.'

As we reflect on remembrance this week, and on moving on from Afghanistan after 12 years here, and having sacrificed much in blood and treasure, many wonder quite what will happen to the dust on the paw, those humble souls and innocents who have suffered and sought to build a brighter future. What of Shabib, the six-year-old girl, minus a limb, some fingers, an eye? What of a woman called Rooh Gul Hizard, a lawmaker and politician whose eight-year-old daughter was killed in an attack? What of those locally employed civilians who have humbly supported the campaign of the International Security Assistance Force?

Holy Scripture reminds us that even those considered dust on the paw are important in God's eyes.

Lord God, we pray for the peoples and the future peace of Afghanistan. We remember those who have given all and suffered much. Remind us of Your grace and help us all to continue to work for the glory of Your Kingdom, a Kingdom where the dust on the paw has a future and a hope. Amen.

BROADCAST SATURDAY 9 NOVEMBER 2013

November 10

Nigel McCulloch

For the last few years, on this Saturday before Remembrance Sunday, it's been my privilege to conduct the worship that concludes the Royal British Legion's Festival of Remembrance, to be broadcast tonight from the Royal Albert Hall.

This year's festival includes St Richard's famous prayer (which I'll use as today's prayer), favourite hymns ('How Great Thou Art', 'When I Survey the Wondrous Cross', 'Eternal Father, Strong to Save') and the traditional act of remembrance itself, when during the two minutes silence in poignant memory of the Fallen, from high up in the Albert Hall, countless poppies are released – many of them coming to rest on serving members of today's forces mustered below.

The Legion is the guardian of the nation's remembrance. Not everyone knows that it's also one of our largest welfare organizations, caring not only for bereaved families, but also for the men and women who survived, many with physical and mental injury. In fact over 20 million people are eligible for help from the Legion – including, of course, the bereaved and survivors of the many conflicts since 1945 to today's action in Iraq and Afghanistan.

May our acts of remembrance this weekend blend with prayer for our troops out there who, in the face of war and terror, as so many before them, bravely put service before self.

Teach us, good Lord, to serve Thee as Thou deservest; to give and not to count the cost; to fight and not to heed the wounds; to toil and not to seek for rest; to labour and not to ask for any reward, save that of knowing that we do Thy will. Amen.

BROADCAST SATURDAY 10 NOVEMBER 2007

November 11

Jasdeep Singh Rahal

This year, Armistice Day falls on the same day as Diwali, the Indian festival of light. Many people of Indian descent will be lighting lamps for Diwali, which will also commemorate their ancestors among the Commonwealth and Indian troops who served and died alongside the British during the Great War. It's a role that's not widely known and that's sometimes overlooked, although the British Indian Army served in all major theatres of World War I, including the Western Front, Gallipoli, East Africa, Salonika and Mesopotamia – with 11 Indian soldiers being awarded the Victoria Cross.

A century ago, undivided India comprised modern-day India, Pakistan, Bangladesh, Burma and Sri Lanka. Soldiers in the British Indian Army were recruited from the so-called 'martial races', including Sikhs, Gurkhas and Punjabi Muslims, as well as Hindu Dogras and Rajputs. They came from a variety of religions and cultures, and spoke many languages.

At the outbreak of the war, the Indian Army had 240,000 men. By the war's end, more than 1.5 million Indians had volunteered for service – a larger number than from the rest of the dominions and colonies combined, and second only to those enlisting from the British Isles.

Today we mark the contribution of all those who served as brothers in arms during the Great War – from the British 'Tommy' to the Indian sepoy. This was truly a world war, fought in all areas by men from across the globe.

Let us remember the dead, injured and bereaved of all wars. The contribution of those who served and fell in the Great War knows no boundaries of race, class or religion, and their sacrifice has lit the way for our society today.

BROADCAST WEDNESDAY 11 NOVEMBER 2015

November 12

Anna Magnusson

Everyone remembers their childhood bedroom. Because I'm from a big family, I shared a room for many years with my older sister. At night we used to lie in bed and talk about television programmes, hockey and food. Then my sister would switch off her light, snuggle down and announce, 'I think I'll dream about Captain Kirk tonight', and she'd describe the latest storyline she'd made up, which featured her in a starring role in *Star Trek*.

I remember the sounds of sharing a bedroom. On dark winter mornings, if I was ill and staying off school, I'd hear my sister get up in the dark and I could follow every step of her getting dressed just by the sounds, until, finally, she'd brush her hair violently, with several big rasping, scratchy noises, and clatter downstairs.

I remember the posters above my bed, and the ones my sister had. I remember when we got a new purple carpet and purple bedspreads – it was the 1970s, after all. I remember hearing the creak on the stair as Mum came up to say goodnight to us.

The grandchildren stay in my old bedroom now when they visit my mother. The posters, and the desks where my sister and I did our homework, are gone. All kinds of stuff from other parts of the house are stored in the room now, but in my memory it's unchanged and intact. The *real* room, and that part of my life with my sister, is inside me. That is the beautiful, wondrous gift of memory: to be able to live beyond the present, and understand more than this moment.

God, who is timeless and yet near, be in our present and in our past today, as we experience both. Amen.

BROADCAST WEDNESDAY 12 NOVEMBER 2008

November 13

Nigel McCulloch

It's a sobering fact that none of the world's major religions began in Europe. The main faiths in this country have been imported. The result: a rich mix that gives opportunities for people whose faiths are different to get to know one another, and to bring about a style of dialogue that helps differences to be honoured and shared values strengthened.

As a Christian I've made good friendships with people of other faiths, and certainly learned and gained from them, without compromising the truth of my Christian faith.

I still believe that Jesus is the Way, the Truth and the Life. But my own experience of personal dialogue has helped me to see that God also makes himself known beyond Christian boundaries. William Temple, the 20th-century Archbishop of Canterbury, wrote: 'There is only one Divine Light and every person in their measure is enlightened by it.' In other words, God doesn't confine himself to one religion; though for me the distinctively Christian insight about the nature of God is clear. What is he like? God is Christ-like – and every Christian is called to be like Christ.

If only we were! As the Hindu Mahatma Gandhi said: 'If all Christians really were like Christ, the whole world would become Christian.'

Last week, at the Festival of Remembrance, when young people of different faiths happily took part in the service, I thought how much better it would be if many more people of different faiths, without losing their separate integrity, could cross boundaries to engage personally with one another. Given the make-up of our 21st-century society, not to do so is such a shame.

O Lord our God, help us to see that we make Your love too narrow by false limits of our own. Amen.

BROADCAST THURSDAY 13 NOVEMBER 2014

November 14

Anna Magnusson

When my nephew was five, he said to me one morning as I looked out his clothes, 'Is it a school day?' He had forgotten – or rather, school was only one possibility in a world as yet fluid and unformed. In that instant I realized how distant my childhood was, like a far-off planet.

How glorious to wake up in the morning and not know everything about what the day is likely to bring. To be free of the memory of the habits and repeated patterns of living that adhere like barnacles as we grow older. It makes me smile to think of how much unfilled memory-space children have, and how they can revel in the open ranges of their imaginations – what Wordsworth called 'the might of heaven-born freedom'.

We grow up, we get older. We shrink the world to fit us, to something we can cope with. Sometimes we're weighed down by our past and fearful of the future, and the childhood planet of infinite possibility and unconscious hopefulness has vanished. But deep inside us the mysterious experience of childhood survives. It flits through us in sudden, powerful memories, and lingers around us like a breath. It is not lost.

Wordsworth's lines from 'Intimations of Immortality' are a kind of prayer to that inextinguishable life:

> *'Those shadowy recollections,*
> *Which, be they what they may,*
> *Are yet the fountain-light of all our day,*
> *Are yet a master-light of our all seeing;*
> *Uphold us, cherish, and have power to make*
> *Our noisy years seem moments in the being*
> *Of the eternal Silence: truths that wake,*
> *To perish never.' Amen.*

BROADCAST FRIDAY 14 NOVEMBER 2008

November 15

Mary Stallard

Is it 'scon(e)s' or 'scones'? You say 'tomatoes' – I pronounce them correctly!
We're all familiar with the humour that comes from words that are said
differently; and the embarrassment, annoyance and confusion when a different
usage or pronunciation leads to miscommunication or even causes offence.

Words are immensely rich in the quest to find meaning and to express
ourselves. Different cultures, their dialects and language, add to the range and
depth of understanding.

My teenage daughter recently discovered this in a light-hearted conversation
with a German friend she met on a school trip. They keep in touch online and
recently simultaneously 'liked' something on a social networking site. 'Two great
minds think alike!' commented Joanna. Her friend instantly responded that in
German they'd say, 'Two idiots and a single thought!' – an opposite reflection,
each culture opening up an alternative perspective. This is surely one of the gifts
of language.

Words, as signposts to fresh ideas, reveal much about our underlying
thoughts and judgements: the tone of voice, the accent and inflection, as well
as the actual terms we choose, contribute to a bigger conversation about who we
are, where we're from and what we value.

There's something holy about language for Christians for whom God is
revealed as 'the Word' in Jesus, and who, as creator, brings everything into
being through speaking. The Bible urges us to use language with reverence.
According to the Book of Proverbs, the 'words of the wise soothe and heal'
and the letter of James identifies our untameable tongues as the most powerful
organ of our bodies.

*Gracious God, thank You for the gifts of words and language. Help me to speak with care
today, to listen to those I meet, and notice opportunities to learn and grow. Amen.*

BROADCAST SATURDAY 15 NOVEMBER 2014

November 16

Frances Finn

A few months ago I took a good look at my, well, 'fleshy' excesses and, like so many others this year, embarked upon the fashionable regime of fasting. Two days each week of eating very little, and five days of eating sensibly. And it worked. In the absence of scales, the ends of the knotted piece of string I was using round my waist began to overlap, and an inch or two later, I felt much better.

Those days of fasting gave me a couple of new insights. The first was how much more I tend eat than I *need* to in order to feel sated. The second was how cold I felt when my body hadn't had enough food. At night I'd often get out of bed and put my dressing-gown on, and then sausage-roll myself in the duvet to keep warm. I found that without fuel my body struggles to heat itself.

With high energy and food prices, I'm now a little more conscious of what some might be going through behind closed doors — those who are becoming steadily exhausted by meagre meals and cold rooms.

In my city of Nottingham, churches running food banks are working together to make sure there's at least one open *somewhere* in the city every day of the week. And what I call 'pop-up' shelters are being run in church halls for five months until March. Thanks to volunteers, air beds are put on floors and hot meals are served.

But that will only scratch the surface of need. And when so much suffering is happening in silence, it's hard to reach. Especially if pride or embarrassment get in the way of asking for help.

Father God, help us to see the needs in our communities. Give us a heart that cares, the energy to respond and the inspiration to know how. Amen.

BROADCAST SATURDAY 16 NOVEMBER 2013

November 17

Jeremy Morris

One of my favourite words is 'ordinary'. That's not because I'm uninterested in the dramatic, or the unexpected, or the unusual. It's because I want to see the ordinary things of life as transfused with the beauty and richness of the God who made the world — because, after all, if I can't see God in the ordinary things of life, I'm condemned to live in a very bleak and boring world, relieved only by an occasional interruption, an occasional outburst of the surprising or remarkable.

The poet George Herbert knew about this all too well. In his poem 'Prayer', among a succession of images in which he tries to describe what prayer is like, he has the lines 'Exalted Manna, gladness of the best, Heaven in ordinarie, man well drest'. Prayer for Herbert is the presence of Heaven itself in the ordinary speech of human life.

If we follow George Herbert, prayer is like the coming of Christ into the world, the Word made flesh. For Christians, the central fact of the drama of redemption is God's sending of His Son into the ordinary conditions of human life. God comes into the world in Christ. He descends to ordinary human life, and makes it extraordinary.

Our lives, then, are touched at every point by the presence of God. Often it doesn't feel like that, it's true. Yet nothing in all creation, St Paul says, can separate us from the love of God in Christ Jesus. Not even ordinary life.

Guide us, Lord, as we struggle to make sense of our world. Be with us as we face a new day, and teach us to understand Your will and to see the miracle of Your presence in the ordinary and the extraordinary alike. Amen.

BROADCAST WEDNESDAY 17 NOVEMBER 2010

November 18

Tony Macaulay

Mark Twain's story 'The Celebrated Jumping Frog of Calaveras County' was published on this day in 1865. It was his first great success as a writer and brought him national attention. He went on to be lauded as the greatest American humourist of his age and his words of wit and satire are much quoted to this day. One of my favourite Mark Twain quotes is 'Writing is easy. All you have to do is cross out the wrong words.' It's clear that the great teller of the stories of Tom Sawyer and Huckleberry Finn understood the power of words.

I believe in the power of stories to change the world. Since earliest times, human beings have sat down in a circle around a fire and told each other stories. And the stories they told defined who they were, what they believed, what was right and what was wrong. I recently led a storytelling workshop with international students in Germany. We explored the role of storytelling in peace building in countries experiencing conflict.

It was remarkable to hear people from Syria, Bosnia, Nigeria and Iran describe the ancient storytelling tradition in their own culture and to hear how today's generation around the world is using digital media to share their stories. The students shared their own compelling stories of peace and reconciliation.

There's a Native American saying that 'It takes a thousand voices to tell a single story.' I believe we can create a web of stories on a massive scale to change the accepted narrative from war to peace, and without dropping a single bomb. That's the power of words.

Lord God, inspire us today to share stories of hope and forgiveness that move us away from war and toward peace. Amen.

BROADCAST WEDNESDAY 18 NOVEMBER 2015

November 19

Martyn Atkins

Personally, I'm not one for buying lottery tickets. Perhaps it's because my wider family has had its fair share of problems with gambling down the years. So I know I'll never win the National Lottery, which began this day in 1994, whatever the odds!

Lotteries do give millions of pounds away, of course. A while ago I went to a meeting where a winsome speaker informed us of the multiple millions that had been given to undoubtedly good causes. And I'm deeply aware that many churches have successfully bid for money raised through lotteries in order to do some stunningly good work in localities around the country. One minister said to me recently that he'd prefer it wasn't money sourced from gambling, 'but if money's there, we'll take it and use it for good'. Holy pragmatism or a Christian lack of integrity? – discuss.

Someone I know who works for a big charity is clear in his opinion that, alongside the effects of recession, large amounts of money previously given directly to such charities are now spent on tickets for various lotteries.

What is clear, whether it be a large lottery for many millions of pounds or a church tombola for a packet of pasta, is that we stand to get something rather than nothing. We are not, in the deliberately jumbled words of the great prayer of St Ignatius, 'giving and not seeking any reward'.

The scriptures are quite clear about giving generously to the poor and needy, but also clear about the motives for giving: the gift benefits others; the motive benefits the giver.

Generous God, who urges us to love mercy and act justly, to give as we have received, to do good and love our neighbour, guide our giving and our motives as we live out our lives today. Amen.

BROADCAST MONDAY 19 NOVEMBER 2012

November 20

Mary Stallard

My family often teases me about the huge bunch of church keys I carry around like a stereotypical gaoler, but at least keeping them all together makes them harder to lose. Keys may be small in size, but they're hugely important for the smooth running of our lives.

They're often seen as a symbol of power: I once knew a parish where a member of the congregation wielded tight control over her village by closely guarding access to the church key; so every baptism, wedding and funeral depended upon her willingness to unlock the doors. When a new vicar arrived, and opened another church building, lots of keys were cut for the new door and given to many people in the community. The previous idea that, the building needed to be protected above all, was suddenly transformed by a new understanding of the church as a place of welcome.

Jesus says to Peter in Matthew's Gospel, 'I will give you the keys of the kingdom of heaven', and gives him power to 'bind and loose things on earth and in heaven'. These words are symbolized by two crossed keys used in papal coats of arms and in the heraldic shields of dioceses including my own in St Asaph. Although these keys have different functions — one unlocks, the other binds — intriguingly they're both the same shape.

We start or stop engines and open or lock doors with the keys in our pockets. But we also figuratively open and close spaces and commence or halt activity by the way we allow and prevent people from having their say, coming close to us or contributing to whatever's happening.

Living God, help me make wise choices today. Make me aware of the effect of what I say and do upon others, and enable me to be more responsive to the needs of those around me. Amen.

BROADCAST THURSDAY 20 NOVEMBER 2014

November 21

Martyn Atkins

I give blood but I'm not a blood donor — yet. You see, I *have* to give blood two or three times a year in order to rid myself of excessive and destructive iron. Trips to my local hospital aren't exactly the highlight of my year, but I'm grateful to the wonderful staff there for their endless patience toward a squeamish patient!

But what has always annoyed me is that my iron-rich blood is just destroyed: my condition has meant it can't be used. I've been in the day ward more than once next to a pallid patient receiving blood for severe anaemia. We've joked about just setting up a line between the two of us. He'd feel better, and so would I, realizing that this precious, life-giving commodity was not heading straight for the incinerator.

But just the other day, I learned something wonderful from a senior person in the NHS blood services. The authorities have recently decided that people with my condition can become blood donors. And given that we need ever more blood donors in order to help and heal each other, I'm really thrilled.

I could launch into deep theology — but it's far too early in the morning! But what a difference it makes to know that rather than being wasted, my blood can be used for good. Because blood given for others, enabling new life, is at the heart of our Christian faith, demonstrating God's love for us all in Christ.

Gracious God, who in Jesus pours out his life that we might live, have mercy on those whose blood is shed in violence today, those who donate and receive blood, and those who organize and administer these processes of gift and life. Amen.

BROADCAST WEDNESDAY 21 NOVEMBER 2012

November 22

Stephen Shipley

I've just spent a few days in the vibrant, bustling city of New York, its streets teeming with diverse life — be it a focused crowd of financial traders marching with anxious faces toward the Stock Exchange district or a carefree group of teenagers rollerskating round the leafy bridleways of Central Park. It's a city that also prides itself on being the cultural capital of the world. And certainly this will be apparent in this coming week, when Americans celebrate Thanksgiving Day — together with a new optimism evident after the recent presidential election. Despite the credit crunch, there's a sense of wellbeing that is both buoyant and infectious. It's also St Cecilia's Day today, the patron saint of music, so my daily reflections this week take a musical theme and reflect the variety of sounds I experienced in that restless metropolis.

The American conductor and composer Leonard Bernstein would have been 90 years old this year — and the prestigious Carnegie Hall in New York is at the moment presenting a tribute to the man who feared that posterity would remember him solely as the composer of *West Side Story*. Toward the end of his life, though, he wrote a huge *Concerto for Orchestra*, which was played last Sunday afternoon. What was so telling was the influence of the Hebrew scriptures on Bernstein, and particularly his setting in the last movement of the familiar words, 'May the Lord bless you and keep you; may He make His face shine upon you.' It reminded me that behind this beautiful world is a benevolent creator. And even when that beauty is disfigured — so often by selfishness and greed — God still immerses himself in our humanity.

So thank You, Lord, for those moments of sudden understanding and joy, a blink of heaven, especially through Your gift of music. Keep us trusting in You — even when discords shake our security. Amen.

BROADCAST SATURDAY 22 NOVEMBER 2008

November 23

Ibrahim Mogra

In the past I might have thought of any scruffy but reasonably healthy-looking person asking for change in the high street as lazy and not bothered to work or find work. But now, with the lack of jobs and the continuing loss of jobs, I try to be careful not to dismiss those who genuinely deserve and require some help. At the same time, I also want to be careful not to be encouraging, along with many other kind people, a habit of begging and dependency.

But then what help is there for the millions of street-dwellers who genuinely have no choice but to roam the cities of the world in search of scraps of food by day and shelter by night? The Qur'an says: 'Woe be to the one who does not encourage or organize the feeding of the poor and needy and refuses even the smallest help.' I remember how Muhammad (peace be upon Him) had helped a beggar. He had made him sell his last possessions and instructed him to purchase an axe with the money. Muhammad then sent him to the woods to collect firewood for sale. The man returned after a few days to thank him that he was now self-employed and self-sufficient and was able to look after his family. Muhammad said, 'It is more honourable for you to work than to beg and depend on others.'

Dear God, give us the strength and the opportunity to earn our daily bread by our hands in an honest way. We ask You to feed the poor, clothe the naked, grant shelter to the homeless, secure people's jobs and help the unemployed find work. Amin.

BROADCAST WEDNESDAY 23 NOVEMBER 2011

November 24

Glenn Jordan

Freddie Mercury, the lead singer with the rock band Queen, died on this day in 1991 just one day after he announced he was HIV positive.

I remember it was Paul, my neighbour, and just a year older than me, who introduced me to Queen and Freddie's wonderful voice. Paul had the full collection of all the vinyl albums and talked endlessly of the band to all who would listen.

And I think of the Live Aid concert in 1985. Mercury's career had stalled a bit by that stage but was re-energized by his performance that day. I remember him beginning their set on the piano playing the opening chords of 'Bohemian Rhapsody'. I remember him prancing across the stage leading the 72,000-strong crowd in the chorus of 'Radio Gaga'.

It is said that Queen's sound engineer switched off the limiters that had been installed on Wembley Stadium's sound system to ensure that Queen's performance was the loudest. Their 20-minute set has been voted the most stunning live performance ever.

Freddie Mercury once said, 'Success has brought me world idolization and millions of pounds. But it has prevented me from having the one thing we all need: a loving, ongoing relationship. Love is Russian roulette for me.' But I love the fact that, when faced with a second chance on that stage at Wembley, a chance to reignite his career, he grabbed it with both hands and blew us all away.

God of the second chances, give us the chance today to do and say the things we should have done and said yesterday. Give us the courage to start anew, to forgive those who have hurt us. Amen.

BROADCAST MONDAY 24 NOVEMBER 2014

November 25

Rebecca Pippert

I'm an American. My husband and I have lived predominately in the UK for several years and of course we love the history, the beautiful buildings and English manners! We've learned important lessons: I no longer say 'I'm mad!' when I'm actually cross, and I've learned the hard way to ask for 'jam' and not 'jelly' on my toast at breakfast.

Today is a special day for Americans. It's Thanksgiving, when families celebrate and feast on turkey, sweet potatoes, cranberry sauce and pumpkin pie. Thanksgiving is a holiday where the sole purpose is to be grateful for our blessings.

The Bible is filled with calls to be grateful. Why is gratitude so important? Because life is a gift and God is good. 'Give thanks to the Lord for He is good and his love endures forever.'

The Bible says the path to gratitude lies in 'remembering'. We remember the good things of the past and we express gratitude for our present blessings. When we fill our minds with gratitude it makes it almost impossible to be ill-tempered, anxious or self-pitying.

Entitlement and envy will block gratitude. We become resentful because we feel we deserve better. We look over our shoulder and believe someone has what we should have. But no one's life is as it appears. We all have our own unique pressures and pain. It's foolish to want to be someone else — that's simply exchanging our set of problems for theirs.

Lord, we thank You for Your goodness to us in the past. We're so grateful for Your blessings today. And we trust You for our future. Amen.

BROADCAST WEDNESDAY 25 NOVEMBER 2015

November 26

Karen Smith

Sojourner Truth died on 26 November 1883. Born into slavery in New York, at nine years of age she was taken from her parents and sold at auction and then sold a further three times before she was able to gain her freedom. She was abused, beaten and forced to bear children who were taken from her and in turn made slaves.

After gaining freedom, and prompted by a religious experience in which she claimed to have been 'overwhelmed with the greatness of the Divine presence', Sojourner travelled to tell others the truth about slavery. Fearless in her desire for freedom, she believed with the Apostle Paul that there is neither male nor female, slave nor free, but in Christ we are all one. In 1851, Sojourner Truth attended a convention on women's rights in Akron, Ohio. When she heard that men claimed that women were too weak to vote, she delivered her famous 'Ain't I a woman?' speech:

'I have plowed, and planted, and gathered into barns … And ain't I a woman? I could work as much and eat as much as a man (when I could get it), and bear the lash as well! And ain't I a woman? I have borne 13 children and seen most all sold off to slavery and when I cried out with my mother's grief, none but Jesus heard me! And ain't I a woman?'

When she finished, people were stunned by her words. Although unable to read and an ex-slave, Sojourner Truth was a voice for freedom for all.

Thank you, Lord, for all those who refused to allow adversity to break their spirit. Give us courage to work for equality for all people. We ask it in the name of Jesus Christ who came to bring good news to the poor, to proclaim release to the captives and to let the oppressed go free. Amen.

BROADCAST FRIDAY 26 NOVEMBER 2010

November 27

Rebecca Pippert

The Czech author Milan Kundera wrote a novel agreeing with Nietzsche that it makes no sense to claim moral meaning in a world without God. Without God, Kundera says, our condition is at best 'the unbearable lightness of being' — the title of his brilliant novel.

The writer of Psalm 1 agrees! Without God, he says, we are like the chaff over corn that is so light, it is weightless.

But, he adds, the person who knows God is like 'a tree planted by the streams of water which yields its fruit in season and whose leaf does not wither.' God's intention is to make us like trees that grow near the ocean. They are strong because they have endured gale-force winds. Consequently their roots grow deep and their branches are sturdy.

We wonder if surrendering our lives to God will make us boring and dull. But the Bible reveals that knowing God gives us lives bursting with vitality!

Yes, life is difficult. But instead of blaming God for our difficulties, let's turn to God for help — for that will make all the difference. The real surprise in the biblical story is God. The God who seeks us. The God who sent His Son, Jesus. The God who loves us. The God who will not let us go.

When we read the biblical story of David, we see a man so utterly human. He danced, he cried, he made mistakes and he loved God with every fibre of his being. And what was God's verdict on David's passionate expression of humanity and faith? He said: 'Now there's a man after my own heart.'

Oh Lord, create in us a new heart and give us a heart like Yours. Amen.

BROADCAST FRIDAY 27 NOVEMBER 2015

November 28

Alison Twaddle

Yesterday marked the beginning of Advent, although to look at the shops and the television adverts, you'd think we'd been anticipating Christmas for quite a while already. For some, the journey toward Christmas can be fraught with financial worries as the shopping bills mount up — and with complicated family arrangements about whose turn it is to visit whom. For others, the relentless pursuit of fun and the round of parties serve to highlight their own loneliness and lack of social connections. Getting *to* Christmas, and getting *through* it, can become a bit of a slog. And that's rather sad because it's the opposite of what Advent is meant to be. The first Advent candle, lit this week in many churches, is a symbol of hope and expectation as a dark world waits for the coming of the light.

As I try to keep that perspective in mind, I think of parents bombarded by requests for this year's 'must have' presents, who face going into debt and are worried about the consequences. I think of families where there's conflict and jealousy; where children have divided loyalties because Mum and Dad no longer live together; and where old wounds are still keenly felt. I remember those facing a lonely time while everyone else is making plans, especially those who will be alone for the first time at Christmas, feeling their grief more keenly as memories come flooding back.

Loving God, who searches and knows us beyond any understanding we have of ourselves, hear the unspoken prayers of each heart, and comfort all those who find it hard to share in the joy of this season. We pray for all in pain — physically, mentally and emotionally — that ours may be the welcoming smile, the comforting word or the gentle touch that is the light they need in the darkness. Amen.

BROADCAST MONDAY 28 NOVEMBER 2011

November 29

Steve Williams

I've always subscribed to the motto, 'It's better to light a candle than curse the darkness.' And in the Jewish neighbourhood where I live, my friends were proving this right last night by lighting candles whose appearance in their front windows marked the beginning of the Feast of Hanukkah – the Festival of Lights or the Feast of Dedication. For eight nights, candles will be lit on a distinctive candelabra of eight branches, a menorah, which also has an extra ninth branch from which the others will be lit – one more for each successive night until they're all burning.

It's to remember the re-dedication of the Temple in Jerusalem in the year 165 BCE. It had been overrun by Jerusalem's Greek rulers four years earlier, and then liberated by Judas Maccabeus for worship according to the purpose for which it had been built. Only one night's worth of oil was left for the light in the Temple to burn through the night, yet, in what's celebrated as a miracle, it burned for eight nights – just the time needed for new oil to be prepared. And the celebrations included games, the exchange of gifts and potato cakes.

For me, as a Christian neighbour looking in, it's a reminder of my own season of Advent, where I too am waiting for God's light to shine in the darkness – and it's an encouragement too that when I'm seeking to follow God and have come to the end of my natural strength, there are spiritual resources I can draw upon which will see me safely through.

God of love, Your light shines in the darkness – and the darkness has not overcome it. Where life is dark today, help me to trust in You for the light I need to find my way. Amen.

BROADCAST FRIDAY 29 NOVEMBER 2013

November 30

Kevin Franz

Today is a special day for Scots – and for Russians and Greeks too – as our very different nations mark the festival of our patron saint, Andrew. Quite how a saint becomes the patron of a nation is a mysterious process. In Scotland's case, Andrew came late onto the scene. In earlier times Columba was the best known among the Scottish saints, but as Scotland established her independence against her powerful southern neighbour, Andrew, the brother of Peter and so closely linked to Rome, seemed a good choice. Soon the city on the coast named after him, with its cathedral and university, became a focal point for Church life, and Andrew's cross, the saltire, became the national flag.

All of this is a long way from the life of the fisherman called by Jesus to follow him. Yet there is, in the little we hear of Andrew in the Gospels, a spirit which any nation, indeed any of us, could base our life on. Andrew offers a witness to generosity of heart. We see it in the way he shares with his brother Peter what he learns from his encounter with Jesus. Peter was to play such a dominant role among the disciples, while Andrew, who the Greeks call the 'first chosen', seems content to step back and to lay no claim to power or prestige. And later, at the miracle of the feeding of the 5,000, it's Andrew who finds the boy with the five fish and two loaves and brings him to Jesus.

So today is worth marking, a celebration of Andrew's quiet virtues.

May that spirit be ours. May God today be a bright flame before you, a guiding star above you, a smooth path below you, a kindly shepherd behind you, today, tomorrow and forever. Amen.

BROADCAST TUESDAY 30 NOVEMBER 2010

December 1

Alex Robertson

When I was a student in Manchester in the late 70s, I have to confess I didn't like the city at all. Drab, grey, boring and bleak – I couldn't wait to get away from it. And as a music student I did get the chance to escape – opportunities arose to travel to far distant places for concerts, festivals, competitions and exchanges. I jumped at every opportunity – and dreaded returning each time. I vowed I'd move away as soon as possible.

Thirty-four years later, I'm still here. What happened? Well, I do think Manchester is a different place: a great deal of it has been regenerated and transformed, and it's now a vibrant and colourful city. But it isn't only Manchester that's changed: I'm also a very different person. I probably imagined that my problems would all be solved when I moved to a better place. But it's unwise to think that our surroundings are the sole cause of our inward state. For myself, I found that as my inner issues were dealt with, so was my view of the outside world; and while it wouldn't be quite honest to say that I'm just as happy to be in Hulme as in Honolulu, I think I've actually 'moved to a better place' – a place of contentment, and a sense of purpose in being wherever I am. Happiness really is a state of mind.

Lord, Your desire for each one of us is that we might know a sense of purpose, fulfilment and contentment in all our situations. Grant us the grace to identify and enter into that purpose, so that our lives can be rich and fruitful wherever You have placed us. Amen.

BROADCAST SATURDAY 1 DECEMBER 2012

December 2

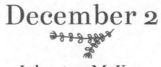

Johnston McKay

I don't want to make things worse for those who are mourning the passing of the weekend and who are perhaps less than enthusiastic about the start of a new week at this time of the day. The truth is, though, that I don't have any difficulty with the early morning. I am usually up and about, and waiting to take our dog for a walk as soon as (in the phrase the Greek poet Homer used a lot) 'the rosy fingers of dawn appear'.

Down by the shores of the River Clyde, where the dog takes me, it's part of my daily routine to watch as the streaks of light begin to appear above the hills; and slowly the features on our walk that occasionally frighten the dog — a litter bin moved from its accustomed place, a piece of scrap paper blowing threateningly across the grass, or the snapping of a fallen branch underfoot — take their place in a familiar landscape.

Religious faith is neither a matter of groping in the dark nor of blinding flashes of inspiration, but much more often, as Cardinal Newman understood, the glimpsing of a kindly light in encircling gloom. And the word 'kindly' matters. The 19th-century Scottish minister Robert Murray M'Cheyne once asked a colleague what he had preached about on the previous Sunday and got the answer, 'The wicked shall be turned into hell,' and M'Cheyne asked, 'Were you able to preach affectionately from that text?'

So on my early morning walk, the first streaks of dawn become a visual symbol of the God who guards us each night and guides us each day.

So it is, loving God, that for us and for all, Your love is an offer which is new every morning. Amen.

BROADCAST MONDAY 2 DECEMBER 2013

December 3

Michael Mumisa

In 1868, the Russian composer Rimsky-Korsakov wrote his symphony *Antar*, alluding to Antar Ibn Shaddad al-'Absi, who was a black slave and one of 'The Seven' great Arabic poets of the pre-Islamic era. Antar was one of the composers of the famous *Seven Golden Odes*, which are considered by scholars to be the finest poems ever to come out of Arabia.

Although Antar was celebrated by all pre-Islamic Arabs as a great warrior who also possessed all the noble traits they greatly valued, they could not allow him to marry the woman he loved because of his race. His poems deal with the themes of lost love and racial identity. The story of Antar has long been retold to Arab children. The Prophet of Islam, Muhammad, is reported to have said: 'I continued to hear the stories about the Bedouin Antar so much that I wished I had met him!'

Our religious traditions are based mostly on narratives about the past. All narratives, depending on how they are transmitted and received, have the potential either to bring people together regardless of their beliefs or to separate them. Antar's story reflects a pre-Islamic culture, and yet both Muslims and non-Muslims can be united in their appreciation of his life and achievements.

O Lord, grant us knowledge, wisdom and the courage to act according to the good that we know. Amen.

BROADCAST WEDNESDAY 3 DECEMBER 2008

December 4

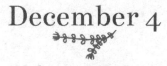

Johnston McKay

I want to introduce you to my friend Mary. She belongs to a church in the centre of Edinburgh, a very historic church, but I suspect that when the story of the Church of Scotland today comes to be written, it's what is happening there now that provides the story.

For the last ten years, Mary's church has raised over a million pounds for a Christian charity through a book sale every May. It's been held every year since 1974 and now is one of the biggest charity book sales in the world.

Last year a very prominent Scottish journalist was moving house – 'downsizing', he said – and he donated a large part of his very valuable library to the book sale. Now Mary has inspired a picture sale, and last week paintings donated either by generous collectors or by some of Scotland's most celebrated artists raised thousands of pounds. Mary would say that she wasn't doing anything special – just what she could do to help an important cause she believed in.

Anyone who is tempted to think that small in scale means insignificant hasn't been stung by a mosquito, as I was in Spain not so long ago. The pain in my arm was still there long after I'd returned home. If a wee mosquito could have that effect on me, there's a place still for stinging determination in a somewhat complacent world.

So, loving God, help us to see the transforming change to the world which only we can make. Amen.

BROADCAST WEDNESDAY 4 DECEMBER 2013

December 5

Noël Vincent

Are you a SAD person? I don't mean, do you spend your time moaning about life being unfair, sitting in a corner sobbing and feeling sorry for yourself. I'm talking about people who suffer from SAD, or Seasonal Affective Disorder.

The beneficial effects of sunlight have been in the news recently. Usually it's the opposite, we're being warned of the dangers of too much exposure to the sun. But now we're told it's important actually to enjoy some sunshine on the skin to top up the vitamin D.

People who suffer from SAD find that their health and sense of wellbeing deteriorate in the winter. They miss sunshine pathologically, so the treatment is to sit in front of lights to compensate for the shorter days and the winter skies.

Although most of us don't have this clinical condition, there's no doubt the sun does cheer us up. Life just seems more full of possibilities when the skies are bright and the birds are singing. Daylight is a positive benefit to us all.

Throughout history, non-Christian religions have often seen the sun as having divine properties. Things and people thrive better under its influence.

And within most mainstream religions, light is a precious symbol of God and His presence. The recent Hindu festival of Diwali celebrates light, Jewish rituals often involve the lighting of candles, especially Hanukkah around this time, and the same is true for Christianity. The Christmas lights we enjoy in our streets and houses signify that light and darkness are a central theme of devotion as we approach the Nativity, celebrating God's light coming into the world in the person of Jesus.

God of the morning, may the dawning of a new day lead us from darkness to light. May we enjoy the benefits it brings and joyfully celebrate the coming of Your light in the birth of Jesus as we spread good will to all we meet. Amen.

BROADCAST WEDNESDAY 5 DECEMBER 2007

December 6

Alex Robertson

Times change! A generation ago, Britain's industrial cities were regularly subject to smog — the acrid, filthy mixture of water vapour and soot that created the famous 'pea souper' fogs. The Great Smog of 1952 claimed an astonishing 4,000 lives in London over a period of just a few days. It wasn't just an outdoor problem. The smog seeped into homes and public buildings. An evening performance of *La Traviata* at Sadlers Wells had to be stopped, because the audience could no longer see the stage.

After the Clean Air Act was passed by Parliament, things improved somewhat, but most people still had open fires at home, huge power plants like the one at Battersea continually belched smoke over London, and the city continued to suffer from choking smogs that reduced visibility to near zero. Hospitals were put on alert, people were advised to wear masks and told not to bank up their fires at night.

That was 50 years ago. Times have changed. Coal fires have long since gone, and we live in a far more environmentally conscious world, though the challenges have shifted rather than disappeared.

Times change, perceptions change, for better or worse. Something once put up with or taken for granted can become an issue that demands urgent change or eradication, and other things that were once frowned upon can gain acceptance. Standards change, but truth doesn't.

Lord, in a changing world, help us to keep an open mind. May we not be confined to the status quo of our circumstances and standards, but may we see through Your eyes, and have the discernment to perceive what needs to change and the capability to change it. Amen.

BROADCAST THURSDAY 6 DECEMBER 2012

December 7

Naftali Brawer

During the eight days of Hanukkah, the lights are kindled just after sunset, and there is something about dusk and candlelight that I find particularly evocative. Dusk is not day but it is not entirely night either. Soft candlelight illuminates and at the same time conceals, unlike harsh electricity that leaves little to the imagination.

That the Hanukkah ritual is framed in this half-light says something about faith that is all too often overlooked. For many, faith and religion are about certainty in a world of uncertainty. We seek clear boundaries and delineations, immutable truths, and yet our experience is one of turbulence and disorientation.

Some turn to religion to find a bedrock. They want a world that makes sense in black-and-white terms, and fundamentalist religion provides this oversimplification of life. But this is a distortion of what real faith is about. Real faith does not seek to escape from life's complexities by providing simple answers but rather heightens the complexity and makes demands on the adherent to navigate a moral life with nuance and sensitivity. Religion is like the soft light of candles or the natural light of dusk when day mingles with night; it holds opposites in awareness and assumes a stance of wonder and awe toward the deep mysteries of our existence without trying to reduce them to simplistic schemes.

While fundamentalists march through life, a person of true faith treads gingerly, attuned to the subtlety and complexity of life. As the prophet Micah says: 'What does God require of you, but to act justly, to love mercy and to walk humbly with your God.'

Father in heaven, help us to navigate our complex reality with faith, grace and humility so that we may bring blessing wherever we go.

BROADCAST MONDAY 7 DECEMBER 2015

December 8

Andrew Graystone

At the Windsor Celebration of Faiths and the Environment last month, leaders of the great world religions gathered to offer their varied perspectives on our relationship with the environment, so this week I'm drawing inspiration from some of those different faith traditions. Today is celebrated in many Buddhist traditions as Bodhi Day. It marks the day the young prince Siddhartha Gautama is said to have found enlightenment while contemplating under a Bodhi Tree. Thereafter he was referred to as the Buddha – the 'enlightened one'.

As we search for sustainable ways to share the planet, one of the distinctive contributions that Buddhism brings is the challenge of simplicity. The Buddha taught his followers to fall in with the rhythms of the planet and not to fight them. The desire for more, better, faster can never be fully satisfied – because it only leads to a desire for even more, even better and even faster. So if a solution is to be found to the environmental crisis, it will have to begin with the individual.

Buddhists in Japan tell a story that I find inspiring. Receiving a donation of 500 new robes for his followers, the Buddha considered what to do with the old ones. He decided they should be used for bed sheets. The old sheets would become towels. And the old towels would be used as cleaning rags. Everything should be used and re-used. Nothing should be wasted. This is not simply a matter of economics but of respecting our place within the order of being. As a Christian, I, too, can echo the sentiments of this Buddhist affirmation:

May all beings be filled with joy and peace.
May all beings everywhere,
Seen and unseen,
Dwelling far off or nearby,
Being or waiting to become –
May all be filled with lasting joy.

BROADCAST TUESDAY 8 DECEMBER 2009

December 9

Calvin Samuel

This Christmas I'm looking forward to the visit of one of my oldest friends from the British Virgin Islands. We've known each other since our teenage years but have lived at least 3,000 miles apart for most of our lives since then.

He's never been to Britain, so in the last few months my wife and I have been canvassing opinions on Britain's must-see sights.

Some suggestions cropped up regularly: Edinburgh Castle, Holy Island, Hadrian's Wall, Durham Cathedral, the Tower of London, Buckingham Palace, Stonehenge, Land's End and numerous museums, art galleries, cathedrals and castles in between. Unsurprisingly, we received far more suggestions than will fit into a ten-day visit.

The exercise made me more aware of two things. First, it reminded me of the rich history that has shaped these islands, for good and ill, leaving an indelible mark on them for the future.

Second, it also reminded me that the primary purpose of my friend's visit is not to conduct a tour of Britain's best tourist attractions. Rather, the primary purpose is to renew friendship, to talk, to laugh, to pray. These too leave a mark, which, though less obvious, is just as indelible.

Who are the people with whom you will spend time this Christmas, and among whom you will leave your mark?

I am always deeply impressed by those who give generously of their time to charity over Christmas, whether serving the homeless, housing vulnerable children or supporting the lonely. Their efforts, often unseen and unsung, nonetheless leave a mark on the lives they touch.

Gracious God, thank You for all whose lives intersect with ours. May we recognize in each we meet another who bears the image of God. Amen.

BROADCAST TUESDAY 9 DECEMBER 2014

December 10

Naftali Brawer

When trying to turn around a bad situation, should one's focus be on eradicating the negative or introducing the positive? Should changing the negative culture of an organization concentrate on punishing bad behaviour or accentuating good behaviour? In my personal life, should my focus be on refraining from bad habits or on introducing good ones?

Both perspectives are symbolized in the Hanukkah lights, which can represent either fire or light. Fire signifies eradication; it consumes and reduces to ash. It is often used to symbolize the eradication of evil, as the passage in our High Holiday liturgy proclaims: 'All wickedness will dissipate like smoke.'

But the Hanukkah flames can also signify light, and light represents the power of good, as Isaiah declared: 'The people that walked in darkness have seen a brilliant light', which refers to a new world order of goodness.

So which is it? Fire or light? Like so much in Judaism, it is the subject of an argument, which is underpinned by two opposing philosophical viewpoints. According to the school of Shammai, we kindle eight flames on the first night of Hanukkah and reduce one flame each night. The school of Hillel holds the opposite: we start with one flame on the first night and work our way up to eight. Shammai sees the kindling as representing the consumption of evil by fire and so each successive night there is symbolically less evil and so less fire is required. Hillel, however, sees the ritual in terms of adding positive light, and the more one accentuates the positive, the greater its influence and the darkness dissipates on its own. And this is the view we follow in our family.

Father in heaven, help us to change for the better by simply bringing a little more light into our lives each day.

BROADCAST THURSDAY 10 DECEMBER 2015

December 11

Calvin Samuel

Last week, the preacher leading the service in my local Methodist church made a startling confession. 'I hate the run up to Christmas,' she said. For her, as it is for many, the preparation for Christmas is a whirlwind of busyness.

There are Christmas gifts to buy, scores of Christmas cards to write, Christmas parcels to post, Christmas decorations to put up, a Christmas tree to secure and to dress. Then there is Christmas dinner to prepare, holiday visits to organize, and carol services and Christmas parties to attend.

By the time she gets to Christmas, she is exhausted and less than convinced that it has been worthwhile. Her challenge to us this year is to do less, to move slowly, to contemplate the important, to have a horizon that is further away than the next fortnight.

Some will surely say, 'Slow down? Contemplate? At Christmas? Chance would be a fine thing. Where would you find the time?'

It is at our times of greatest busyness that we are in greatest need of learning how to move slowly. One of my favourite prayers begins with the line, 'God of snails and tortoises, and of those things that move slowly in the world ...'

It is when we are busy that we are in most need of a reminder that fulfilment is not to be found in frenetic activity. Rather it is only when we take time to move slowly, to savour God's good creation, to create space for reflection, refreshment and joy, that fulfilment may be found.

Unhurried God, teach me the art of moving slowly; free me from my guilt when my tasks are incomplete and renew in me the joy of Your salvation. Amen.

BROADCAST THURSDAY 11 DECEMBER 2014

December 12

Stephen Shipley

I was travelling by train in south London a couple of weeks ago and found myself having to change at Clapham Junction. Each day, I'm told, about 2,000 trains, most of them stopping, pass through that station – more than through any other station in Europe. And it was there on this day in 1988 that the worst rail accident in recent times happened. Thirty-five people died and a hundred others were injured after three trains were involved in a collision during the morning rush hour. What made the incident even more tragic was the third empty train that later ran into the wreckage, killing some passengers who had survived the first crash.

Any transport accident is, of course, desperately sad, and there are always stories of heroic efforts as the emergency services come to the rescue and people respond in remarkable ways. But there's also a feeling of helplessness, as was expressed only last month by witnesses to the horrific motorway pile-up in Somerset. The emotional scars take a long time to heal and they will never completely disappear. And then there's the inevitable question which is so hard to answer: why did it have to happen?

In this Advent season, Christians prepare for the coming of God into our broken world as a vulnerable newborn baby. It's to the darkness of the suffering *Jesus* experienced as he grew up that we bring our struggles – the suffering that caused even *him* to question God's purposes.

Dear God, awaken the springs of goodness in our hearts and strengthen our society with the bond of love, affection and good neighbourliness. God, grant us Your love, and the love of those whom You love, and the love of those who would bring us closer to Your love and make Your love dearer to us than cool water on a hot day. Amen.

BROADCAST MONDAY 12 DECEMBER 2011

December 13

Patrick Thomas

Some people are hit by tragedies that are so sudden and cruel and apparently pointless that they generate the numbness of shock and disbelief, followed by understandable anger and bitterness. On such occasions it is only natural to turn in on ourselves, entering a spiral of depression.

I knew a farmer's wife, a kindly, lively, intelligent woman, who had been hit by just such a tragedy. Her life, which had been full and satisfying, suddenly seemed barren and empty. She sank deeper and deeper into the darkness – and there was nothing that any of her friends could to do to bring her out of it.

And then she found her own solution. She became a home help, looking after some of the elderly housebound people in our scattered rural community. And as she turned outward toward these often vulnerable and lonely men and women, looking after them with patience and kindness, her inner wounds began to heal. The scars would always be there, of course – but her life acquired new purpose and meaning.

One day I called in to see a blind woman with a wonderful sense of humour, called Hannah, who lived in the old people's bungalows. The farmer's wife was there, gently washing Hannah's feet. As I saw her kneeling there, wholly absorbed in the task of caring for someone else, I felt that somehow I was in the presence of Christ himself.

Heavenly Father, through Your Son You understand the depths of pain and anguish into which we are sometimes plunged. Be with all those who have to face bereavement, depression and despair. In our darkest and most desperate moments, draw us out from getting lost within ourselves, and help us to respond to the needs of those around us. Amen.

BROADCAST THURSDAY 13 DECEMBER 2007

December 14

Stephen Shipley

Perhaps the most celebrated and reproduced religious painting of the last century is Salvador Dalí's *Christ of St John of the Cross*. It's based on a drawing by the 16th-century Spanish friar and mystic whose feast day is today. When it was purchased by Glasgow Art Gallery 60 years ago for a mere £8,000, there was an outcry that it was a waste of money, yet it's rumoured that the Spanish government recently offered over £80 million for the picture – an offer which was turned down. Dalí painted it in 1951, and it depicts Christ on the cross in a darkened sky floating over a body of water complete with a boat and fishermen. What's unusual, though, and what provoked so much strong reaction, is the dramatically different interpretation that Dalí gave it from the Spanish monk. For St John of the Cross, the crucified Christ was primarily a focus for compassion, a tortured and murdered man. Dalí aimed instead for an image of perfection and transcendence – no blood, nails or crown of thorns.

So how do we reconcile these seemingly opposite views? Maybe by remembering that we view the Crucifixion from the perspective of the Resurrection. That doesn't take away from the horror of Jesus giving himself up to death, nor God, his Father, feeling the pain, the agony, the injustice and the rage of it all. But it does show that in this ultimate solidarity with humanity, God reveals himself as the God of love, who opens up hope and a future through the most negative side of history

Lord God, guide and strengthen us as we prepare to celebrate again the coming of Your Son Jesus into the world. Keep us faithful that we may be helped through life and brought to the joy of Your salvation. Amen.

BROADCAST WEDNESDAY 14 DECEMBER 2011

December 15

Michelle Marken

As the car slid toward the kerb last week, controlled by ice, not me, I knew my luck was out – this was going to be the day of the weather monster. One severe jolt and the steering was rendered practically useless. Not injured, except in pride, it did not help to have the damage diagnosed as a bent wishbone! A wishbone – what an insult! Seconds before I had been wishing I'd let my husband drive.

We've had a lot of weather monster days in Northern Ireland recently, and they have raised almost equal amounts of glee and gloom. Glee among happy school-free snowballers, some of whom couldn't resist targets like skidding cars, while gloom consumed those of us who have moved on through the snow-tolerance levels to 'gritted teeth' stage, owing mostly to lack of grit on aforementioned slippy-slidey roads!

In this new ice age I may expect that my son will, like last year, in attempting to travel home for Christmas, miss a plane because the train to the airport wasn't running owing to ice on the tracks, and anyway he was marooned in a house far from the station; then miss a ferry because he thought he could have an extra little sleep before heading for the boat terminal; and finally, miss another plane on account of an ice-bound airport. I am sustained by the memory of my snow-friendly son letting me hear the crunch of the ice down his mobile phone as he sought to persuade me he was manfully struggling down a six-foot-deep ice trench that was once a road. To welcome him late on Christmas Eve, knowing that home really was where he wanted to be, was worth the waiting – the perfect gift.

Lord, we pray that each of us may have the gift of a warm place to travel to this Christmas, and that we may be among people who are waiting to welcome us. Amen.

BROADCAST WEDNESDAY 15 DECEMBER 2010

December 16

Judy Merry

Just about a year ago, I was told I was seriously ill. I'd had various tests and was waiting for the diagnosis. If you've ever been in that position — perhaps you are now — you'll know just how agonizing the wait is. Every hour is like a day and every day like a week. While I was waiting for the diagnosis, I said to a friend that I wasn't looking forward to Christmas with this uncertainty hanging over me and that I was going to cancel the treat I'd planned for the following day. It wasn't anything very grand — just a day out doing some Christmas shopping and going to a favourite café for lunch. But how could I enjoy that when the future was so uncertain — even though I could do nothing about it?

My friend had been in a similar situation a few years ago and she said, 'I don't think you should let worry about tomorrow spoil today.' I wasn't really in the mood to take her advice, but in the end I did and when I look back on that day, I realize it gave me a disproportionate amount of pleasure.

There's nothing new about this advice. It's really what Jesus told his followers 2,000 years ago. He said: 'Don't worry about tomorrow — tomorrow will have enough troubles.' But knowing that and doing it are two different things. What helped me was to try to change my thinking the same way you might try to change the focus of your eyes — instead of looking into the distance, you focus on something just in front of your nose. So I tried to keep my thoughts firmly in the present, and when I did that, I found I could enjoy momentary pleasures: that first cup of tea when you come home from hospital, a friend taking me to buy a new pair of shoes when I couldn't drive, even sharing a dark joke with a fellow patient. Small pleasures, but they get you through the bad times.

Lord, instead of always fretting about a future that we cannot change, help us to live each moment in the present. May we learn to live with our worries and realize that there are moments of light in the darkness. Amen.

BROADCAST TUESDAY 16 DECEMBER 2014

December 17

Dónal McKeown

I spent 23 years as a school teacher and principal. It's an often stressful job —
but it's also a privilege. Young people are fascinating as they grow and dare, ask
and struggle.

Life in modern competitive society requires qualifications and technical
know-how. A good education seeks to promote the whole person. In the words
of Viktor Frankl, the Austrian psychiatrist and Holocaust survivor, it will
help the young person to develop means by which to live and a meaning for
which to live. Teachers know that they don't teach subjects: they teach pupils.
They seek to nourish fragile buds of great potential beauty. They aim not merely
to measure how smart the children are according to some external standards:
they want *the children* to see how smart they are. In the spirit of the Olympics and
the Paralympics, they believe that greatness is not found in possessions, power,
position or exam grades. It is discovered in goodness, humility, service and
courage.

For Christians, the birth of Jesus marks the irruption of generous hope into
the corners of life where too many people labour in uncertainty and distress.
He came to witness to the power of truth and to the meaningfulness of human
life in all its imperfection. He taught about a God who always remains faithful.

This morning I pray ancient prophetic words about the one who accepted the
title of 'Teacher':

*O wisdom, you come forth from the mouth of the Most High. You fill the universe and
hold all things in a strong yet gentle manner. O come to teach us the way of truth. Amen.*

BROADCAST MONDAY 17 DECEMBER 2012

December 18

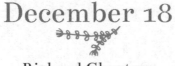

Richard Chartres

The office party season is in full swing and there seems to be a desire to take the waiting out of wassailing well before the Christmas festival proper begins at the end of next week. For the Christian Church, however, we are in the final phase of Advent, the season of preparation.

Most of us try to approach the future with some degree of planning, but the word 'Advent' stands not for the future we have planned but for the future that is coming to meet us. The first phases of Advent encourage us to look into the dark and to confront our fears. There is a progressive stripping away of illusions. We need to be clear about what is wrong with ourselves and with the world, but not get stuck there.

The message that comes at the heart of darkness and silence is that we are created to live toward God and our neighbour. To lose the attraction to others and to God is to suffer the inertia of self-absorption.

Advent is a time for deepening our thirst for the life that we are meant to enjoy with God and with our neighbour. The dark time of the year is the season for uncovering the attraction to the light which is at the heart of every being.

Psalm 42 expresses this Advent hope:

Like as the hart desireth the water brook,
so longeth my soul after Thee, O God.
My soul is athirst for God,
yea even for the living God. …
Why art thou so full of heaviness, O my soul?
and why art thou so disquieted within me?
O put thy trust in God;
for I will yet give him thanks for the help of his countenance.

BROADCAST SATURDAY 18 DECEMBER 2010

December 19

Vincent Nichols

At this time we're well into preparations for Christmas, preparations that may include travel plans, or plans for family parties or guests, or just the prospect of a time for rest and a change from tough routines.

But our thoughts should go wider. I think of those whose Christmas will be full of sadness and grief and who will celebrate even in deprivation and exile. My thoughts go out to them: to those who have been driven from their homes across the Middle East; communities that are even now being persecuted for their Christian faith. Yes, my thoughts are with others who are suffering dreadfully, too. But at this time, and unambiguously, we think of Christians slain because they believe in Jesus, driven from their homes because they value their faith more than their property.

I have met them in Erbil in Iraq. I've stepped inside their makeshift homes, marvelling at their courage and their devotion to Jesus, their Lord and God, the one in whom they trust. They're to be found in refugee camps in Jordan, in Syria, in Lebanon. How can we celebrate Christmas without thinking and praying for them?

And I think, too, of the victims of human trafficking, some held here in our midst, who will grieve profoundly this Christmas. I thank all who work to bring this evil trade to an end.

Lord God, in the birth of Your Son in our flesh, you embraced all our human suffering, taking it into the heart of Your merciful love. In the midst of our Christmas celebrations, whatever they may be, help us to remember all who are on the precipice of despair, that through our prayers and actions they may find new hope. Amen.

BROADCAST SATURDAY 19 DECEMBER 2015

December 20

Dónal McKeown

Exactly 18 years ago today, my first niece Anna was born. And since then she has been a blessing on her family and far beyond it. Of course, she has always had to battle to ensure that her birthday wasn't overshadowed in the preparations for Christmas. But Jesus's birth was intended to give us our place in the sun, not to steal it away.

That name Anna appears in different forms in the Bible. Hannah was the mother of the great Jewish leader Samuel. Anne is traditionally the name given to the mother of Mary, who would give birth to Jesus — and as such she is revered by both Christians and Muslims. St Luke tells us that an old widow and prophetess, Anna, greeted the child Jesus at his Presentation in the Temple.

The name Anna comes from the Hebrew word meaning 'grace' or 'favour' — and yet all the lives of all these biblical women were marked with enormous challenges. As someone said, it's not so much your position in life that matters, it's your disposition. It's easier to tramp the hard roads of our journey when we know where we're coming from and can believe that the steps have value.

Birthdays are important stages on the journey. They help us to remember that living is not about what we achieve or do, what we acquire and who we know — but about who we are and who we are becoming through the unexpected twists on the road.

God of life and of birthdays, free those who sit in our manmade prisons of pain and despair. Enable us to hear our name call us into freedom, and help us believe that, in the turns of life, we too are blessed with grace and favour. Amen.

BROADCAST THURSDAY 20 DECEMBER 2012

December 21

Vincent Nichols

Christmas is soon upon us! A holiday, a feast day, a family occasion. This week there's so much to get done!

My childhood memories of the week before Christmas are clear: planning the shopping trips, preparing the house for visitors and getting together the figures for the crib that tell the story of the birth of Jesus Christ in the stable at Bethlehem.

Our visitors were a funny lot. One I remember well was an old friend of the family who came round only for Christmas and funerals. He was a retired docker, rough, quiet, immensely kind. After a meal he would sit by the fire, missing nothing, loving the music and emptying all the bottles of whisky.

I'm sure most families gather such friends at Christmas, people who turn up out of the dark blue yonder and stake a claim to a welcome and warmth. Sometimes they might be living lonely lives and feel it most keenly at Christmas.

I'm glad that our visitor came. He kept our feet on the ground and our conversation spicy.

Something similar happened at Bethlehem. The first people who turned up were the shepherds, a rough old lot who probably smelled. They had a poor reputation and probably criminal records, if such things existed in those days.

They're the first to go into our family crib.

Lord God, as we prepare to welcome the feast day of Your Son's birth, help us to open our hearts and our homes to all those who turn up, especially the awkward ones. They were the first to be called to Your side. In fact, You still have a soft spot for them. So should we. Give us the grace to welcome them, and patience with their special ways. Amen.

BROADCAST MONDAY 21 DECEMBER 2015

December 22

Stephen Wigley

'Enter his gates with thanksgiving and his courts with songs of praise.' These words from the 'Jubilate', Psalm 100, will be well known to many who say them as part of their daily devotions in praying the Office. They're also very familiar to me from my time in Aberystwyth, as this was the inscription greeting visitors at the entrance of our new church there.

These ancient words also have a contemporary resonance, as today we mark the 25th anniversary of the re-opening of the historic Brandenburg Gate in Berlin. It was originally commissioned by King Frederick William II as a symbol of peace; however, during the 19th century it was redesigned as a triumphal arch and came to represent instead Prussian military power and prestige, an impression reinforced by its prominence during the Nazi regime. The gate was badly damaged in the war and then closed in 1961 as Berlin, along with the rest of Germany, was divided and Europe entered a new phase of the Cold War. Its re-opening in December 1989 was part of that climactic series of events that began with the Berlin Wall coming down and ended in the reunification of Germany. And so, as the West German Chancellor walked through the gate on this day 25 years ago, he was greeted by the East German Prime Minister with the words, 'It must be a gate of peace.'

This is a powerful image to carry into our prayers at the start of this week, reminding us that even in our conflicted and divided world, it is possible for walls to come down and gateways to be opened, as we prepare for the coming of Christ, the Prince of Peace.

So we pray:

Merciful God, as we prepare for the coming of the Prince of Peace to our divided world, may Your Holy Spirit encourage us to open the gates of our hearts and guide us, and all people, in Your way of peace. For Christ's sake, Amen.

BROADCAST MONDAY 22 DECEMBER 2014

December 23

Richard Chartres

Today we come to the end of the series of Advent chants in the daily worship of the Church, which prepare for the birth of the Christ-child.

The focus today is on the virgin birth. I wonder: when a baby is born, do you feel optimism or pessimism?

Pessimism seems to be the luxury of people who have done rather well out of history. It is certainly profoundly uncreative.

Optimism, on the other hand, seems to contradict experience and to shrink from acknowledging the reality of what threatens us as a human race.

But the story of Christmas in the Bible is full of light and hope. 'Fear not: for, behold, I bring you good tidings of great joy, which shall be to all people' and 'the people that walked in darkness have seen a great light'.

The God of infinite creativity does not offer us a blueprint for utopia or a problem-solving formula. He comes among us as a child menaced by the dark but with an inner light which has never been overcome.

If we have really made the Advent journey, then it is possible that the new birth will take us away from our fears and worries, and renew within us the transforming light which it is fatally easy to cover up.

There is immensity cloistered in the dear womb of the Blessed Virgin Mary, and as Christmas Day approaches, we pray, Almighty God, as we prepare with joy to celebrate the gift of the Christ-child: embrace the earth with Your glory and be for us a living hope in Jesus Christ our Lord. Amen.

BROADCAST THURSDAY 23 DECEMBER 2010

December 24

Stephen Wigley

I expect that many thoughts are now turning toward this evening, when people will be putting Christmas stockings out and attending midnight services to welcome the birth of the Christ-child. And for our family this is a very special Christmas Eve, as it marks the 21st birthday of our twin sons.

Looking back, it's hard to imagine where the last 21 years have gone. The consultant who looked after Jenny during her pregnancy was always sure they would be Christmas babies, but I don't think that even he expected they would be born as our respective churches were starting their midnight communion, so that news of their birth would be relayed to colleagues, choir and congregations just after the service in the early hours of Christmas morning. I also suspect that our now grown-up lads, who no longer look quite so cute as they did when Christmas babies, will be making their own alternative plans for their 21st celebrations as well.

However, our two are not the only ones to have since grown up. All those gathering to greet the Christ-child, in services up and down the country, are also meeting to remember how this baby grows up into a man: Jesus of Nazareth. And it will be Jesus's role to announce the coming kingdom, no longer the cute and cuddly baby but the Christ who proclaims God's kingdom of justice and peace. So our Christmas Eve communion reminds us that there is no rejoicing at the cradle without also turning to the cross.

Let us pray:

Almighty God, the angels call us to rejoice in the birth of Your Son at Bethlehem. Help us to remember how he grows up the son of a carpenter, the one who lays down his life on the cross to bring healing and hope for all the world. We ask this in Christ's name, Amen.

BROADCAST WEDNESDAY 24 DECEMBER 2014

December 25

Vincent Nicols

In my childhood home, Christmas Day had its clear routines and its unique excitement. We went to church, of course we did! We opened presents in a frenzy of excitement and wrapping paper. We opened our door to all the colourful family circle. And we placed the figure of the infant Jesus into our crib. He is born today! Rejoice and be glad!

I have to admit today, with a little regret, that on Christmas Day my mother did most of the work. It was in part because she wanted us all to be surprised by what was in store, but also because we were engrossed in so much else. Her name was Mary, and she made this day full of graciousness, welcome and generosity. That's what mothers do. Not only mothers, of course, but so much that mothers do for their families has something special about it. They give tangible reality to the love that lies at the heart of creation, the love that is God, that holds all things in being. The rhythm of every day, of food, rest and play, watched over by a loving parent, no matter its simplicity, is a parable of that great truth. In the eyes of faith this is the work of God, achieved through loving hands and hearts, even if often they are pushed to their limit.

Lord God, as we greet Your Son made flesh, Your love in our midst, we thank You for all mothers, and for all who parent children. May their selfless love be sustained throughout this day of celebration so that its true meaning may linger long in our hearts, reverberating round our family circle and reaching out to the forlorn and the lonely.

BROADCAST FRIDAY 25 DECEMBER 2015

December 26

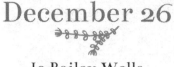

Jo Bailey Wells

Today is St Stephen's day, when, as the carol tells us, the snow lies all deep and crisp and even.

And, as the carol tells us, Good King Wenceslas not only *looked* out but also *went* out, bringing both food and fuel to the poor. One theory suggests that it's because of this habit that St Stephen's day is known as Boxing Day – the day when food is parcelled up and alms boxes are shared, so as to give whatever we can spare and share to those in need.

There are many in our society who are forced to choose between food and fuel this winter, as well as plenty of people who have neither. Thankfully, there are just as many who, recognizing that they have plenty, have shared what they have with incredible generosity. Some of the charities that feed the homeless report record numbers of volunteers. A food bank I know has been swamped with gifts of food to share. The Radio 4 Christmas Appeal with St Martin-in-the-Fields (a community to which I have links) reports the highest-ever level of giving. It's impressive to realize how times of serious economic hardship are also times of phenomenal personal generosity.

Generous God, this Boxing Day we ask You to open our eyes and our hearts, to discover afresh what we might share and with whom we might share it. Nurture in each of us the goodness of Good King Wenceslas — so that those who are hungry may find food, and those who are cold may find warmth; and all of us may find joy in sharing together what You first shared with us. Amen.

BROADCAST THURSDAY 26 DECEMBER 2013

December 27

Steven Croft

There is a lovely story told about John the Evangelist whose feast day is today. John lived to a great old age. Toward the end of his life, his sermons became shorter and shorter until they were reduced to just one line. Whenever he was invited to speak to the church as a very old man, John would repeat over and over again a single line. 'Little children, love one another.'

It is good today to think of what it means to love. Many families will have exchanged harsh words over Christmas. Others may be hurting and disappointed or alone today. You may have discovered as I do every year that we are not really that good at loving even those who are close to us.

Loving other people can sometimes be about grand gestures and promises. But more often it's very practical and down-to-earth and everyday. Love is about being there and turning up and keeping going. It's about forgiving others and being able to forgive yourself. It's about small thoughtful words and actions. Love is about imagining yourself in someone else's shoes and then doing something that will help them or bring a smile to their faces. As one person has said, love often consists of random acts of unseen kindness. Love can be fierce in its commitment but love is always gentle in its working out.

On St John's Day, let's listen to the Apostle's sermon and put it into practice:

Almighty God, You have taught us that all our doings without love are worth nothing. Fill our hearts and minds this day with charity to others and fill our every action with kindness. In the name of Jesus Christ, the king of love, Amen.

BROADCAST TUESDAY 27 DECEMBER 2011

December 28

Mary Stallard

Today's Feast of the Holy Innocents marks one of the most disturbing commemorations of the Christian calendar.

It recalls the slaughter of male infants by the King some called 'Herod the Great'. According to Matthew's Gospel, this murderous act was part of an attempted plan by Herod to kill the Christ-child.

Questions have been raised about whether this event actually took place because of a lack of supporting evidence from other sources; although scholars acknowledge that other information attests that ruthless brutality was a hallmark of Herod's rule. But whether it's historically accurate or not, this story is part of a greater message that sadly still has resonance with the treatment of many children today.

Throughout the Bible, there's a recurring narrative about the importance of showing concern for the vulnerable. One of the central messages of Christianity is that the little ones — the meek and needy — are those for whom we should show the greatest concern, for as Jesus himself said, these are the ones who 'shall inherit the earth'.

At Christmas, remembering a story of violence and brutality directed at children may seem to be starkly at odds with the joy of the season. But at the heart of the story Christians celebrate is a God who chose to be born in vulnerability, among the poor and marginalized. This God identifies with the weak, and the Feast of Holy Innocents reminds us that those who sometimes seem to count the least in human conflicts are precisely the ones who are most important to God.

Heavenly Father, as we recall the loss of innocent lives and remember the continuing violence of our world, we ask Your blessing on all who work to protect children and keep them safe. Fill every heart with Your hope and love. Amen.

BROADCAST MONDAY 28 DECEMBER 2015

December 29

Martyn Atkins

I remember clearly the first time I came across a satellite navigation system — a 'sat nav' — in a car. Now very common but then quite rare, this technological marvel identifies where you are, then you key in where you want to go, and it works out how to get there. This sat nav was built into the dashboard of a luxury car and my friend proudly showed it off, the silky voice of a famous actress giving instructions — 'Turn right; take the second left' — as we headed home.

Revealing myself as a rebellious sinner, I asked my friend, 'What happens if you don't do what she says?' A glint came into his eye: 'Watch this,' he said. And as we approached a roundabout and the silky voice said 'At the roundabout, turn left,' he went straight on. The sat nav voice was quiet a moment, as if thinking, and then spoke these wonderful Gospel words: 'I have worked out a new route for you.'

Now, that's what God does for us. In spite of our disobedience and going our own way, God, full of grace and endless possibilities, makes a new way for us, gives us yet another chance to change the direction of our lives and travel the way God desires. As we fast approach the turn of a year, a time of personal stocktaking and resolve to make new starts, that's a marvellous promise.

Thank you, wonderful God, that in spite of our repeated disobedience we are never in a place where You are unwilling or unable to work out a new route for us. As this year nears an end, lead and guide our lives, as You choose. Amen.

BROADCAST TUESDAY 29 DECEMBER 2009

December 30

Steven Croft

A friend taught me this quotation from the early Quaker Isaac Penington: 'Our life is love, and peace, and tenderness; and bearing one with another, and forgiving one another, and not laying accusations one against another; but praying one for another and helping one another up with a tender hand.'

Today's an excellent day for stocktaking. We can almost guarantee that whatever we are doing with our time, we will all be taking stock of the year. The news bulletins will look back over the year that is coming to an end. Most of us will take time to look through our diaries, our photographs, our bank accounts and our memories.

However you do your stocktaking, I hope it's good news. But here is a question to think about as you look back on this year. Where are you storing your treasure? On earth or in heaven?

According to Jesus in the Sermon on the Mount, it's not good to store up treasure on earth. It doesn't last. Moths and rust consume it and thieves can break in and steal. Instead, says Jesus, store up for yourselves treasure in heaven. For where your treasure is, there your heart will be also.

We all know what it means to have treasure on earth. What does it mean to store up treasure in heaven? Read it again in the Sermon on the Mount. Deeds of kindness, secret charity, forgiving others, speaking the truth, faithfulness in marriage, gentle words, humility, mercy and peacemaking: all of these things store up treasure in heaven.

Lord, let our life indeed be love, and peace, and tenderness; and bearing one with another, and forgiving one another, praying one for another and helping one another up with a tender hand. Amen.

BROADCAST FRIDAY 30 DECEMBER 2011

December 31

Mary Stallard

It's New Year's Eve and many of us will be busy today making preparations to mark the occasion in some way. Some enjoy a party and look forward to exuberant celebrations with friends and family; others may prefer something rather quieter.

There can be mixed emotions at such liminal moments of change and transition. For some it's a magical time: midnight on New Year's Eve can feel like a gateway between the past and the future. A time to take stock of the year that's ending, perhaps to remember previous years, and an opportunity to dream about things we hope the future may hold.

All of this may fill us with excitement or it might leave us feeling rather unsettled. Standing on a threshold can be scary; there can be such a mixture of challenges and blessings both from the past and from things that may lie ahead.

There's a lovely Jewish tradition that recognizes this, in the fixing of words of scripture on doorposts as a reminder of God's presence. Those who pass through are encouraged to touch these as a way of acknowledging that God is our constant guardian, watching over all the comings and goings of life.

Christian faith teaches that Jesus spoke about doors and gateways as places of hope, invitation and opportunity. He even described himself as 'the door' or 'the gate', reminding us that there can be something holy about change and transition. 'Knock and the door shall be opened,' he said. These words might spur us on to welcome whatever the new year may bring with hopeful and expectant hearts.

Be with us, God, as we look back on days past and as we move forward into the future. Fill our hearts with thankfulness for all that we've known and received and bless us with courage for the next chapter in our lives. Amen.

BROADCAST THURSDAY 31 DECEMBER 2015

Biographical Index of Contributors

The Reverend **Liz Adenjunle** is the Archdeacon of Hackney and a member of the Archbishops' Task Group on Evangelism. She read theology at Birmingham University before training for the ministry at Ridley Hall, Cambridge. She was formerly Chaplain at St John's College, Cambridge. **Page 214**

Bishop Dr **Joe Aldred** is a broadcaster, ecumenist, speaker and writer. He is responsible for Pentecostalism and Multicultural Relations at Churches Together in England, Honorary Research Fellow at Roehampton University and a Bishop in the Church of God of Prophecy. **Pages 279, 310, 315**

Pastor **Lindsay Allen** was born and grew up in Belfast, and worked for FEBA (Far Eastern Broadcasting Association) before becoming Pastor of Carrickfergus Baptist Church in 1996. He retired in 2013. **Pages 155, 158, 161, 260, 266,**

Padre **David Anderson** is a Church of Scotland Minister. Ordained in 2002, he served as a Parish Minister before joining Her Majesty's Land Forces in 2007. He has undertaken three operational tours of duty; the most recent in Afghanistan with The Royal Scots Dragoon Guards. **Page 335**

Bishop **Angaelos** was consecrated a monk in 1990 and served as Papal Secretary until 1995. He is General Bishop of the Coptic Orthodox Church in the UK. Active ecumenically, he works extensively in inter-religious relations, youth, advocacy and development work in Britain and internationally. **Page 15**

The Reverend Dr **Martyn Atkins** is the Superintendent Minister and Team Leader at Methodist Central Hall Westminster, and formerly the General Secretary of the Methodist Church in Britain. **Pages 120, 123, 125, 345, 347, 387**

The Right Reverend **Nick Baines** is the Anglican Bishop of Leeds. A Liverpudlian, he worked as a linguist at GCHQ before ordination training at Trinity College, Bristol. Formerly Bishop of Croydon, he is an experienced broadcaster and the author of six books. **Page 215**

The Reverend **Peter Baker**, former Senior Pastor of Highfields Church, Cardiff, took over as Senior Minister of Lansdowne Baptist Church, Bournemouth, in 2013. **Pages 135, 149, 164, 167**

Canon **Noel Battye** spent 30 years as Rector of two Belfast parishes. He now enjoys leading worship in the country parishes of Co Armagh, as well as producing and presenting his own weekly programme of sacred music for BBC Radio Ulster. **Pages 183, 186, 312**

The Very Reverend **Mark Beach** is Dean of Rochester and formerly Team Rector at Rugby, having served at several parishes in Nottinghamshire. **Pages 38, 42**

Tina Beattie is an author and the Director of the Digby Stuart Research Centre for Religion, Society and Human Flourishing at the University of Roehampton. **Pages 54, 58, 173, 300, 304**

The Reverend **Chris Bennett** is Church of Ireland Chaplain to the Titanic Quarter in Belfast. He is a leading light at The Dock, a café and community hub. He is also Priest-in-Charge of St Clement's Church in Belfast. **Pages 216, 219**

The Reverend **Derek Boden** was Presbyterian Chaplain to the University of Ulster in Coleraine from 1975 until 1978, when he became a Minister in Dublin. From 1981 until 2012 he was Minister of Malone Presbyterian Church in Belfast. **Page 220**

The Very Reverend Dr **Ian Bradley** is a British academic and Church of Scotland Minister. He is Reader in Practical Theology and Church History at the University of St Andrews, where he is Principal of St Mary's College and a university Chaplain. **Pages 109, 254**

Rabbi Dr **Naftali Brawer** was ordained as an Orthodox Rabbi aged 22, and for over two decades has served as the spiritual leader of congregations in the USA and Britain. He is Rabbi and co-founder of Mishkan, a trans-geographical Jewish community, as well as a columnist and published author. **Pages 365, 368**

David Bruce is Executive Secretary of the Presbyterian Church's Board of Mission in Ireland. He lives in Lisburn and worships at Elmwood Presbyterian Church. He worked with the University and Colleges' Christian Fellowship and Scripture Union International. **Pages 238, 241**

The Reverend Dr **Nicholas Buxton** is Priest-in-Charge of the Parish of St John the Baptist, Newcastle upon Tyne, and author of *The Wilderness Within: Meditation and Modern Life*. **Page 271**

Claire Campbell Smith worked for many years as a producer and director for the BBC Religion and Ethics and Classical Music TV departments. She now teaches academic music at Chetham's School of Music in Manchester. **Pages 212, 217, 269, 273**

The Reverend Dr **Lesley Carroll** has been a Presbyterian Minister in Belfast for over 30 years, closely involved in cross community work. In 2016, she stepped back from her position at the Northern Ireland Equality Commission to campaign for a seat in the Stormont Assembly as an Ulster Unionist MLA. **Page 89**

The Right Reverend and Right Honourable **Richard Chartres** KCVO DD became Bishop of London and The Dean of Her Majesty's Chapels Royal in 1995. Previously, he was Gresham Professor of Divinity and Area Bishop of Stepney. He is a notable environmentalist and Joint Chair of the Christian University, St Mellitus College. **Pages 107, 376, 381**

The Most Reverend **David Chillingworth** is Bishop of St Andrews, Dunkeld and Dunblane and Primus of the Scottish Episcopal Church. Born in Dublin, he was ordained in 1976 and served in Northern Ireland before moving to Scotland in 2005. **Pages 112, 298**

Mark Coffey is a teacher of religion and philosophy at The Manchester Grammar School, and a regular presenter of *The Daily Service* on Radio 4. **Pages 22, 26, 49, 248, 250, 252**

Canon **Edwin Counsell** is Director of Education for the Diocese of Llandaff and Lead Education Officer for the Church in Wales. Ordained in 1988, he has since been a regular contributor to local and national radio. **Page 43**

Dr **Catherine Cowley** is a member of the Congregation of the Religious of the Assumption. She has been Assistant Director for the Heythrop Institute for Religion, Ethics and Public Life and Secretary to the Association of Teachers of Moral Theology. **Pages 200, 246**

George Craig is a retired senior civil servant, and a Methodist local preacher in Cardiff. **Pages 168, 170, 205, 240, 259, 305**

The Right Reverend Dr **Steven Croft** became the Anglican Bishop of Oxford in 2016. He was formerly Bishop of Sheffield. A theologian specializing in mission, he helped found the Fresh Expressions' initiative. **Pages 385, 388**

Shaunaka Rishi Das is Director of the Oxford Centre for Hindu Studies. He is a Hindu cleric, writer and lecturer, and Hindu Chaplain to Oxford University. Born an Irish Catholic, he joined a Hare Krishna ashram in Dublin in 1979. **Pages 78, 236, 239, 311, 316, 318, 328**

Maggi Dawn is an author and songwriter, as well as Associate Professor of Theology and Literature, and Dean of Marquand Chapel at Yale Divinity School. Before moving to Yale in 2011, she served as Chaplain and taught theology at the University of Cambridge. **Pages 143, 146**

Ranjit-Singh Dhanda is Lead for Faith Inclusion across the Nishkam Schools (Sikh ethos multi-faith schools), guided by Bhai Sahib Bhai Dr Mohinder Singh Ji. Previously, he was a member of Birmingham SACRE and the Sikh Chaplain to Wolverhampton University. **Page 185**

The Reverend Canon **Simon Doogan** is the Rector of St Columbanus Church, Ballyholme in Bangor. He is also Prebendary of Wicklow, representing the Diocese of Down and Dromore, on the Chapter of the National Cathedral of St Patrick in Dublin. **Pages 41, 296**

Anna Drew is Director of Communications for the Anglican diocese of Canterbury. She was formerly lead media officer at Methodist Church House in London. A freelance writer and broadcaster, she is passionate about theology and social justice. **Pages 261, 264**

The Right Reverend **Chris Edmondson** was Bishop of Bolton from 2008 until his retirement in 2016. Ordained in 1973, he has worked in a variety of parish and diocesan posts, and was Warden of Lee Abbey, Devon, from 2002 to 2008. **Pages 139, 306**

Frances Finn is a journalist and presenter for TV and radio. She is a BBC Radio 4 *Daily Service* presenter and fills in on *The Sunday Hour* on BBC Radio 2. She can be seen on local TV channel Notts TV, and heard on BBC Radio Nottingham at the weekend. She has written movingly about a serious motorbike accident that hospitalized her in 2009. **Page 342**

The Very Reverend Dr **Graham Forbes** CBE is an Episcopalian Priest. A former Provost of St Ninian's Cathedral in Perth, since 1990 he has been Provost of St Mary's Cathedral, Edinburgh. Also, among other posts, he is Chair of the Mental Welfare Commission for Scotland and Chair of Court, Edinburgh Napier University. **Page 11**

The Reverend Dr **Michael Ford** is an ecumenical deacon, developing a contemplative ministry between and beyond denominations. He is a

BBC religious broadcaster and author of many books on contemporary spirituality including biographies of Henri Nouwen and Mychal Judge. **Pages 19, 136, 138, 140, 191, 247, 249, 251**

The Reverend Dr **Kevin Franz** is Head of the Department of Pastoral and Spiritual Care for Mental Health in the Greater Glasgow and Clyde Health Board. He served as a curate in Edinburgh before becoming Rector of St John's, Selkirk, and Provost of St Ninian's Cathedral, Perth. **Pages 188, 356**

The Reverend Dr **Richard Frazer** is Parish Minister at Greyfriars Kirk, Edinburgh. He is also Convener of the Church and Society Council of the Church of Scotland and is involved with the Green Pilgrim Network. **Pages 28, 307**

The Reverend Dr **Craig Gardiner** teaches theology at South Wales Baptist College and is an Honorary Senior Tutor at the Cardiff School of History, Archaeology and Religion. He is a member of the Iona Community. **Pages 132, 258**

The Reverend **Neil Gardner** is Minister at Canongate Kirk, Edinburgh. He has served with the Royal Army Chaplains' Department in Germany, Hong Kong, Northern Ireland, Surrey and Hampshire. **Pages 232, 234, 297, 301, 327**

The Very Reverend **Martin Graham** is a Catholic priest of the Diocese of Down and Connor and Administrator of St Peter's Cathedral, Belfast. He is involved in a number of catechesis initiatives in the Diocese. **Pages 88, 309**

The Reverend Dr **Gordon Gray**, after being Minister of a Church Extension charge in Belfast, was Youth Secretary to the Presbyterian Church in Ireland from 1966 to 1973, when he became Minister of First Lisburn Presbyterian Church. He retired in 2001. **Pages 23, 91, 115**

Andrew Graystone worked for BBC Religion and Ethics for more than a decade as a TV and radio producer. He continues to present radio programmes and researches and writes on Christian faith and digital culture. **Pages 13, 25, 141, 147, 231, 366**

The Reverend **Sharon Grenham-Thompson**, a former solicitor, is Team Minister in the Watling Valley Ecumenical Partnership, Milton Keynes. She also contributes regularly to BBC Radio 2's *Pause for Thought*. **Pages 14, 16, 45, 64, 79, 82, 85**

The Reverend Dr **Leslie Griffiths**, Lord Griffiths of Burry Port, is a British Methodist Minister and a Labour Life Peer. He served as President of the Methodist Conference from 1994 to 1995. He is President of the Boys' Brigade. **Pages 9, 47, 50, 110, 202, 204, 207, 330, 332**

Becky Harris is a teacher at The King David High School in Manchester. **Page 152**

Richard Hill MBE served as a Presbyterian Minister in County Antrim and in Belfast, and in a former Chair of Northern Ireland Screen Commission and on the Northern Ireland Consumer Council. He is currently a film and media consultant and a member of the Independent Press Standards Organisation and Ofcom Communications Consumer Panel. **Pages 18, 21, 24, 222, 244**

Canon Dr **Ann Holt** OBE is an expert in education, as governor of several schools and consultant to Local Education Authorities, the DFE and independent schools. Since 2002 she has been Director of the Programme Team at Bible Society. **Page 93**

The Right Reverend **Nicholas Holtam** is Bishop of Salisbury and previously was Vicar of St Martin-in-the-Fields, London. He is the lead Bishop on the environment and for ministry with and among deaf and disabled people. **Page 319**

The Reverend Dr **Rosa Hunt** is Pastor of Salem Baptist Chapel in Tonteg, Pontypridd, South Wales. **Pages 72, 74**

Imam **Monawar Hussain** is the Imam of Eton College and Muslim Chaplain to Oxford University Hospitals NHS Foundation Trust. He is also the founder of The Oxford Foundation and the national initiative United for Peace: Communities United Against Extremism. **Pages 281, 286, 308**

Dr **Musharraf Hussain** OBE is a scientist, educator and religious scholar in Nottinghamshire. He is Chief Executive of the Karimia Institute, Chief Editor of *The Invitation*, and Vice Chair of the Christian/Muslim Forum. **Page 303**

The Reverend **Roger Hutchings**, a Methodist Minister, was Editor of BBC's *Songs of Praise*, and later of ITV's *Morning Worship*. He lives in retirement in Wiltshire and near Carcassonne, Languedoc, France. **Pages 80, 86, 116, 121, 325, 331**

Father **Nicholas James** is Parish Priest of St Mary's Roman Catholic Church in Monmouth and also Parish Priest for the Parish of St Frances of Rome, Ross-on-Wye. **Page 268**

The Reverend **Clair Jaquiss** was ordained in 2008, having worked for many years as a radio producer for BBC Religion and Ethics. She is also Assistant Priest at All Saints Church, Hale Barns, not far from Manchester Airport. **Pages 46, 144, 226, 229**

Glenn Jordan has 30 years of leadership in the Northern Ireland voluntary sector, mostly in the areas of peace building, social justice and urban regeneration. He is Director of Law Centre NI, a not-for-profit legal practice using the law for social change. **Pages 87, 350**

Sarah Joseph lectures on Islam both within the UK and internationally. A convert from Roman Catholicism, she was editor of the Muslim lifestyle magazine *emel*. In 2004 she was awarded the OBE for services to interfaith dialogue and the promotion of women's rights. **Pages 218, 221**

Dr **Krish Kandiah** is the founder and director of 'Home for Good', a charity that finds adoptive and foster homes for vulnerable children. A vice-president of Tear Fund, he also lectures at Regents' Park College, Oxford University. He is the author of ten books, including the award-winning *Paradoxology*. **Page 17**

Gopinder Kaur combines motherhood with postgraduate research in education. Formerly in children's publishing, she has written on Sikh heritage and participates in faith-inspired civic engagement projects fostered by the Nishkam Civic Association, under the tutelage of Bhai Sahib Dr Mohinder Singh. **Pages 114, 118, 182**

Dr **Edward Kessler** MBE is an author and the Founding Director of The Woolf Institute, Cambridge. He is a notable thinker in interfaith relations and Fellow of St Edmund's College. **Pages 34, 36, 284, 288, 290**

Monsignor **Mark Langham** has, since 2013, been Chaplain at the Cambridge University Catholic Chaplaincy. He is a Priest of the Archdiocese of Westminster and former Administrator of Wesminster Cathedral. **Pages 51, 53**

Cathy Le Feuvre is a writer, journalist and media consultant. She worked as a print and radio journalist in Jersey before moving to the UK, where she joined the media office of the Salvation Army. **Pages 127, 131, 209**

The Reverend **Richard Littledale** is Pastor of Newbury Church, having previously served at churches in Hertford, Purley and Teddington. He trains preachers and writes books for adults and children. **Pages 48, 52**

Leon Litvack is Professor of Victorian Studies at Queen's University Belfast, a Dickens scholar and the author of books on 19th-century literature. He has frequently contributed to BBC radio and television on arts and culture, and religion and ethics. **Pages 29, 32, 35**

Sister **Jane Livesey** CJ is the Congregational Leader of the Congregation of Jesus, which has 1700 members in 23 countries. Her background was in education, first as a teacher and subsequently as a head teacher. **Pages 171, 283**

Tony Macaulay is a Northern Ireland writer, management consultant and peace-builder. Raised on the Shankill Road in West Belfast, he has worked with hundreds of youth and community groups to break down barriers of mistrust, hatred and division. **Page 344**

The Reverend **Gillean Maclean** is a Church of Scotland minister serving two rural parishes – Udny and Pitmedden – in Aberdeenshire.

She was formerly a Chaplain at the University of Aberdeen where she had been a divinity and ministry student. She is a writer, poet and radio presenter. **Pages 178, 181**

The Reverend Dr **Marjory MacLean** is a Church of Scotland Parish Minister in East Perthshire, and a Chaplain in the Royal Naval Reserve. She has previously served in an Orkney parish and as a Clerk of the Church's General Assembly. **Pages 177, 233, 240**

Anna Magnusson has produced, written and broadcast programmes for the BBC for more than 25 years. She has been in charge of Religion and Ethics programming for BBC Radio Scotland. She is the author of three books of non-fiction. **Pages 60, 66, 95, 108, 113, 157, 159, 338, 340, 388**

Michelle Marken OBE completed her teaching career as Principal of St Joseph's College, Belfast. She is a regular contributor to BBC Radio Ulster programmes, an enthusiast for amateur drama and a passionate educationalist, and is now volunteering with a range of charities. **Page 373**

Father **Andrew Martlew** is a former Army Chaplain who is now Vicar of St Martin's, Womersley, in North Yorkshire, and an Honorary Chaplain of York Minster. He is one of the regular presenters of *The Daily Service* on Radio 4. **Pages 128, 256**

The Reverend Prebendary **Edward Mason** was appointed Rector of Bath Abbey in 2004. He was previously Director of Music at a Gloucestershire comprehensive school and then spent six years in Uganda with his family as Mission Partners with the Church Mission

Baroness Neuberger is a former chief executive of the King's Fund. **Page 33**

Vincent Nichols received the red hat of his office from Pope Francis in St Peter's Basilica on 22nd February 2014. He is Archbishop of Westminster and President of the Catholic Bishops' Conference of England and Wales. He served as Archbishop of Birmingham from 2000 to 2009. **Pages 377, 379, 383**

Father **Eugene O'Neill** is a Priest of the Diocese of Down and Connor, and is also a spiritual director. He works near Belfast and contributes regularly to broadcasting and print in the UK, Ireland and United States. **Pages 145, 163, 169, 189, 193 195**

The Right Reverend **Stephen Oliver** is the retired Anglican Bishop of Stepney. A former Head of BBC Religious Programmes, he has also been a Canon of St Paul's Cathedral. **Page 162**

The Reverend Canon **Nick Papadopulos** worked as a barrister before doing his theological training. A former Vicar of St Peter's, Eaton Square, London, he is now Canon Treasurer of Canterbury Cathedral. **Page 20**

Rebecca Pippert is a global conference speaker and author of 11 books. She equips Christians to engage effectively as witnesses in the 21st century. The founder of Becky Pippert Ministries, she and her husband divide their time between the UK and USA. **Pages 351, 353**

The Reverend Dr **Michael Piret** is Rector of Christ Church, Oyster Bay, in the Episcopal Diocese of Long Island, New York. Until 2016 he was Dean of Divinity at Magdalen College, Oxford, where he is now an Emeritus Fellow. **Page 228**

The Reverend **George Pitcher** is a journalist, author and cultural commentator, and serves as an Anglican priest in the Dioceses of Chichester and London. He is chairman of change-management consultancy Jericho Chambers. **Pages 323, 329**

Andrea Rea is a freelance writer and broadcaster working with the BBC Religion and Ethics and Classical Music departments in Belfast. She plays the viola and is Director of Music at St Nicholas Church in Belfast. **Pages 137, 142, 148, 151, 225, 292**

The Reverend **Ernest Rea** is a former Head of BBC Religious Broadcasting. He presents *Beyond Belief* on Radio 4. He is the recipient of the Gold Medal of the International Council of Christians and Jews for his contribution to interfaith understanding. **Pages 90, 235**

Dr **Pritpal Kaur Riat** is a Sikh from Leeds. She has extensive experience of interfaith work, including her association with the Faith Guiding and Faith Encounter programme in Birmingham. She was part of a Sikh delegation to visit Israel and Palestine in 2005. **Page 180**

Pastor **Alex Robertson** is one of the Pastors at The Lighthouse, an Elim Pentecostal church in Salford. He is also a musician and teaches viola at the Royal Northern College of Music. **Pages 359, 364**

Monsignor **Tony Rogers** is a Catholic Priest, currently working in Aldeburgh in Suffolk. Previously he was Priest at Our Lady and the English Martyrs Church, Cambridge. He is a regular presenter of *The Daily Service* on Radio 4. **Pages 59, 119, 122**

The Reverend Canon Dr **Sarah Rowland Jones** LVO OBE is Priest-In-Charge of St John's

Church in Cardiff city centre. She was formerly research adviser to Archbishops of Cape Town. Before ordination she worked as a diplomat in London, Amman and Budapest. **Pages 67, 71**

Rabbi **YY Rubinstein** splits his time between the US and UK. He is one the most sought-after Jewish speakers in the UK and abroad. He is a columnist in several Jewish magazines and the author of eight books. **Page 39**

The Reverend Dr **Calvin Samuel** is a Methodist Minister, currently Director of Wesley Study Centre and Academic Dean of Cranmer Hall, St John's College, Durham University. Previously he was New Testament Tutor at Spurgeon's College and Chaplain to Farringtons School in Kent. **Pages 31, 83, 92, 94, 98, 367, 369**

The Right Reverend Dr **Frank Sellar**, a Presbyterian Minister, served a congregation in Dublin from 1990 until 2007, when he became Minister of Bloomfield Presbyterian Church in East Belfast. He was elected Moderator of the General Assembly in June 2016. **Pages 190, 192**

The Reverend Canon **Stephen Shipley** is a Priest in Buxton, Derbyshire, and Honorary Canon of Derby Cathedral. He is a producer for BBC Radio Religion and Ethics. **Pages 174, 243, 245, 270, 272, 320, 322, 348, 370, 372**

Dr **Gemma Simmonds** CJ is a sister of the Congregation of Jesus. After a teaching career, she worked as Chaplain in the University of Cambridge. She has worked with street children in Brazil. She now teaches theology at Heythrop College, London, and is a volunteer Chaplain at Holloway Prison. **Pages 150, 154**

Jasdeep Singh Rahal is a British Sikh. He is Project Officer for 'Brothers in Arms' at the National Army Museum in London. Working closely with British Asian Communities, he is helping to research, catalogue and digitize 60,000 artefacts from the Indian Army over the past 200 years. **Pages 333, 337**

The Reverend Dr **Karen Smith** is Tutor in Church History and Christian Spirituality at South Wales Baptist College, Honorary Senior Tutor in the School of History, Archaeology and Religion at Cardiff University, and Pastor of Orchard Place Baptist Church, Neath. **Pages 291, 295, 321, 324, 352**

The Most Reverend **Peter Smith** is Archbishop of Southwark. He has also served as Bishop of East Anglia, Archbishop of Cardiff, and has been Chairman of the Catholic Truth Society. **Page 153**

The Most Reverend **George Stack** was installed as Archbishop of Cardiff in 2011. He was ordained Priest in 1972, later serving in Wood Green and Kentish Town, London, among other places. He has also been Administrator of Westminster Cathedral, and Bishop in the Archdiocese of Westminster. **Pages 81, 101, 124**

The Reverend **Mary Stallard** is Chaplain of St Joseph's Catholic and Anglican High School, Wrexham, as well as Director of the St Giles Centre for Religious Education and Faith Development in the same town. **Pages 68, 76, 130, 299, 302, 341, 346, 386, 389**

The Reverend **Mike Starkey** is a former commercial radio journalist and newsreader who became an Anglican vicar and worked in parishes. He is now a Tutor for Church Army

398

in Sheffield and a freelance broadcaster for the BBC. He is the author of eight books, as well as the popular Faith Pictures online course for church home groups (www.faithpictures.org). Pages 253, 255, 257

The Reverend Canon **Patrick Thomas** is the Vicar of Christ Church, Carmarthen, and Chancellor of St Davids Cathedral, Pembrokeshire. An honorary member of the Gorsedd of Bards, he has published works in both English and Welsh. **Pages 224, 371**

The Reverend Dr **Bert Tosh** was ordained to the Presbyterian ministry in 1973 and worked with congregations in Belfast, Londonderry and County Donegal before joining the BBC Religious Broadcasting Department in Belfast in 1984. He retired in 2013 but continues to produce worship programmes. In 2013 he was made an honorary Doctor of Divinity by the Union Theological College, Belfast. **Page 265**

The Venerable **Peter Townley** is Archdeacon of Pontefract, in the Anglian Diocese of Leeds. He spent the first 16 years of his ministry in the Manchester area. Before moving to Pontefract, he was Vicar of St Mary le Tower, Ipswich. **Pages 176, 179**

Pádraig Ó Tuama is a poet and theologian who works as the leader of the Corrymeela Community (corrymeela.org), a Christian witness to peace in Northern Ireland working with over 10,000 people a year. His poetry and prose are published by Canterbury Press and Hodder & Stoughton. **Page 30**

The late **Alison Twaddle** was General Secretary of the Church of Scotland Guild, and served that church in many ways before her death in 2013. She was a full-time mother before joining the Guild. She was a member of BBC Scotland's Scottish Religious Advisory Committee. **Pages 274, 277, 280, 354**

The late Reverend Canon **Noël Vincent** was Canon Treasurer of Liverpool Cathedral and before that a notable religious broadcaster, who was Chief Assistant to the Head of Religious Broadcasting at the BBC. Throughout the 1980s he produced hundreds of radio and TV programmes across the north of England. **Page 363**

The Reverend Dr **Mark Wakelin** has served for more than 30 years with the Methodist Church as Minister in various appointments. He was President of the Methodist Conference from 2012 to 2013 and is currently a Minister at Epsom Methodist Church, Surrey. **Pages 84, 97, 100, 156**

The Right Reverend Dr **David Walker** is the Anglican Bishop of Manchester. He was previously Bishop of Dudley in the West Midlands. He is a member of the Third Order of the Society of St Francis. **Page 117**

The Reverend Dr **Sheila Watson** is a priest in the Church of England. She served as Archdeacon of Canterbury and Archdeacon of Buckingham. On 21 March 2013, she enthroned Justin Welby as the 105th Archbishop of Canterbury, the first woman to carry out the ceremony. **Page 103**

The Reverend Canon Dr **Jo Bailey Wells** is Bishop of Dorking. A former Dean of Clare College, Cambridge, she was Associate Professor of Bible and Ministry at Duke Divinity School in North Carolina, before serving as Chaplain to the Archbishop of Canterbury. **Page 384**

The Reverend Dr **Sam Wells** is the Vicar of St Martin-in-the-Fields, London. He is also Visiting Professor of Christian Ethics at King's College, London. He is the author of 25 books on ethics, ministry, faith, mission, liturgy and discipleship. **Page 334**

The Reverend **Peter Whittaker** is a retired Methodist Minister, and formerly Chair of the West Yorkshire Methodist District, and Chair of the Trustees and the Enabling Group of Churches Together in England. **Page 56**

The Reverend Canon **Jenny Wigley** is Rector of Radyr and Area Dean of Llandaff. She is a former teacher. All her ministry has been in the Church in Wales, including university chaplaincy and theological education. **Pages 10, 12, 73, 75, 172, 175**

The Reverend Dr **Stephen Wigley** is Chair of the Wales Synod of the Methodist Church, having previously ministered in circuits in Swansea, Ceredigion and Cardiff. He has also written books about the 20th-century theologians Barth and von Balthasar. **Pages 313, 317, 380, 382**

The Reverend Canon **Steve Williams** is Priest-in-Charge of St Gabriel's, Prestwich (in the Prestwich Mission Partnership). He is Interfaith Advisor in the Diocese of Manchester and Co-chair of the Manchester branch of the Council of Christians and Jews. **Page 355**

Rabbi **Jonathan Wittenberg** is the Senior Rabbi of Mosorti Judaism UK, and Rabbi of the New North London Synagogue. He is a leading writer and thinker on Judaism and is currently working to establish a multi-faith school in London. www.jonathanwittenberg.org **Pages 37, 287, 289**

The Reverend Dr **Janet Wootton** is Director of Learning and Development for the Congregational Federation. Ordained in 1979, she has served in rural and city churches. She is on the editorial team for *Feminist Theology Journal* and *Worship Live*, among other publications. **Pages 61, 63, 65, 105, 263, 267, 276, 278, 282**

The Right Reverend Professor **Tom Wright** is one of the world's leading New Testament scholars, and from 2003 until his retirement in 2010 was Bishop of Durham. He is now Research Professor of New Testament and Early Christianity at St Mary's College in the University of St Andrews. **Page 104**

Acknowledgments

The Publishers would like to thank Bishop James Jones for providing the Foreword. Many thanks to Mike Ford and to Vanessa Ford at the BBC for their invaluable help in producing this book.